Workplace Bullying

Symptoms and solutions

Edited by Noreen Tehrani

Routledge
Taylor & Francis Group

LONDON AND NEW YORK

First published 2012 by Routledge
27 Church Road, Hove, East Sussex BN3 2FA

Simultaneously published in the USA and Canada
by Routledge
711 Third Avenue, New York NY 10017

*Routledge is an imprint of the Taylor & Francis Group, an
Informa business*

British Library Cataloguing in Publication Data
A catalogue record for this book is available from the
British Library

Library of Congress Cataloging in Publication Data
Workplace bullying : symptoms and solutions / edited by
Noreen Tehrani.
    p. cm.
  ISBN 978–0–415–61707–9 (hardback) —
  ISBN 978–0–415–61708–6 (pbk.) I. Bullying in the
  workplace. I. Tehrani, Noreen.
HF5549.5.E43W6717 2012
658.3'82—dc23

                                            2011032511

ISBN: 978–0–415–61707–9 (hbk)
ISBN: 978–0–415–61708–6 (pbk)
ISBN: 978–0–203–13011–7 (ebk)

Typeset in Times
by RefineCatch Limited, Bungay, Suffolk
Paperback cover design by Andrew Ward

Printed and bound in Great Britain by
TJ International Ltd, Padstow, Cornwall

Contents

Illustrations

Tables

Figures

Text box

Contributors

Alicia Arenas is an Assistant Professor in Work and Organisational Psychology at the University of Seville (Spain). She has worked as a researcher for the Spanish Institute of Safety and Health at Work, a position that also involved the elaboration of instruction materials in health promotion, development of new publications, and evaluation of different projects on OHS. Since 2007, she has been working in the research group INDRHO directed by the Professor Lourdes Munduate, where she is involved in a research project to evaluate the effectiveness of organisational strategies to cope with bullying.

Charlotte Bloch is an Associate Professor, Department of Cultural Sociology, University of Copenhagen. She has researched and published articles and books within the field of Sociology of Emotions. Her main research focus is on the complex relationships between structures, cultures, emotions and social relations. Within this framework she has studied quality of life in terms of flow and stress in everyday life and emotions and emotional culture in academia. At present she is exploring bullying at the workplace. Her focus is in particular on emotional processes in the interaction between perpetrator, victim and bystander.

Sandra L. Bloom, MD is a board-certified psychiatrist, Associate Professor of Health Management and Policy and Co-Director of the Center for Nonviolence and Social Justice at the School of Public Health of Drexel University in Philadelphia. Dr Bloom is the founder of the Sanctuary Institute, Distinguished Fellow at the Andrus Children's Center and a Past-President of the International Society for Traumatic Stress Studies. She is author of *Creating Sanctuary: Toward the Evolution of Sane Societies* and co-author of *Bearing Witness: Violence and Collective Responsibility*. A new book, co-authored by Andrus Children's Center COO Brian Farragher and titled *Destroying Sanctuary: The Crisis in Human Service Delivery*, will be published soon by Oxford University Press to be followed by *Restoring Sanctuary: A New Operating System for Organizations*.

Thelma Butts Griggs is a conflict management consultant and mediator. She holds a degree in law from the Ohio State University, where she also studied international relations and political science. She teaches courses and university seminars in mediation, negotiation, facilitation, and organisational restructuring in the United States, Spain, Mexico, and South America. Thelma has worked internationally developing and evaluating court-based and community-based mediation programmes. She is an international consultant to government agencies, healthcare systems, and private firms that are implementing programmes in conflict management; including dispute systems design, organisational conflict reduction, and work team training. She mediates disputes in a variety of arenas, from international situations, to healthcare issues, to commercial disputes and workplace conflict.

Laura Crawshaw founded the Executive Insight Development Group, Inc. in 1994 which provides coaching services exclusively for abrasive leaders. In 2009 she founded The Boss Whispering Institute, dedicated to research and training in the field of coaching leaders who engage in bullying behaviours. Originally a clinical social worker, she holds a doctorate in organisational behaviour. Author of *Taming The Abrasive Manager: How To End Unnecessary Roughness In The Workplace* (Jossey-Bass, 2007), she publishes in academic journals and speaks internationally. Dr Crawshaw is a member of the International Society for the Psychoanalytic Study of Organizations, the American Psychological Association, The British Psychological Society, and the International Coach Federation.

Barbara Davey is a Senior Research Officer at Acas and has a background in social policy research. Before joining Acas, she worked in academia and voluntary bodies as a Department of Health funded researcher. Barbara's particular research interest was in the careers and working lives of social care workers and nurses, focusing on race and gender discrimination at work. Barbara has written reports, book chapters and journal articles on these areas and publications include *Social Services: Working Under Pressure, Management, Social Work and Change, Social Policy Review, Work, Employment and Society, Research Policy and Planning* and *Journal of Inter-Professional Care* among others.

Since joining Acas, Barbara's role in managing research into Acas conciliation and mediation services has facilitated an extension of her research interests into conflict management in the workplace.

Gill Dix is Head of Research and Evaluation at Acas. She has a background in social and public policy research, working in academia and voluntary and public sector bodies prior to joining Acas. Gill has written on a wide range of industrial relations subjects including contributing to the 1998 and 2004 Workplace Employment Relations Surveys, an internationally recognised survey mapping patterns of industrial relations in Britain. Within Acas, Gill has a particular interest in employee engagement and consultation arrangements, and in the legal infrastructure of both individual and collective relations. She has written reports and papers on conflict at work and the conciliation roles of Acas, including an important study on the mechanisms involved in the conciliation process.

Debbie Dunn is an accredited mediator and has a long history of working in and with organisations. She has been a general manager of a multinational company, a company secretary, a human resources manager and operated her business Accord Facilitation Services for some ten years before moving to Hobart in 2005 where she works as a human relationships manager. She holds a postgraduate diploma in narrative therapy and it is these proposals that now inform her work with individuals, couples, groups and organisations. Debbie has a long-held interest in the practices in which organisations engage and the effects of these practices on people, their lives and their relationships. This has led her work into the area of workplace bullying.

Åse Marie Hansen is a senior researcher at the National Research Centre for the Working Environment (NRCWE) and adjunct lecturer at the Department of Public Health, University of Copenhagen (Denmark). She has worked as a senior researcher for NRCWE, a position that involved biological monitoring and the development of methods for determination of the bodily response of stress reactions. These methods cover a number of biological measures in blood and saliva (e.g. cortisol and saliva), mental arousal, and sleep disturbances. These techniques have been used in occupational health research on, for example, workplace bullying and mental diseases in both field studies and experimental settings.

Marie-France Hirigoyen is a practising psychiatrist, psychoanalyst and family psychotherapist, with French and American training in victimology, and she has pioneered research in workplace bullying in France. Her book, *Stalking the Soul: Perverse Everyday Violence* (1998), which described the phenomenon for the first time, sold over 450,000 copies and has been translated into 24 languages. She coined the term 'moral harassment' (*harcèlement moral*), which has been since used by legislators in France and Belgium and been broadly adopted in Spain and Japan. Her book sparked interest and drew attention to the reality and gravity of the phenomenon and led to civil and penal provisions being made in French law against moral harassment. She works essentially supporting and counselling targets of bullying, but also intervenes at the corporate level and European level in the area of moral and sexual harassment.

Annie Hogh is an Associate Professor in Work and Organisational Psychology at the University of Copenhagen's Department of Psychology. Annie's interests are primarily in researching and teaching work psychology. Prior to joining the University of Copenhagen in April 2009 she did her research at the National Research Centre for the Working Environment (NRCWE) in Copenhagen. Her research has focused on exposure to negative behaviour, such as bullying, violence and harassment at work and individual consequences and coping as well as investigating how employers and employees can work together in order to prevent workplace bullying and harassment. She is also involved in research on how to develop an effective treatment programme to deal with the individual consequences of adult bullying. Annie has published her research in a number of national (Danish) and international journal articles in refereed journals such as *Work & Stress*, *European Journal of Work and Organizational Psychology*, *Scandinavian Journal of Psychology*, *Journal of Psychosomatic Research* and *Scandinavian Journal of Public Health*. She has also presented a number of conference papers at international conferences.

Adrienne Hubert is the managing director of a consultancy firm in the Netherlands which specialises in policy research and implementation related to workplace bullying, sexual harassment, discrimination, aggression and violence. Her company is involved in training managers, confidential supporters and grievance committees in tackling unwanted workplace behaviours. Her master's degree (1996) explored 'mobbing' and she followed this with two years working as a scientific researcher in the University of Leiden where she undertook the first major studies into workplace bullying in the Netherlands.

She has presented the results from her studies at national and international conferences and in a number of (inter)national journals and books.

Paul Latreille is Professor of Economics at Swansea University. He currently holds a visiting position at Westminster Business School's Centre for Employment Research and is a Research Fellow of the IZA, Bonn; during 2008–9 he was the ESRC Visiting Research Fellow at Acas. His research interests focus on workplace conflict, mediation and the economics of employment tribunals; disability; economic inactivity; vocational training; and self-employment. Journal publications include *Oxford Economic Papers*, *Oxford Bulletin of Economics and Statistics*, *Economics Letters*, *The Manchester School*, *Applied Economics*, *Industrial and Labour Relations Review*, *British Journal of Industrial Relations*, *Regional Studies*, *Industrial Law Journal*, *Industrial Relations Journal*, *Labour: Review of Labour Economics* and *Human Resource Management Journal*. He has also undertaken funded work for various bodies including the Department for Business, Innovation and Skills, the Ministry of Justice, the Welsh Assembly Government, the Low Pay Commission, the Sector Skills Development Agency and Acas.

Jose M. León-Pérez is a researcher in the Department of Social Psychology, University of Seville. He holds an MS degree in Human Resource Management from the University of Seville and is a Health and Safety Technical Expert (according to the Occupational Health Law in Spain). In that sense, he has been working with a number of public and private organisations in the assessment of psychosocial risks factors at work. Currently, his research focuses on the evaluation of training programmes in order to prevent workplace violence from a conflict perspective.

Andreas Liefooghe is Assistant Dean and Course Director at Birkbeck College. His main research areas are the interactions between human frailty and the organising and disciplining pressures of work. He has interests in bullying, violence and harassment, managing difference, power and politics, with an emphasis on the role of discourses and interpenetration in the above. Andreas has published in *Human Relations*, *Journal of Occupational and Organizational Psychology*, *Child Development*, *Journal of Organizational Behaviour*, and the *European Journal of Work and Organizational Psychology*, amongst others. In 2002, he organised the first International Conference on

Bullying and Harassment at Work in London, and has been instrumental in informing the workplace agenda on bullying, violence and harassment.

Eva Gemzøe Mikkelsen is an occupational psychologist in the Danish consultancy firm CRECEA, working primarily in organisational development and the prevention and management of conflicts and bullying at work. In 2001 Eva completed her PhD thesis 'Workplace Bullying: Its Prevalence, Aetiology and Health Correlates' since which time she has continued her research into bullying. Her early scientific interest was in the health consequences of exposure to bullying. She is now also looking at intervention research and the evaluation of the effectiveness of psychosocial rehabilitation for severely traumatised victims of bullying. Together with Annie Hogh, she heads a research project into developing, implementing and evaluating organisational strategies aimed at preventing conflicts and bullying at work. Eva has presented papers at a number of international conferences and in international books and journals. Eva is the primary author of a comprehensive Danish book on bullying at work.

Joan Popovic is a human resources consultant with over 20 years experience working at an operational level in a major insurance company. In addition to specialising in the management of long-term absence cases, her experience also includes 12 years advising and investigating complaints of alleged bullying, harassment and victimisation. Joan has helped develop policies and best practice guidelines in the management of such cases and has also had responsibility for the recruitment, training and development of a team of dignity at work advisors across the UK. She qualified with the Open University, where she majored in sociology and psychology.

Siriyupa Roongrerngsuke is Professor of Human Resource Management at the Sasin Graduate Institute of Business Administration of Chulalongkorn University, Bangkok, Thailand. For many years she has researched international HRM practices, and is regarded as one of the most influential women in the field of organisational behaviour in Asia. Her work on negative behaviours in the workplace and toxic leadership has led her to co-operate with Andreas Liefooghe, and they are now conducting the first pan-Asian research programme on workplace bullying.

Angelo Soares is Professor of Organizational Behaviour in the School of Management (ESG) of the University of Quebec in Montreal

(UQAM). He received his PhD on Sociology of Work from Laval University. He is a member of the Centre for Research and Intervention on Suicide and Euthanasia (CRISE) at UQAM.

Noreen Tehrani is a chartered occupational, health and counselling psychologist with an international reputation for her work in dealing with disasters, crisis and trauma. She works with a number of police forces, fire services and commercial organisations in the development of integrated trauma support programmes. Noreen is the consultant psychologist with the Child Exploitation and Online Protection Centre, providing support for the organisation and its workers, and where she is involved in undertaking research into the prevention of compassion fatigue, burn-out and secondary trauma.

Maarit Vartia is a senior specialist in the Finnish Institute of Occupational Health. She has undertaken research on workplace bullying for over 20 years. She works as an expert, consultant and trainer. Maarit is particularly interested in the strategies for the prevention and management of bullying and harassment in organisations where she supports and assists organisations at different levels to deal with bullying. During the last few years, she has worked on several international projects looking at the psychosocial factors involved in bullying, harassment and violence at work including the Psychosocial Risk Management – European Framework (PRIMA-EF) – project. This project has provided a framework to promote policy and practice in relation to psychosocial risks of bullying, harassment and violence at national and enterprise level within the European Union. Maarit has written a number of books, reports and articles on conflicts and bullying at work.

Sarah Vaughan is a lecturer in intercultural communication and management with a business school in France and is currently investigating corporate social responsibility (CSR) education in France for her DBA at Grenoble Ecole de Management and the University of Newcastle. Her interest is particularly in the human resource implications of CSR and in the role of French management education in changing a culture of compliance to regulation with regard to workplace violence and conflict towards a culture of well-being at work.

Chapter 1

Introduction to workplace bullying

Noreen Tehrani

Introduction

Human beings have the potential to abuse one another with physical violence, verbal abuse, threats of violence, back-stabbing, undermining and a range of other bad behaviours. History is littered with examples of the individual and group cruelty meted out on unfortunate victims by victorious armies, vicious leaders, violent masters and vindictive family members. However, attitudes and responses to these behaviours are strongly influenced by the culture, social climate and meaning of the behaviour to the target. In this chapter we look at the names that people have used to describe negative interpersonal behaviours, the history and development of the construct of bullying in the workplace, the features of individual, group and organisational bullying and ways to differentiate between healthy conflict, strong management and workplace bullying.

What's in a name?

> 'When I use a word,' said Humpty Dumpty in a rather scornful tone, 'it means just what I choose it to mean – neither more nor less.'
>
> (Carroll, 1998)

Harmful interpersonal behaviours have largely been defined by people who perceive themselves as targets or victims of this behaviour. Adjectives such as abused, victimised, coerced, harassed, terrorised, mobbed, undermined and bullied are everyday descriptions of how these negative behaviours are experienced by victims. The phenomenon of workplace abuse has been give a number of names. Generally these negative behaviours are divided into two groups: (a) harassment for behaviours involving discrimination on the grounds of race, sex, religion, nationality, ethnic origin, sexual orientation, disability, age, language, social origin or other status (UN, 2008); (b) the more generalised behaviours that can affect anyone are called emotional abuse or petty tyranny by the French (Bukspan, 2004), bullying in the English-speaking world (Lewis *et al.*, 2008), while in other countries, particularly Scandinavia, Germany and Italy, there is an additional term used to describe bullying involving a number of people attacking an individual (Leymann & Gustafsson, 1996).

Evil by nature or intent?

It is not surprising that people having experienced bullying use terms like evil, bully, tyrant and oppressor to describe the person they view as having treated them harshly or unfairly. Whilst it is possible that some people get pleasure out of hurting others (Vickers, 2002), people should recognise that not everyone who engages in bullying is wicked or evil. Damasio, a neurobiologist, has studied the interactions between the body, emotions and feelings and suggests that positive social behaviours have significant evolutionarily benefit and without these altruistic attitudes humankind would have become extinct long ago (Damasio, 2003). Instead of regarding the person who bullies as intrinsically evil, a more useful approach would be to see their behaviour as an aberration caused by an absence of positive attributes and an arrested state of development (Esselmont, 1980).

Workplace bullying

It is difficult to be precise in identifying the origin of workplace bullying. There are early descriptions of coercive and destructive behaviours within armies, monasteries, households and guilds. However, it is only with the industrial revolution and the move away from the cottage industries to labour intensive factories, foundries and offices that bullying has had the opportunity to develop within the workplace. Some of the earliest working communities were attached to the monasteries; 1500 years ago St Benedict recognised the negative effect of bullying and cautioned the following: 'If a brother, without the abbot's command, assumes any power over those older or, even in regard to boys, flares up and treats them unreasonably he is to be subjected to the disciple of the rule' (Benedict, 1982). Roman legions were well known for dealing with soldiers harshly, with floggings, breaking of bones and death sentences being used to enforce discipline, particularly among those in lower ranks (Fields, 2006). In the sixteenth century Machiavelli (2001) wrote his influential political treatise *The Prince*, dealing with the acquisition and maintenance of power. Machiavelli posed the following question: 'Is it better for a leader to be loved or feared?' His response was 'It is far safer to be feared than loved when one could not do both.' In Britain, Mrs Beeton (2000) provided nineteenth-century women with advice on how to manage their households. She criticised the abuse of servants and advised her readers that servants should be treated as reasonable human beings with no excuses being made for their shortcomings. At the beginning of the twentieth century Robert Tressell (2008) described the plight of a young woman in domestic service as a series of petty tyrannies, insults and indignities and years of cruelly excessive work which began two or three hours before the rest of the household were awake and only ended when she went exhausted to bed, late at night. Tressell also drew on his own experiences of working as a house painter in his description of bullying and oppression suffered by building workers where the older workers were constantly in fear of losing their jobs. An even more extreme bullying was found in the experiences of children working down mines, in textiles and other manufacturing industries. Interviews undertaken in the mid-nineteenth century by the Earl of Shaftsbury showed that the children were regularly beaten and bullied as they toiled by day and often at night in conditions of Dickensian squalor (Barkham, 2007). Up to 50 years ago fear was still a predominant feature of working life, with workplaces being hierarchical and autocratic, exposing workers to demeaning and oppressive behaviours with impunity (Snook, 2008). It is only during the past 30 years that western society has begun to recognise that bullying in the workplace is unacceptable and a cause of distress, illness and reduced productivity (Vega & Comer, 2005).

Bullying defined

Throughout this book the term bullying is used to cover the range of negative interpersonal behaviours observed in the workplace. There are many definitions of bullying, but one of the most useful was developed by Einarsen and colleagues:

> *A definition of workplace bullying*
> Bullying at work involves repeated negative actions and practices that are directed at one or more workers. The behaviours are

unwelcome to the target and undertaken in circumstances where the target has difficulty in defending him or herself. The behaviours may be carried out as a deliberate act or unconsciously. These behaviours cause humiliation, offence and distress to the target. The outcomes of the bullying behaviours have been shown to cause clinically significant distress and impairment in social, occupational, and other areas of functioning.

(Einarsen et al., 2003: 15)

In this definition of bullying there are four main features: (a) the behaviours need to be perceived as negative and unwelcome; (b) they have to be persistent and long-term; (c) they need to involve an imbalance in power; (d) they do not have to be intentional to cause bullying to have taken place.

Negative behaviours

The negative behaviours found in bullying fall into four main types:

1   *Personal derogation*: this includes the use of humiliation, personal criticism, ridiculing or demeaning comments to undermine the standing or integrity of the target.
2   *Intimidation*: where threats of physical violence or psychological intimidation, the misuse of power or position are used to create a situation where the victim feels unable to defend themselves or to take other forms of action.
3   *Work-related bullying*: in which the withholding of information, removal of responsibilities, work overload or where the credit for work undertaken is 'stolen' or not recognised as being undertaken by the target.
4   *Social exclusion*: where the target is cut off, isolated, scapegoated or sidelined by other employees.

Persistent and long term

To be classified as bullying the negative behaviours need to be repeated and persistent. Whilst it is unpleasant to be the target of someone's occasional aggressive behaviour, occasional behaviours are generally excluded from the bullying criterion. However, a single incidence of extreme bad behaviour can be regarded as bullying when the intimidating behaviour is of such a severity that the target is left in a permanent state of fear and anxiety. In some instances the bullying is subtle. Whilst it may be reasonable for a target to ignore or forgive an occasional expression of unwarranted irritation, when this occurs on a regular basis it should be regarded as bullying. As most of the bullying behaviours are commonplace it is not unusual for some bullying behaviours to continue for weeks or months before their true nature is recognised.

Imbalance of power

Whilst two or more workers of equal power having a difference of opinion may experience the exchange of views as a conflict, it is unlikely that this exchange would be regarded as bullying. However, when there is an inequality in the balance of power and this is used by the more powerful individual or group to undermine or subjugate another individual, this is bullying. Managers tend to be the main source of power in an organisation. However, there are more sources of power including the following:

- *Positional power*: this power is derived from the person's role or position. Managers and supervisors can abuse their power to impose unfair restrictions or rules affecting one or more people.
- *Relationship power*: this power relates to groups which may be established in order to usurp the rights and freedoms of workers outside the group. In some situations this group will be based on characteristics such as race, gender or ideology.
- *Resources power*: having access to resources is important, be it having the required technology, contact with senior management or the time to complete a piece of work. Removing scarce resources essential to the achievement of objectives can be an abuse of power.
- *Psychological power*: some people have the power to recognise a target's psychological vulnerabilities and then to exploit this knowledge to the target's detriment.
- *Knowledge power*: the abuse of this power can be observed when important information is delayed or withheld.
- *Delegated power*: this is an abuse of power at second hand. The abuser uses the power of their relationship with a second person to persuade them to undermine and/or threaten a target by proxy.
- *Personality power*: some people have a personality and presence which makes it difficult for others to challenge them or their

behaviours. These personality-driven behaviours can then be used to bully and intimidate.

Intent

The decision on whether bullying has taken place is not determined by the intention of the offender but rather by the nature of the behaviour. The defining principles used in establishing whether bullying has occurred are (a) was the behaviour unacceptable by normal standards of behaviour? (b) has this behaviour been disadvantageous or unwelcome to the target? However, intentionality does become relevant in understanding the impact of the behaviour on the target and in choosing the most effective intervention for the offender and target. There are three levels of intent:

- *Wilful intent*: where the behaviour was directed at the target with the intention of causing actual occupational, physical or psychological harm.
- *Instrumental intent*: where the negative behaviour was an unintended side-effect of a behaviour that was directed at achieving another goal.
- *Unintentional*: where the offender has a lack of sensitivity or awareness of the negative impact of his or her behaviour.

On occasions, the bullying associated with instrumental behaviours can be intentional. In these circumstances, the offender may attempt to hide his or her personal responsibility for the negative behaviours by blaming it on organisational policy or procedures or on other factors.

Individual bullying

Much of the literature on bullying, particularly that produced by support groups, has focused on individualised bullying involving a single bully bullying and one or more targets. In these accounts the descriptions are written by people who perceive themselves as being the innocent targets with the bully being described as behaving in ways that are at best dysfunctional and at worst psychopathic. Although some researchers have suggested that there are bullying and victim personality types (Randall, 1997), this is not a conclusion which has gained universal support (Einarsen, 1999). The more commonly held view is that there are important situational factors including culture, organisational change, poor training and an excessive use of competition that lead to higher rates of bullying (Hodson *et al.*, 2006). There are several types of individualised bullying: predatory, dispute related or escalating.

Predatory bullying

Predatory bullying occurs when the target of the bullying has done nothing to warrant the negative behaviour. The bully may be using the innocent victim to demonstrate their power to others or perhaps the victim belongs to an outgroup and is attacked because they are different and not part of the group. Predatory bullying occurs more often in organisations where the culture permits this kind of behaviour as the bully recognises they are unlikely to be punished for their negative activities. Targets of predatory bullying often find it difficult to understand what they have done to warrant the negative behaviours. This is not surprising as they do not need to do anything wrong to become targeted.

Predatory bullying – case notes

A secretary joined a media organisation working for a senior manager. Within a few days, she found that he was behaving very badly towards her. He would criticise her work pointing out errors in front of visitors. He would become angry whenever he was kept waiting. The secretary found out that he had behaved in the same way with all his secretaries and that no one had stayed long.

Dispute-related bullying

Dispute-related bullying develops out of a perceived slight or conflict that has been allowed to get out of hand with the result that the social climate in the workplace has become soured. Each participant in the dispute-related conflict comes to perceive the other person as having caused them harm. The attacks and counter-attacks escalate until the destruction of the opponent becomes the overriding goal. Dispute-related conflict can involve intense emotions leading individuals on both sides to experience feelings of fear, suspicion, resentment, contempt and anger.

Dispute-related bullying – case notes

Two research scientists had been working on a project. When one of the researchers made a breakthrough, he wrote a paper that failed to recognise the work undertaken by his colleague. From that time the two men would not work together and at every opportunity they would undermine each other. This attitude spread to their teams with the resultant loss of co-operation and support.

Escalating bullying

Escalating bullying can be explained by the way people attribute the reasons for their own and others' behaviours. When people consider their own behaviour they tend to attribute positive aspects to their personality and values and negative aspects to external circumstances such as their health or pressure at work. Typically, people looking at the behaviour of others see it the opposite way round. Negative behaviours are seen as due to personal characteristics and positive behaviours the result of external circumstances. In an escalating conflict, neither person is passive. As each perceived negative act occurs, the other player will respond according to their attribution of the intentions behind the act. As the atmosphere deteriorates, it is possible that both players come to believe that the other person is responsible for the breakdown of relationships and either may accuse the other of bullying.

Attribution of intention – case notes

A supervisor was walking down a corridor talking to a colleague. As they came to a door the supervisor held the door open for the colleague but let it close as Jill, another member of his team, walked up. Jill saw this as a deliberate act and felt upset. During the next week Jill thought about what had happened and began to notice more things about the supervisor and started to behave negatively towards him. This continued for a few weeks during which time the supervisor and Jill only noticed the negative behaviours of the other. Independently they went to human resources, Jill complained that the supervisor was bullying her and the supervisor said that Jill was being obstructive.

Complex bullying

While there are complexities in understanding the origin and processes involved in the development of bullying between two people, the situation becomes much more complex in an organisational setting where there are a number of players, a range of motivations, hidden agendas and old scores to be settled. The following four examples describe some aspects of complex bullying in organisations.

Delegated bullying

Sometimes the person perceived as undertaking the bullying is unaware of the role that they are playing on behalf of someone else, generally their manager. In order for this kind of bullying to occur the target has to be painted in a poor light by the manager. The target will be described to the naive bully (NB) as lazy, unco-operative, ineffective or difficult. Having established this expectation in the mind of the NB, the manager exerts pressure on the NB to bring the target into line. Common corrective measures might include close monitoring, isolation and the setting of unreasonable goals. The NB would be expected to report their actions on addressing the target's 'failures' to the manager. If the target experiences the NB behaviour as bullying it is not uncommon for the NB to be identified as a bully and the manager to escape criticism.

Bystander bullying

It is not always the primary target of bullying that is most affected by the behaviours of a bully. In some instances, the bully creates a situation where one person is picked upon unfairly and other people stand by watching helplessly but on occasions may take part in the taunting of the target. Research (Tehrani, 2004) has shown that bystanders can experience a high level of distress as a result of their feelings of guilt at being unable to support the victim and fear of standing up to the workplace bully.

Bystander – case notes

A CEO insisted on total unquestioning support. Anyone who raised issues or foresaw problems in his ideas was verbally attacked in management meetings and described as inflexible and resistant to change. Meetings of the senior team were characterised by personal attacks and anxiety about when their turn would come. Efforts to assist the target were rare with most of the senior managers sitting silent, waiting for the tirade to end.

Merry-go-round bullying

Merry-go-round bullying is a variant of bystander bullying. In this case the bully selects one member of a team at a time to bully; after a while the attention moves on to another team member. The team is constantly on edge wondering when it will be their turn to be bullied.

Mobbing or gang bullying

Mobbing involves gang bullying where the target is typically a team member or a manager. As mobbing is group behaviour, the bad behaviour from a single member of the mobbing group need not be particularly bad or frequent for the impact of the group behaviour to have a major impact on the target. If challenged it is much easier for individual mobbers to justify their infrequent bad behaviours.

Mobbing – case notes

Elaine could not drink alcohol due to a medical condition. Her job required her to attend residential events with colleagues. One of her colleagues kept drawing attention to her sobriety and over time others would join in insisting she have a drink and commenting that it could not possibly be bad for her. Elaine found this situation difficult and started to stay in her room or travelled home whenever possible. Her colleagues began to see her as odd and descriptions like 'kill-joy' and 'party-pooper' became commonplace.

Good guy/bad guy bullying

There are occasions when two or more individuals become involved in the bullying process. The good guy will befriend and appear concerned about the target while passing on information to the bad guy who uses the information to refine their bullying behaviour.

Good guy/bad guy – case notes

Judy was a homeworker, she had a good relationship with her previous boss but when a new manager joined the company she found his style brash and critical. She was having personal problems with her son who was playing truant from school. Sometimes she would talk to a colleague about how upset and vulnerable she was feeling. Her relationship with the manager grew worse and he seemed able to pick the most difficult times to put added pressure on her. After a few months her manager mentioned something that Judy had told her colleague in confidence. She then realised that he had been given personal information by the colleague and was using it against her.

Subordinate bullying

Although the power of the role or position can protect the jobholder from bullying, around 12 per cent of bullying in the UK is by subordinates (CIPD, 2004). Subordinate bullying can be subtle and may remain hidden for some time. Subordinates have the power to undermine, procrastinate, block, withhold information and fail to pass on important messages.

Subordinate – case notes

Sally joined an organisation as a middle manager. An internal candidate, George had been unsuccessful. A female subordinate

(Jenny), who was responsible for a key area of work, held back information that Sally needed to do her job. When Sally asked why information had not been given she would say 'I thought you would know that.' Sally also missed important meetings because messages were not passed on. Jenny and George began to talk to colleagues and others giving untrue examples of how Sally was unreasonable and incompetent.

Passive aggressive bullying

People use passive aggression as a way of undermining and manipulating others. Instead of being open in disagreeing, they will resist undertaking any tasks allocated to them and covertly sabotage or undermine the efforts of their manager and others. Passive aggressive bullies resist undertaking routine social or occupational tasks and constantly complain about being misunderstood or unappreciated. They can demonstrate a wide range of emotions depending upon what they wish to achieve. To a peer or subordinate they may be sullen or argumentative as a way of avoiding work. On the other hand, they may be playful and charming to get the attention of their manager. Passive aggressive bullies alternate between hostile attacks and contrition. They tend to emphasise their personal misfortunes, difficulties and needs as a way of manipulating others to provide them with help and support or to deflect blame.

Passive aggressive – case notes

Anne worked in a small office with Emma, another personal assistant. Some days Emma would be pleasant and cheerful but at other times she would not speak for days. Emma would put Anne under pressure to help her but when Anne did the work Emma would be on the internet doing her shopping. The situation got worse after Anne had booked a half-day's holiday and Emma left early leaving the office without cover. Emma insisted that Anne had deliberately failed to tell her that she was taking a half-day. A senior manager found Anne crying and met with Emma to discuss what was happening. Emma responded by raising a grievance against Anne.

Personality disordered bullying

Personality disorders are long-standing disturbances in personality that commonly begin in late adolescence and continue throughout life. People with personality disorders engage in repetitive patterns of behaviour in their occupational and other relationships. Usually the people suffering from personality disorders are unaware of the impact that their behaviour is having on others and frequently they do not believe that they have a problem. There are many types of personality disorder and some of the milder versions of the disorder are sometimes valued in the workplace where a single-minded approach can be viewed as an advantage. However, people with more developed personality disorders are difficult to handle due to the nature of their condition. They have difficulties in sustaining relationships with other people and see their own negative behaviours as virtues or strengths.

Organisational bullying

In recent years, it has been recognised that organisations can behave in a bullying manner (Liefooghe & MacKenzie Davey, 2001). Organisational bullying occurs in situations in which organisational practices and procedures are used to oppress, demean or humiliate the workforce. There are a number of different ways in which organisations can employ bullying tactics as a management style.

External pressure

Sometimes organisations are bullied by outside bodies including shareholders, customers and government agencies. Profit or performance targets may be set at a level that cannot be achieved without placing significant stress and pressure on the employees. A chief executive, managing director, head teacher or other leader required to bring about the changes is put in the difficult position where any failure to achieve the targets may result in some form of censorship whilst working to achieve the targets will cause extreme pressure and distress to the workforce.

History and culture

Organisational cultures tend to develop over time and are made up of shared beliefs, assumptions and behaviours. When organisational cultures are based on negative beliefs and assumptions then institutionalised bullying can occur. The following are examples of cultures that lead to bullying: blame cultures, gossip cultures and victimising cultures.

Senior team tactics

In some organisations, the chief executive may appoint a henchman or woman whose job it is to carry out harsh and uncaring actions, leaving the CEO with clean hands. When challenged, the CEO may even appear genuinely concerned about the negative behaviours, and may decide to punish the henchman/woman if things go too far. This process results from the CEO's difficulty in handling the harsh and the caring requirements of the role and splitting the role, allowing him or her to be caring while leaving his or her subordinate to hand out all the difficult and punishing messages (Hirschhorn, 1999).

Process bullying

When oppressive organisational practices are employed frequently and consistently, employees feel victimised by them. Examples of organisational bullying can include organisations excessively using statistics to manage workflow, or punishments such as withdrawal of overtime for failing to reach unreasonable performance targets. In organisational bullying, employees often recognise that their line manager is not the source of the problem but rather the bullying is related to the way in which the organisation goes about its business.

Strong management, healthy conflict and bullying

Many managers accused of bullying find it difficult to recognise themselves as behaving in a bullying or aggressive way. When line managers need to deal with a low performing team their role is to motivate the team to perform more effectively. The process of bringing about changes in the ways of working involves action in a number of areas such as agreeing standards, identifying and dealing with errors and mistakes, increasing productivity, achieving greater flexibility of roles, changing priorities and reducing unreasonable expenditure. If these changes are introduced and managed correctly they can achieve the required business improvements with little or no employee distress. However, if the line manager fails in his or her handling of the change accusations of bullying can occur (see Table 1.1).

Table 1.1 Strong management versus bullying

Addressing poor performance in teams	Strong management	Bullying
The performance issue is identified.	The identification involves looking at all the potential reasons for the performance deficit.	There is no attempt to identify the nature or source of the poor performance.
The views of the team or individual are sought to identify the causes.	The team/individual takes part in looking for the source of the problems.	There is no discussion of the cause of the poor performance.
New standards of performance are agreed.	Standards of performance and behaviours are set and agreed for the team and manager.	New standards imposed without discussion of what might be appropriate.
Failures to achieve the standards are handled as performance improvement issues.	Support is provided for individuals who are struggling. Where there is an unwillingness to comply, action is taken.	Ridicule, criticism, shouting, withholding benefits, demotion, teasing and sarcasm are used to deal with failure.
Recognition of contribution.	Improvements are rewarded.	No monitoring leading to a lack of recognition for efforts and arbitrary rewards.

Healthy conflict and bullying

A certain amount of disagreement and conflict is unavoidable in working life. When handled well conflict can lead to interesting and creative solutions. Healthy conflict occurs when people clash over their wish to pursue differing goals, competition for scarce resources or through a misunderstanding. It is important that differences of view are not suppressed as unless differences are brought into the open and dealt with they can fester and cause problems in the future.

One of the ways to distinguish between healthy and destructive conflicts which may lead to bullying is to identify the underlying reason for the conflict. Conflicts can either be related to an issue, idea or task or to personal values and beliefs. The resolution of issue-related conflicts is generally easier to achieve than a conflict related to a strongly held value or belief, although both could lead to bullying. Destructive conflict and bullying are more common in organisations where there is role ambiguity, a lack of co-operative working, a failure to share goals and objectives, a low level of trust, poor communication and a lack of respect (WHO, 2003). Bullying differs from healthy conflicts in that bullying always involves an abuse of power whereas in healthy conflict the participants are able to discuss the issue without wishing to undermine or show a lack of respect towards the person holding a different view on the issue.

Discussion

This introduction to *Workplace Bullying: Symptoms and Solutions* briefly sets the scene for the rest of the book, providing the reader with an indication of the nature and extent of workplace bullying. However, the main focus of this book is not to describe workplace bullying as a phenomenon but rather to show the negative impact that it has on workers and their organisations, and then to provide the reader with some well-tested and proven interventions and techniques to deal with workplace bullying. One of the most challenging aspects of working with bullying is the need to reflect on the nature of human relationships and to explore whether it is ever helpful to regard one party in a conflict as wholly evil or guilty and the other as totally innocent and blameless. Organisations and employees need to move beyond bullying and to deal with the antecedents, triggers and pressures which can lead to bullying.

References

Barkham, P. (2007) Beaten and bullied, Victorian child workers remain uncomplaining. *The Guardian*, Friday 7 September.

Beeton, I. (2000) *Mrs Beeton's Book of Household Management.* Oxford: Oxford University Press.

Benedict, St. (1982) *The Rule of St. Benedict in English*, ed. T. Fry. Collegeville. MN: Liturgical Press.

Bukspan, E. (2004) Bullying at work in France. *British Journal of Guidance and Counselling*, 32(3): 397–406.

Carroll, L. (1998) *Through the Looking Glass.* London: Penguin (first published 1872).

Chartered Institute of Personnel and Development (2004) *Managing Conflict at Work – A Survey of the UK and Ireland.* London: CIPD.

Damasio, A. (2003) *Looking for Spinoza – Joy, Sorrow and the Feeling Brain.* London: Heinemann.

Einarsen, S. (1999) The nature and causes of bullying at work. *Journal of Manpower*, 20(1/2): 16–27.

Einarsen, S., Hoel, H., Zapf, D., & Cooper, C. L. (2003) *Bullying and Emotional Abuse in the Workplace: International Perspectives in Research and Practice*. London: CRC Press.

Esselmont, J. E. (1980) *Bahaullah and the New Era*. Wilmette; IL: Baha'i Publishing.

Fields, N. (2006) *Roman Auxiliary Cavalrymen AD 14–193*. Oxford: Osprey Publishing.

Hirschhorn, L. (1999) *The Workplace Within – Psychodynamics of Organizational Life*. London: MIT Press.

Hodson, R., Roscigno, V. J., & Lopez, S. H. (2006) Chaos and the abuse of power: workplace bullying in organizational and interactional context. *Work and Occupations*, 33(4): 382–416.

Lewis, D., Sheehan, M., & Davies, C. (2008) Uncovering workplace bullying, *Journal of Workplace Rights*. 13(3): 281–301.

Leymann, H., & Gustafsson, A. (1996) Mobbing at work and the development of post traumatic stress disorders, *European Journal of Work and Organizational Psychology*. 5(2): 251–275.

Liefooghe, A. P. D., & Mackenzie Davey, K. (2001) Accounts of workplace bullying: the role of the organization. *European Journal of Work and Organizational Psychology*, 10(4): 375–392.

Machiavelli, N. (2001) *The Prince*. London: Penguin.

Randall, P. (1997) *Adult Bullying – Perpetrators and Victims*. London and New York: Routledge.

Snook, S. A. (2008) Forethought: a survey of ideas, trends, people and practices on the business horizon. *Harvard Business Review*, January: 16–17.

Tehrani, N. (2004) PTSD and bullying. *British Journal of Guidance and Counselling*, 32(3): 357–366.

Tressell, R. (2008) *The Ragged Trousered Philanthropist*. Oxford: Oxford University Press.

United Nations (2008) Prohibition of discrimination, harassment, including sexual harassment, and abuse of authority. Available at: http://daccess-dds-ny.un.org/doc/UNDOC/GEN/N08/238/36/PDF/N0823836.pdf?OpenElement (accessed October 23 2010). UN.

Vickers, M. H. (2002) Bullying as unacknowledged organisational evil: a researcher's story. *Employee Responsibilities and Rights Journal*, 13(4): 205–217.

Vega, G., & Comer, D. R. (2005) Sticks and stones may break your bones, but words can break your spirit: bullying in the workplace. *Journal of Business Ethics*, 58(1–3): 101–109.

World Health Organization (2003) *Raising Awareness of Psychological Harassment at Work – Advice to Health Professionals, Decision Makers, Managers, Human Resource Directors, Legal Community and Workers*. Geneva: WHO.

Part I

Impact and symptoms

Chapter 2

Impact of bullying on workers

Annie Hogh, Eva Gemzøe Mikkelsen and Åse Marie Hansen

Introduction

Four decades ago Carol Brodsky described how workers developed severe stress reactions following exposure to harassment or *bullying* at work (Brodsky, 1976). The harassed workers in Brodsky's interview study portrayed symptoms such as nervousness, irritability, chronic fatigue, insomnia, tension, memory problems, physical pains, aggression, depression and self-hatred. As such, the study presented a comprehensive description of the health damaging effects of bullying/harassment at work while at the same time introducing a new field of research. A decade later, the legacy was taken up by Leymann (1987). Since then the field of research has expanded greatly as have the number of studies documenting the detrimental effects of workplace bullying on targets' health and well-being (Hogh *et al.*, 2011). The primary aim of this chapter is to review the literature on individual consequences of bullying and to relate findings to the methodological developments that have taken place since Brodsky wrote his pioneering book. The second aim is to explain the negative health effects of bullying using the cognitive activation theory of stress (CATS) developed by Ursin and Eriksen (2004) as well as Williams's theory of social ostracism (Williams, 1997).

Psychological and psychosomatic stress reactions

Both quantitative and qualitative methods have been used to document the health effects of bullying at work. Also, in quantitative studies, bullying has been measured by means of either self-labelling (i.e. inquiring about exposure to bullying preceded by a definition) and/or by exposure to different negative acts (Nielsen *et al.*, 2011).

Very early quantitative research found correlations between self-labelled exposure to bullying and psychosomatic, psychological and physical symptoms (Einarsen & Mikkelsen, 2003). For instance, symptoms such as musculo-skeletal complaints, insomnia, anxiety, irritability and depression were reported by targets in different European countries (Einarsen *et al.*, 1996; Niedl, 1996; Zapf *et al.*, 1996b; O'Moore *et al.*, 1998).

In later quantitative studies measuring exposure to negative acts, researchers have reported symptoms of burnout (Meliá & Becerril, 2007; Mathisen *et al.*, 2008), and psychological and psychosomatic stress symptoms (Agervold & Mikkelsen, 2004; Meseguer de Pedro *et al.*, 2008) in different occupations. Other studies have found symptoms of anxiety, depression, mental strain and job-induced stress (Bilgel *et al.*, 2006; Niedhammer *et al.*, 2006; Meliá & Becerril, 2007; Nolfe *et al.*, 2008; Hauge *et al.*, 2010).

Using both self-labelled bullying and exposure to negative acts, a British study in 70 organisations found a strong correlation between frequency of bullying and physical and mental well-being; slightly more among men than among women. Larger correlations were found between frequency of negative behaviours and health effects than between self-labelled bullying and health effects (Hoel *et al.*, 2004). In this study, the authors also explored how different negative acts of a personal or work-related nature may be used as bullying behaviour and that this may have different negative consequences. For instance, women reported more symptoms than men, yet men reacted more strongly to persistent criticism of work and effort, being ignored and attempts to find faults. Women reacted more to negative acts such as hints that they should quit their job, pressure not to claim something to which they were entitled, having allegations made against them and repeated reminders of mistakes (Hoel *et al.*, 2004).

The early qualitative studies (Thylefors, 1987; Kile, 1990; Price Spratlen, 1995; O'Moore *et al.*, 1998; Mikkelsen & Iversen, 2002) demonstrated consequences such as reduced self-confidence, low self-worth, shyness, an increased sense of vulnerability as well as feelings of guilt and self-contempt.

A more recent qualitative study (N = 20) showed that targets had developed psychological and psychosomatic symptoms a few months after the onset of the bullying (Hallberg & Strandmark, 2006). In the beginning, targets were only symptomatic when at work. However, over time the symptoms became more chronic with targets reporting psychological symptoms such as inability to concentrate, mood swings, anxiety, sleep problems, fear and depressive symptoms, as well as psychosomatic symptoms such as headaches, respiratory and cardiac complaints, hypertension and hypersensitivity to sounds, etc. Moreover, if the targets had chronic diseases these tended to worsen.

Social and socioeconomic effects

Being bullied may also have various social and socioeconomic effects. For instance, Leymann (1987) suggested that bullying would inevitably lead to sickness absence. Likewise, Zapf and colleagues (Zapf *et al.*, 1996b) demonstrated that targets may use sickness absence as a means of coping with the bullying. Later studies have confirmed these findings (Kivimäki *et al.*, 2000; Voss *et al.*, 2004; Vingård *et al.*, 2005). For instance, a register-based study showed that the risk of long-term sickness absence (six weeks or more) was twice as high among frequently bullied Danish care workers than among non-bullied (Ortega *et al.*, 2011). In addition, more targets went to work even when they were sick, i.e. presenteeism (Hogh *et al.*, 2007). Hence, while long-term sickness absence puts their at risk of being fired, presenteeism may, in the long run, increase their level of stress, which might again lead to sickness absence and possible unemployment. Indeed, exposure to bullying seems to be associated with a risk of unemployment (Einarsen *et al.*, 1999; Mikkelsen & Einarsen, 2002) and early retirement (Dellve *et al.*, 2003; Matthiesen *et al.*, 1989).

An interview study of 30 targets of bullying (trade and commerce) may shed some light on the relationship between bullying and unemployment. Twenty-one of the targets were unemployed and almost all of them reported that this was due to their exposure to bullying and a resulting poor mental health. In addition, some thought they had lost their ability to work, partly because of an increased intolerance of stress and fear of customers. Moreover, an intense fear of job interviews prevailed – particularly among the recently bullied (Mikkelsen & Iversen, 2002).

Summary

The above cross-sectional studies show that bullying – whether self-labelled or measured by exposure to negative acts – is associated with a variety of both psychological and psychosomatic symptoms and stress reactions. The risk of taking sickness absence as well as going to work when feeling sick (presenteeism) is high and in both instances targets are at risk of being fired or made redundant. Qualitative studies may in this respect yield deeper insight into how exposure to bullying increases the risk of social and socioeconomic effects such as unemployment. Together, the studies show that: (a) there is more diversity in the way bullying/mobbing has been measured in recent years; (b) associations have been found between both self-labelled bullying and exposure to negative behaviour and health effects; and (c) health effects may be different between women and men. However, the presented studies are cross-sectional and cannot determine the direction of cause and effect. Yet, they demonstrate associations, which may be tested in longitudinal studies.

Longitudinal studies

Using a longitudinal design may make it easier to determine cause and effects, even though certain methodological issues must be considered (Zapf et al., 1996a). For instance, all variables should be measured at all time points and other variables should be considered as potential confounders. The time lag should also be carefully considered a well as assumptions of the time course of the variables under study.

Early qualitative studies indicated that bullying may have long-term negative effects on the targets' health and well-being (e.g. Kile, 1990). Later longitudinal studies have confirmed this. As such, long-term stress reactions were found in a five-year follow-up questionnaire study of a representative sample of the Danish working population who had been exposed to nasty teasing. Moreover, gender effects were demonstrated insofar as direct effects were found for women but not men. For both sexes, education, job and social class had no impact on the relationships between nasty teasing at baseline and health at follow-up (Hogh et al., 2005). Furthermore, a one-year follow-up study showed that being bullied during education may have health effects during the first year at work after graduation (Hogh et al., 2007). Symptoms such as mental health problems, somatic stress reactions or fatigue were seen even after adjusting for health problems at baseline.

A much higher risk of cardiovascular disease for targets of prolonged bullying was found in a longitudinal Finnish hospital study of primarily female employees (Kivimäki et al., 2003). The targets also had a four times greater risk of developing depressive symptoms.

A third study followed bullied targets (36 women and 12 men) with no previous significant psychiatric history for a year (Brousse et al., 2008). Interview and questionnaire data demonstrated that targets developed serious mental health problems such as depression and anxiety following exposure to bullying, leading to serious psychiatric pathologies. Around half of the targets reported feelings of shame and guilt for having been bullied. They also presented loss of self-confidence. On the more positive side, the study also showed that creating a distance from the bully seemed to have a positive effect on depressive symptoms.

Summary

These fairly recent longitudinal studies indicate that from a methodological point of view progress has been made in the investigation of bullying and health. Methodologically, the studies follow some but not all of the recommendations of Zapf *et al.* (1996a). The studies show that exposure to bullying at work may result in long-term health effects, and that there seem to be gender differences in the symptoms presented. The studies also indicate that prolonged exposure is highly detrimental to the targets' health and well-being. Lastly, one important although not surprising finding is that distancing oneself from the bullying behaviour, while continuing to work, may be beneficial.

Physiological effects

Bullying also has an impact on the physiology of the targets, affecting for instance sleep and stress hormones.

Sleep problems

Insomnia symptoms covering difficulties falling asleep, maintaining sleep and early morning awakening are widespread complaints (Ohayon & Partinen, 2002; Stewart *et al.*, 2006). Daytime consequences of insomnia symptoms are fatigue, mood changes, cognitive difficulties or daytime sleepiness which may lead to impaired quality of life (Léger *et al.*, 2001; Ohayon & Partinen, 2002; Stewart *et al.*, 2006). Further, lack of sleep is associated with increased risk of diabetes, cardiovascular disease and depression (Perlis *et al.*, 1997; Schwartz *et al.*, 1999; Nilsson *et al.*, 2004; Franzen & Buysse, 2008). One of the mechanisms involved might be an initially increased arousal, which subsequently disturbs sleep (Partinen, 1994). Poor psychosocial working environments, in which bullying and negative behaviour thrive, might create a vicious circle where poor sleep leads to decreased productivity and avoidance of daytime activities in turn leading to more stress (Linton & Bryngelsson, 2000). Sleep has important homeostatic functions, and sleep deprivation is a stressor that may have consequences for the brain, for instance, memory and cognitive functions as well as regulation of neuro-endocrine systems (McEwen, 2006). Studies have shown, that targets of bullying are more likely to have sleep difficulties (Rafnsdóttir & Tómasson, 2004; Hogh *et al.*, 2009), a lower sleep quality (Notelaers *et al.*, 2006), and they more often use sleep-inducing drugs and sedatives (Vartia, 2001) compared to non-bullied respondents. Sleep is a major path for restitution and is vital for health and well-being. The precise pathological processes behind the target's poorer health are not fully understood, but it is commonly perceived that stress reactions including sleep problems play a major role. Thus it seems plausible that sleep problems might provide a link between work-related bullying and poor health.

Physiological reactions

The 'fight-or-flight' response is the classical way of describing the behavioural and physiological response to a threat from a challenging or dangerous situation. The stress response is the activation of the autonomic nervous system and hypothalamo-pituitary-adrenal (HPA) axis. Activation is a normal response and as such not unhealthy. However, inadequate or excessive adrenocortical and autonomic function is deleterious for health and survival. It is when the fight/flight response occurs too frequently or is greatly prolonged that we begin to experience the negative effects of stress. This prolonged elevation may be due to anxiety, to constant exposure to adverse environments involving interpersonal conflict, and to changes in lifestyle and health-related behaviours that result from being under chronic stress (McEwen, 2007).

A few studies have addressed the physiological consequences of workplace bullying with biological measurements among targets who were still working (Kudielka & Kern, 2004; Hansen *et al.*, 2006). These studies have found an altered circadian cycle of cortisol secretion among targets. Similar results were reported among young adults where lower levels of salivary cortisol were found in male targets who reported having no feelings of anger about their experience compared to controls and those who did report anger (Hamilton *et al.*, 2008). A recent study (Hansen *et al.*, 2010) of a large number of occupationally active persons showed that frequently bullied employees, irrespective of gender, had poorer psychological health and a lower level of salivary cortisol compared to a non-bullied reference group. Occasionally bullied employees only had a poorer psychological health compared to a reference group. In conclusion, workplace bullying was associated with a low level of cortisol indicating a chronic reaction.

Coping with bullying in the workplace

Individual coping strategies play a central role in the stress process. Most targets seem to make an effort to stop the bullying by means of various strategies. However, earlier findings indicate that this is usually to no avail and hardly any manage to stop the bullying without help from others (Niedl, 1996; Hogh & Dofradottir, 2001; Zapf & Gross, 2001). A more recent qualitative study (N = 30) demonstrated that targets initially tried to solve the problem by means of confronting the bully or reporting to management (Mikkelsen, 2004). When this failed some attempted to control or suppress their negative feelings and tried to live up to the bully's demands. Others sought support from colleagues and/or superiors. After some time, the targets tried once again to solve the problem. When this approach failed, they contacted the union. This was usually followed by long-term sickness absence and subsequently they were either fired or quit their job.

An Australian study revealed that avoidance was the most common strategy used by targets of bullying, suggesting a perceived inability to defend oneself. Assertiveness was mostly used when the targets were exposed to work-related negative behaviours, where the consequences would lead to a reduction of their ability to perform their jobs (Djurkovic et al., 2005). Nonetheless, although stressing the importance of situational factors in determining coping strategies, the study also shows that many of the targets did not use assertiveness or seek help at all, and many used avoidance as their first and only strategy. Whether this is due to individual general tendencies to use avoidance strategies or fact-based estimations of the particular situation as hopeless remains to be further explored.

Unfortunately, some targets attempt to cope by means of drugs. As such, studies have shown that there seem to be an overuse of drugs among targets of bullying (Vartia, 2001). For instance, 20 per cent of Tyrolean targets took drugs repeatedly because of job problems as compared to 4.1 per cent of the non-bullied employees. The prevalence of drug consumption was even higher (85 per cent) when the employees were discontented with their jobs as well as exposed to bullying at work (Traweger et al., 2004).

Despite methodological limitations such as the use of cross-sectional designs, convenience sample targets, self-report measure and possible self-recall bias, the above studies give a clear indication of massive coping failure, which is likely to be very stressful at least for some individuals in as much as needs such as those of controllability and predictability are not met (Hogh et al., 2011).

Cognitive activation theory of stress (CATS)

The above review of research has shown that exposure to bullying may have highly detrimental effects on targets' psychological and physiological health as well as their social lives and self-esteem. Yet, the studies also show that some targets only exhibit moderate levels of stress reactions while others develop severe symptoms of stress such as depression and anxiety. The fact that many targets fail to put an end to the bullying no doubt contributes to the high level of stress symptoms demonstrated in the reviewed studies.

CATS offers a psychobiological explanation for the assumed relationship between stressful events and health (Ursin & Eriksen, 2004; Reme et al., 2008). The theory incorporates the cognitive evaluation of the situation and subsequent individual coping strategies. A core element in CATS is expectancy. It is the person's experience and evaluation of demands and expectancies of outcomes that determine whether the demands cause a stress response which may affect the health. In CATS, coping with stressors is defined as positive outcome expectancy and is related to psycho-physiology. In a stressful situation, it is not enough to have control. People must expect that this control leads to a good result. If this is not the case they may develop hopelessness (Reme et al., 2008). People have a need for self-esteem and tend to construe events in a way that enhances and maintains self-esteem (Brewin, 1988). Prolonged exposure to acts that the targets cannot cope with is likely to instigate the use of stable, internal causal attributions (Peterson et al., 1981). According to the hopelessness theory, internal, stable and global causal attributions for a negative event such as bullying often lead to feelings of hopelessness, reduced self-worth and depression (Abramson et al., 1978; Nielsen et al., 2005). Internal attributions of causality, however, are more likely when the bully is in a superior position (Nielsen et al., 2005) since this may make it even more difficult to cope.

Since being bullied by definition is associated with loss of control, the CATS theory provides a possible explanation of why exposure to bullying affects targets' health and also why some targets are better able to cope with the negative treatment than others.

A theory of ostracism

Some of the negative acts used in bullying are active and direct and often tend to be aggressive. Also many targets are subjected to the 'silent treatment'. For instance, co-workers and managers stop talking to them or otherwise exclude them from the work group. In some cases they are physically excluded such as when they are given an office or work station far from their colleagues. Indeed, bullying may be a process of social ostracism (Williams, 1997; Williams & Zardo, 2005). According to Williams and Zardo (2005) ostracism threatens four basic social needs that when fulfilled make us able to function in our daily lives and maintain our health and well-being. The first need is to belong to a significant social group. As such, being ignored, isolated and eventually excluded from the work group threatens this need and even more so if the targets do not belong to other social groups. The second need is to maintain a high self-esteem. This is difficult if you are not recognised, seen and appreciated by your colleagues and superiors. If communication with colleagues stops, this may leave the person powerless and helpless essentially conveying that he or she has ceased to exist socially (Einarsen & Mikkelsen, 2003). Bullying also threatens the basic need to feel in control of one's interactions with others and to be able to control the outcome of such an interaction. This may be difficult when bullied, since acting or trying to solve the problems may result in an escalation of the negative treatment (Zapf & Gross, 2001). Finally, people have the fourth need of maintaining a belief in a meaningful existence. According to Williams (1997), social exclusion may be subjectively perceived as a form of social death, especially if you are the only target. The immediate reaction to threats to these needs is pain, outrage, a depressed mood and physiological arousal. If the bullying continues and the target is unable to defend himself or herself, a feeling of resignation and hopelessness will emerge. People who are excluded from the community will feel alienated, depressed, helpless and worthless (Williams & Zardo, 2005).

Williams and Zardo's theory stresses the importance of basic needs, while emphasising the target's ability to cope or change the aversive social interaction. As such, the theory may also be integrated with the CATS theory.

Conclusion

This chapter demonstrates that exposure to bullying may have severely damaging effects on the targets' health and well-being and that their social and socioeconomic lives may also be affected. The recent longitudinal studies as well as the physiological studies yield invaluable contributions to the knowledge of the potential consequences of bullying. Nonetheless, we still need to identify the dynamic interplay between individual, situational and other factors in fully determining the impact of bullying on the targets. In this respect, we suggest that researchers focus even more on individual coping strategies. It is also important to take into consideration how organisational actions may impact on these processes and whether preventive measures in organisations actually reduce bullying at work and diminish the effects on targets and bystanders. Our common efforts are also important with respect to increasing awareness of the phenomenon in companies as well as in society as a whole.

References

Abramson, L. Y., Seligman, M. E. P., & Teasdale, J. D. (1978) Learned helplessness in humans: critique and reformulation. *Journal of Abnormal Psychology*, 87(1): 49–74.

Agervold, M., & Mikkelsen, E. G. (2004) Relationships between bullying, psychosocial work environment and individual stress reactions. *Work & Stress*, 18(4): 336–351.

Bilgel, N., Aytac, S., & Bayram, N. (2006) Bullying in Turkish white-collar workers. *Occupational Medicine*, 56(4): 226–231.

Brewin, C. R. (1988) *Cognitive Foundations of Clinical Psychology*. Hove, UK: Psychology Press.

Brodsky, C. M. (1976) *The Harassed Worker*. Lexington, MA: Lexington Books.

Brousse, G., Fontana, L., Ouchchane, L., Boisson, C., Gerbaud, L., Bourguet, D., *et al.* (2008) Psychopathological features of a patient population of targets of workplace bullying. *Occupational Medicine*, 58(2): 122–128.

Dellve, L., Lagerström, M., & Hagberg, M. (2003) Work-system risk factors for permanent disability among home-care workers: a case-control study. *International Archives of Occupational and Environmental Health*, 76: 216–224.

Djurkovic, N., McCormack, D., & Casimir, G. (2005) The behavioral reactions of victims to different types of workplace bullying. *International Journal of Organization Theory and Behaviour*, 8(4): 439–460.

Einarsen, S., & Mikkelsen, E. G. (2003) Individual effects of exposure to bullying at work. In S. Einarsen, H. Hoel, D. Zapf, & C. L. Cooper (eds) *Bullying and Emotional Abuse in the Workplace: International Perspectives in Research and Practice*. London: CRC Press.

Einarsen, S., Raknes, B. I., Matthiesen, S. B., & Hellesøy, O. H. (1996) Helsemessige aspekter ved mobbing i arbeidslivet. Modererende effekter av sosial stotte og personlighet/The health-related aspects of bullying in the workplace: the moderating effects of social support and personality. *Nordisk Psykologi*, 48(2).

Einarsen, S., Matthiesen, S. B., & Mikkelsen, E. G. (1999) *Tiden leger alle sår? Senvirkninger av Mobbing i Arbetslivet/Time Heals? Late Effects of Bullying at Work*. Bergen: Institutt for Samfunnspsykologi, Universitetet i Bergen.

Franzen, P. L., & Buysse, D. J. (2008) Sleep disturbances and depression: risk relationships for subsequent depression and therapeutic implications. *Dialogues in Clinical Neuroscience*, 10(4): 473–480.

Hallberg, L., & Strandmark, M. (2006) Health consequences of workplace bullying: experiences from the perspective of employees in the public service sector. *International Journal of Qualitative Studies on Health and Well-Being*, 1(2): 109–119.

Hamilton, L. D., Newman, M. L., Delville, C. L., & Delville, Y. (2008) Physiological stress response of young adults exposed to bullying during adolescence. *Physiology & Behaviour*, 95(5): 617–624.

Hansen, Å. M., Hogh, A., Persson, R., Karlson, B., Garde, A. H., & Ørbæk, P. (2006) Bullying at work, health outcomes, and physiological stress response. *Journal of Psychosomatic Research*, 60: 63–72.

Hansen, Å. M., Hogh, A., & Persson, R. (2010) Frequency of bullying at work, physiological response, and mental health. *Journal of Psychosomatic Research*. online.

Hauge, L. J., Skogstad, A., & Einarsen, S. (2010) The relative impact of workplace bullying as a social stressor at work. *Scandinavian Journal of Psychology*, 51: 426–433.

Hoel, H., Faragher, B., & Cooper, C. L. (2004) Bullying is detrimental to health, but all bullying behaviours are not necessarily equally damaging. *British Journal of Guidance & Counselling*, 32(3): 367–387.

Hogh, A., & Dofradottir, A. (2001) Coping with bullying in the workplace. *European Journal of Work and Organizational Psychology*, 10(4): 485–495.

Hogh, A., Henriksson, M. E., & Burr, H. (2005) A 5-year follow-up study of aggression at work and psychological health. *International Journal of Behavioral Medicine*, 12(4): 256–265.

Hogh, A., Ortega, A., Giver, H., & Borg, V. (2007) *Mobning af Personale i Aeldreplejen*. Copenhagen: National Research Centre for the Working Environment.

Hogh, A., Hansen, A. M., Bloch, C., Mikkelsen, E. G., Maier, C., Persson, R., et al. (2009) *Mobning og Negativ Adfærd på Arbejdspladsen*. Copenhagen: National Researchs Centre for the Working Environment.

Hogh, A., Mikkelsen, E. G., & Hansen, A. M. (2011) Individual consequences of workplace bullying/mobbing. In S. Einarsen, H. Hoel, D. Zapf, & C. L. Cooper (eds) *Workplace Bullying: Development in Theory, Research and Practice*, 2nd edn. London: CRC Press.

Kile, S. M. (1990) *Helsefarlig Lederskab. Ein Eksplorerande Studie/Health Endangering Leadership. An Exploratory Study*. Bergen: University of Bergen, Department of Psychosocial Science.

Kivimäki, M., Elovainio, M., & Vahtera, J. (2000) Workplace bullying and sickness absence in hospital staff. *Occupational Environmental Medicine*, 57: 656–660.

Kivimäki, M., Virtanen, M., Vartia, M., Elovainio, M., Vahtera, J., & Keltikangas-Järvinen, L. (2003) Workplace bullying and the risk of cardiovascular disease and depression. *Occupational and Environmental Medicine*, 60(10): 779–783.

Kudielka, B. M. & Kern, S. (2004) Cortisol day profiles in victims of mobbing (bullying at the work place): preliminary results of a first psychobiological field study. *Journal of Psychosomatic Research*, 56(1): 149–150.

Léger, D., Scheuermaier, K., Philip, P., Paillard, M., & Guilleminault, C. (2001) SF-36: evaluation of quality of life in severe and mild insomniacs compared with good sleepers. *Psychosomatic Medicine*, 63(1): 49–55.

Leymann, H. (1987) *Voksenmobning – Om Psykisk Vold i Arbejdslivet*. Copenhagen: Teknisk Forlag.

Linton, S. J., & Bryngelsson, I. (2000) Insomnia and its relationship to work and health in a working-age population. *Journal of Occupational Rehabilitation*, 10(2): 169–183.

McEwen, B. S. (2006) Sleep deprivation as a neurobiologic and physiologic stressor: allostasis and allostatic load. *Metabolism*, 55: S20–S23.

McEwen, B. S. (2007) Physiology and neurobiology of stress and adaptation: central role of the brain. *Physiology Review*, 87(3): 873–904.

Mathisen, G. E., Einarsen, S., & Mykletun, R. (2008) The occurrences and correlates of bullying and harassment in the restaurant sector. *Scandinavian Journal of Psychology*, 49(1): 59–68.

Matthiesen, S. B., Raknes, B. I., & Rokkum, O. (1989) Mobbing pa arbeidsplassen/ Bullying at the worksite. *Tidsskrift for Norsk Psykologforening*.

Meliá, J. L., & Becerril, M. (2007) Psychosocial sources of stress and burnout in the construction sector: a structural equation model. *Psicothema*, 19(4): 679–686.

Meseguer de Pedro, M., Soler Sanchez, M. I., Saez Navarro, M. C., & Garcia, I. M. (2008) Workplace mobbing and effects on workers' health. *Spanish Journal of Psychology*, 11(1): 219–227.

Mikkelsen, E. G. (2004) Coping with bullying at work: results from an interview study. In S. Einarsen & M. B. Nielsen (eds) *Fourth International Conference on Bullying at Workplace* (pp. 90–91). Bergen: University of Bergen.

Mikkelsen, E. G., & Einarsen, S. (2002) Basic assumptions and symptoms of post-traumatic stress among victims of bullying at work. *European Journal of Work and Organizational Psychology*, 11(1): 87–111.

Mikkelsen, E. G., & Iversen, G. F. (2002) Bullying at work: perceived effects on health, well-being and present job situation. In A. P. D. Liefooghe & H. Hoel (eds) *International Conference on Bullying at Work* (p. 31). London: Birkbeck, University of London.

Niedhammer, I., David, S., & Degioanni, S. (2006) Association between workplace bullying and depressive symptoms in the French working population. *Journal of Psychosomatic Research*, 61(2): 251–259.

Niedl, K. (1996) Mobbing and well-being: economic and personnel development implications. *European Journal of Work and Organizational Psychology*, 5(2): 239–249.

Nielsen, M. B., Matthiesen, S. B., & Einarsen, S. (2005) Ledelse og personkonflikter: Symptomer på posttraumatisk stress blandt ofre for mobbing fra ledere. *Nordisk Psykologi*, 57(4): 319–415.

Nielsen, M. B., Notelaers, G., & Einarsen, S. (2011) Measuring exposure to workplace bullying. In S. Einarsen *et al.* (eds) *Bullying and Harassment in the Workplace. Developments in Theory, Research, and Practice*, 2nd edn. London: CRC Press.

Nilsson, P. M., Roost, M., Engstrom, G., Hedblad, B., & Berglund, G. (2004) Incidence of diabetes in middle-aged men is related to sleep disturbances. *Diabetes Care*, 27(10): 2464–2469.

Nolfe, G., Petrella, C., Blast, F., Zontini, G., & Nolfe, G. (2008) Psychopathological dimensions of harassment in the workplace (mobbing). *International Journal of Mental Health*, 36(4): 67–85.

Notelaers, G., Einarsen, S., De Witte, H., & Vermunt, J. K. (2006) Measuring exposure to bullying at work: the validity and advantages of the latent class cluster approach. *Work & Stress*, 20(4): 288–301.

Ohayon, M. M., & Partinen, M. (2002) Insomnia and global sleep dissatisfaction in Finland. *Journal of Sleep Research*, 11(4): 339–346.

O'Moore, M., Seigne, E., McGuire, L., & Smith, M. (1998) Victims of bullying at work in Ireland. *Journal of Occupational Health and Safety – Australia and New Zealand*, 14(6): 569–574.

Ortega, A., Christensen, K. B., Hogh, A., Rugulies, R., & Borg, V. (2011) One year prospective study on the effect of workplace bullying on long-term sickness absence. *Journal of Nursing Management*, 19(6): 752–759.

Partinen, M. (1994) Sleep disorders and stress. *Journal of Psychosomatic Research*, 38: 89–91.

Perlis, M. L., Giles, D. E., Buysse, D. J., Tu, X., & Kupfer, D. J. (1997) Self-reported sleep disturbance as a prodromal symptom in recurrent depression. *Journal of Affective Disorders*, 42: 209–212.

Peterson, C., Schwartz, S. M., & Seligman, M. E. P. (1981) Self-blame and depressive symptoms. *Journal of Personality and Social Psychology*, 41(2): 253–259.

Price Spratlen, L. (1995) Interpersonal conflict which includes mistreatment in a university workplace. *Violence and Victims*, 10: 285–297.

Rafnsdóttir, G. L., & Tómasson, K. (2004). Bullying, work organization and employee well-being. *Laeknabladid*, 90(12): 847–851.

Reme, S. E., Eriksen, H. R., & Ursin, H. (2008) Cognitive activation theory of stress – how are individual experiences mediated into biological systems? *Scandinavian Journal of Work Environment and Health*, 6: 177–183.

Schwartz, S., Andersson, W. M., Cole, S. R., Cornoni-Huntley, J., Hays, J. C., & Blazer, D. (1999) Insomnia and heart disease: a review of epidemiologic studies. *Journal of Psychosomatic Research*, 47(4): 313–333.

Stewart, R., Besset, A., Bebbington, P., Brugha, T., Lindsay, J., Jenkins, R., *et al.* (2006) Insomnia comorbidity and impact and hypnotic use by age group in an national survey population aged 16 to 74 years. *SLEEP*, 29(11): 1391–1397.

Thylefors, I. (1987) *Syndabockar. Om utstödning och mobbning i arbetslivet Scapegoats/About Social Exclusion and Bullying at Work*. Stockholm: Natur och Kultur.

Traweger, C., Kinzl, J. F., Traweger-Ravanelli, B., & Fiala, M. (2004) Psychosocial factors at the workplace: do they affect substance use? Evidence from the Tyrolean workplace study. *Pharmacoepidemiol and Drug Safety*, 13: 399–403.

Ursin, H., & Eriksen, H. R. (2004) The cognitive activation theory of stress. *Psychoneuroendocrinology*, 29: 567–592.

Vartia, M.-L. (2001) Consequences of workplace bullying with respect to the well-being of its targets and the observers of bullying. *Scandinavian Journal of Work Environment and Health*, 27(1): 63–69.

Vingård, E., Lindberg, P., Josephson, M., Voss, M., Heijbel, B., Alfredsson, L., *et al.* (2005) Long-term sick-listing among women in the public sector and its associations with age, social situation, lifestyle, and work factors: a three-year follow-up study. *Scandinavian Journal of Public Health*, 33: 370–375.

Voss, M., Floderus, B., & Diderichsen, F. (2004) How do job characteristics, family situation, domestic work, and lifestyle factors relate to sickness absence? A study based on Sweden Post. *Journal of Occupational and Environmental Medicine*, 46(11): 1134–1143.

Williams, K. (1997) Social ostracism. In R. M. Kowalski (ed.) *Aversive Interpersonal Behaviors*. New York: Plenum Press.

Williams, K. D., & Zardo, L. (2005) Ostracism. The indiscriminate early detection system. In K. D. Williams, J. P. Forgas & W. von Hippel (eds) *The Social Outcast: Ostracism, Social Exclusion, Rejection, and Bullying*. Hove UK: Psychology Press.

Zapf, D., & Gross, C. (2001) Conflict escalation and coping with workplace bullying: a replication and extension. *European Journal of Work and Organizational Psychology*, 10(4): 497–522.

Zapf, D., Dorman, C., & Frese, M. (1996a) Longitudinal studies in organizational stress research: a review of the literature with reference to methodological issues. *Journal of Occupational Health Psychology*, 1(2): 145–169.

Zapf, D., Knorz, C., & Kulla, M. (1996b) On the relationship between mobbing factors, and job content, social work environment, and health outcomes. *European Journal of Work and Organizational Psychology*, 5(2): 215–237.

Chapter 3

Bullying and post-traumatic stress

Noreen Tehrani

> I must Create a System, or be enslav'd by another Man's.
> (William Blake, 1757–1827)

Introduction

Severe and long-term bullying causes psychological distress which impacts the physical and psychological well-being of bullied victims and can cause impairment in all aspects of life. As a clinician experienced in working with victims of terrorist bombings, major rail crashes, armed raids, rape, trafficking, body recovery, armed conflict and other major traumas, it was surprising initially to find that victims of bullying were suffering very similar symptoms and in the most extreme cases the symptoms had a more profound impact on their psychological and physical health and well-being. This chapter looks at the history and need for accurate diagnosis and classification of psychiatric conditions and the development of the diagnosis of post-traumatic stress disorder (PTSD). The controversy that surrounds this unusual diagnosis and the need to maintain boundaries to protect the disorder from trivialisation and overuse is described. The case for enabling severe bullying to be recognised under Criterion A-1 is provided, supported by evidence from research into the impact of bullying. Finally, suggestions are made on ways to look at traumatic exposures and address some of the problems faced in the existing classifications.

What is in a name?

In a world of chaos and uncertainty, one of the roles of the scientist is to create a sense of order through the naming and classification of things. The names chosen inevitably affect the way in which the animal, system or condition is perceived, with membership of a group conveying a status which can help or hinder the way in which the world comes to understand, respond and deal with it (Dorit, 2007). One of the first attempts at classifying diseases can be found in the Bills of Mortality (Woods & Shelton, 1997), which were used in sixteenth-century London to provide a weekly tally of people who had died with their cause of death. By the middle of the seventeenth century William Farr had established an early system for classifying diseases, which eventually developed into the International Classification of Diseases (ICD; Lilienfeld, 2007). The *Diagnostic and Statistical Manual* (DSM) was first published in 1952 by the American Psychiatric Association having been developed from a nineteenth-century census of mental health conditions (Grob, 1991). Since their development, the DSM and ICD manuals have become the touchstones of clinical diagnosis with revised versions; the *DSM-V* and *ICD-11* currently under development. The naming of diagnostic conditions provides significant benefits for clinicians, researchers, insurers, lawyers and patients through the creation of a common language for classifying, describing and treating mental illnesses. However, there have been concerns that the manuals have sought a consistency of diagnosis over the establishment of diagnostic validity and calls have been made for them to do more to capture the underlying mechanisms of dysfunction by reducing arbitrary boundaries between disorders and dealing with co-morbidity (Creamer, 2000; First, 2008). Given the advances in brain imaging technology, molecular genetics and neuro-endocrinology techniques (Yehuda, 1998; Insel *et al.*, 2010) there are calls for the next revisions of the manuals to group disorders not on the similarity of symptoms but rather into families sharing aetiology (McHugh, 2010).

Diagnosis of post-traumatic stress

PTSD has been one of the most contested diagnoses since its appearance in *DSM-III* (American Psychiatric Association, 1980). The current editions *DSM-IV-TR* (American Psychiatric Association, 2000) and *ICD-10* (World Health Organization, 1992) include PTSD, and whilst there are differences between classifications within essential features they are similar (Table 3.1). For a diagnosis of PTSD an individual needs to experience, witness or be confronted by an extreme stressor such as a threat of death, serious injury to self or to others and to have responded to that threat with intense distress, fear or horror (Criterion A). Importantly, PTSD is the only psychiatric condition, apart from alcoholism, with a prerequisite for a specific aetiological event to have

	DSM-IV-TR DSM Category: Anxiety disorders	ICD-10 ICD Category: Neurotic, stress-related & somatoform disorders
Stressor	The person has experienced, witnessed, or was confronted with an event or events that involve actual or threatened death or serious injury, or a threat to the physical integrity of self or others. The person's response involved intense fear, helplessness, or horror.	Arises as a delayed or protracted response to a stressful event or situation (of either brief or long duration) of an exceptionally threatening or catastrophic nature, which is likely to cause pervasive distress in almost anyone.
Pre-disposing factors	Not mentioned in the DSM diagnostic criteria.	Predisposing factors, such as personality traits or previous history of neurotic illness, may lower the threshold for the development of the syndrome or aggravate its course, but they are neither necessary nor sufficient to explain its occurrence.
Re-experience	Recurrent and intrusive distressing recollections of the event, including images, thoughts, or perceptions. Recurrent distressing dreams of the event. Acting or feeling as if the traumatic event were recurring. Intense psychological distress at exposure to internal or external cues that symbolise or resemble an aspect of the traumatic event. Physiological reactivity on exposure to internal or external cues that symbolise or resemble an aspect of the traumatic event.	Episodes of repeated reliving of the trauma in intrusive memories ('flashbacks'), dreams or nightmares.
Hyperarousal	Difficulty falling or staying asleep. Irritability or outbursts of anger. Difficulty concentrating. Hypervigilance. Exaggerated startle response.	There is usually a state of autonomic hyperarousal with hypervigilance, an enhanced startle reaction, and insomnia.

(Continued overleaf)

Table 3.1 Continued

	DSM IV-TR DSM Category: Anxiety disorders	ICD-10 ICD Category: Neurotic, stress-related & somatoform disorders
Avoidance	Efforts to avoid thoughts, feelings, or conversations associated with the trauma. Efforts to avoid activities, places, or people that arouse recollections of the trauma. Inability to recall an important aspect of the trauma. Markedly diminished interest or participation in significant activities. Feeling of detachment or estrangement from others. Restricted range of affect. Sense of a foreshortened future.	Persisting background of a sense of numbness and emotional blunting, detachment from other people, unresponsiveness to surroundings, anhedonia, and avoidance of activities and situations reminiscent of the trauma.
Duration	Duration of the disturbing symptoms is more than one month. Specify acute if duration of symptoms is less than three months, chronic if duration is three months or more and delayed onset if onset of symptoms is at least six months after the stressor.	The onset follows the trauma with a latency period that may range from a few weeks to months. The course is fluctuating but recovery can be expected in the majority of cases. In a small proportion of cases the condition may follow a chronic course over many years, with eventual transition to an enduring personality change.
Associated conditions	There may be increased risk of panic disorder, agoraphobia, obsessive-compulsive disorder, social phobia, specific phobia, major depressive disorder, somatisation disorder, and substance-related disorders.	Anxiety and depression are commonly associated with the above symptoms and signs, and suicidal ideation is not infrequent.
Occupational & social impact	The disturbance causes clinically significant distress or impairment in social, occupational, or other important areas of functioning.	Not mentioned in ICD diagnostic criteria.

occurred prior to a diagnosis being made. The following groups of symptoms are also required:

- the re-experience in flashbacks, dreams or thoughts about the traumatic event
- high levels of arousal including difficulty in sleeping or exaggerated startle response
- an avoidance of the traumatising stimuli and numbing of responsiveness.

These symptoms need to be present for at least a month from the time of onset. In *DSM-IV-TR* there is also a requirement for trauma victims to suffer significant distress or impairment in social, occupational or other important aspects of their life before PTSD can be confirmed.

Since its introduction there have been challenges to the notion that psychiatric disorder could be caused by extreme stress (Summerfield, 2001) with suggestions that the condition is a fad or sociopolitical construction (McHugh & Triesman, 2007). However, the increasing neurobiological and neurological evidence shows post-traumatic stress responses to be fundamentally different to the responses found to everyday stress, social anxiety and phobia (Yehuda & McFarlane, 1995; Etkin & Wager, 2007) and clinicians find this to be a useful diagnosis. Post-trauma responses, like many other disorders (Krishnan, 2005), are complex, exhibiting high levels of co-morbidity with major depressive disorder, anxiety (Shalev & Yehuda, 1998) and alcohol and drug disorders (Breslau, 1998). Clearly, it is impossible to develop a post-traumatic condition without a traumatising event. Over the years the diagnostic manuals have attempted to refine the types of exposures and events believed to be capable of causing PTSD without losing the 'special' features of PTSD. However, what is emerging is not a simple 'trauma-stimulus/trauma-response' relationship (March, 1993), but rather an awareness that exposure to a wide range of precipitating traumatic events can – in the presence of other potentiating factors such as previous traumatic experiences, level of exhaustion, mental health, personality, training and social support (Breslau, 2002; Ozer *et al.*, 2008) – increase the likelihood of PTSD. Nevertheless, Breslau (2009) has shown that some events are more likely to result in the development of post-traumatic symptoms, but regardless of the trauma type the most common response is to recover (McNally, 2004). Studies that compared the trauma symptoms of people who had experienced a recognised traumatic event and/or a distressing life event (e.g. bullying, relationship problems and chronic illness) have consistently shown higher levels of trauma symptoms recorded for life events (Joseph *et al.*, 2000; Gold *et al.*, 2005; Mol *et al.*, 2005; Robinson & Larson, 2010). Not surprisingly, much of the current debate on PTSD diagnosis involves the relative importance of the traumatic exposure and immediate (peritraumatic) responses versus the magnitude and duration of the post-trauma symptoms. Many researchers suggest that any further relaxation of Criterion A will lead to a trivialisation of the disorder (Spitzer *et al.*, 2007) or 'conceptual bracket creep' (McNally, 2003, 2010). However, in a field trial, allowing low magnitude events to qualify as triggers to PTSD had virtually no impact on the prevalence rates (Kilpatrick *et al.*, 1994, 2007) and has shown that broadening the stressor criteria has not led to a higher prevalence rate. An interesting challenge to the PTSD diagnostic criteria comes from the law, with lawyers contending that it is not for clinicians to decide what is trivial or significant in terms of events or causality; this decision should be determined in law (Large & Nielsen, 2010). In the light of the continuing problems with Criterion A, suggestions were made in the *DSM-IV* PTSD committee to abolish the requirement for a particular traumatic event as a prerequisite for the diagnosis of PTSD (McNally, 2004). This has been accompanied by the requirement to strengthen other parts of the diagnosis through focusing on the diagnosis-making process, ensuring that the traumatising experience of a severe threat to physical or psychological well-being is clearly linked to a current re-experience of multisensory intrusions accompanied by feelings of intense fear and horror (Brewin *et al.*, 2009). Consistency of diagnosis should be enhanced with the use of structured clinical assessments, supporting evidence from trauma diaries, observations of psychophysiological reactivity to reminders and where possible objective evidence from neuro-endocrine and neuro-imaging assessments.

Bullying and PTSD

Workplace bulling has been shown to cause a wide range of negative emotional, psychological and physical outcomes affecting the target's social, occupational, cognitive, emotional and other areas of functioning (Einarsen & Mikkelsen, 2003; Hoel *et al.*, 2003; O'Donnell *et al.*, 2010). Research has shown that targets of bullying experience high levels of avoidance, hyperarousal and re-experience responses linked to their bullying experience and indicative of post-traumatic stress disorder (Ravin & Boal, 1989; Leymann, 1990; Leymann & Gustafsson, 1996; Mikkelsen & Einarsen, 2002; Walsh & Clarke, 2003; Matthiesen & Einarsen, 2004; Tehrani, 2004; Balducci *et al.*, 2009; Bond *et al.*, 2010).

Whilst serious bullying is traumatic, the nature of the trauma tends to involve threats, undermining and humiliation rather than physical attacks. The negative acts questionnaire-revised (NAQ-R; Einarsen *et al.*, 2009) lists 22 negative behaviours commonly found in bullying. These behaviours involve work-related, person-related or physically intimidating bullying. The physically intimidating acts included exposure to outbursts of extreme anger, pushing or shoving, threats of violence and physical attacks. In the development of the NAQ-R 5000 UK workers were surveyed. It was found that 70 per cent had not experienced bullying, 5 per cent severe bullying and an additional 3 per cent physical abuse. There are many features of traumatic bullying which are also found in other traumatic events involving relational abuse, e.g. domestic violence (Roberts, 2000), stalking (Kamphuis *et al.*, 2003) and psychological torture (Turner, 2000). In each of these traumatic events the victim is trapped in a relationship where there are prolonged, repeated, negative, threatening behaviours from which it is difficult or impossible to escape. Whilst it may be possible to claim that in these different forms of relational abuse the victims experienced a threat to their physical integrity, this is by no means certain, leaving victims of physical attacks, emotional abuse, neglect, domestic violence and other long-term abusive relationships (Pelcovitz *et al.*, 1997; Roth *et al.*, 1997; Van der Kolk, 2002) feeling that their experiences have been trivialised by the system. In bullying, the traumatic experience is not primarily the events or occurrences but rather the state of fear and dread evoked by a known individual who, through their abusive behaviour and threats, becomes the most powerful person in the victim's life. Perpetrators use their position of power to control and undermine the targets' sense of safety, trust and self-worth, instilling terror and helplessness (Herman, 1992). The harm caused by bullying and other relational traumatic exposures has been given a number of names: complex PTSD (Herman, 1992), disorder of extreme stress not otherwise specified (DESNOS; Van der Kolk, 2002), prolonged duress stress disorder (Scott & Stradling, 2006) and post-traumatic embitterment disorder, (Linden *et al.*, 2007) in an attempt to provide some validation of the victims experiences.

Evidence for PTSD in victims of severe bullying

A number of studies have shown that victims of severe physical and psychological bullying experience symptoms of traumatic stress as measured by recognised traumatic stress questionnaires. The following outline of some of these studies gives an indication of the magnitude of trauma symptoms found in victims of severe bullying.

Leymann and Gustafsson (1996)

This study involved 64 victims of workplace bullying who attended a clinic specialising in the treatment of victims of psychological trauma. The bullied patients were taken through a comprehensive clinical assessment and completed a number of self-report questionnaires including the Impact of Events Scale (Horowitz, 1986); PTSS-10 (Raphael *et al.*, 1989); GHQ-20 (Goldberg, 1985); and Beck Depression Inventory (Beck *et al.*, 1961). The results showed that 81 per cent of the targets of bullying were experiencing intrusions most days and at least once a week, 67 per cent experienced high levels of avoidance symptoms and half the group had at least six symptoms of hyperarousal, with the rest (apart from one person) having at least two symptoms of hyperarousal. There was also a high level of co-morbidity with around three-quarters of the group experiencing moderate or severe depression and high scores on the GHQ. Leymann and Gustafsson found the results for the victims of bullying were higher than those found in train drivers who had run over someone (Malt *et al.*, 1993) and similar to those found in raped women (Dahl, 1989).

Mikkelsen and Einarsen (2002)

The aim of this study was to identify the prevalence and severity of PTSD symptoms in a self-selected group of junior teachers, nurses and trade union members. One hundred and eighteen targets of bullying took part in the study of which 90 per cent were women. Data was collected using a self-report questionnaire which provided a definition of bullying and then asked the participants: (a) whether they had experienced bullying; (b) the duration of the bullying; (c) who bullied them; (d) the nature of the bullying. The subjects were also asked to complete the Post-Traumatic Diagnostic Scale (PDS; Foa, 1995); the Negative Acts Questionnaire (NAQ; Einarsen & Raknes, 1997) and the World Assumptions Scale (WAS; Janoff-Bulman, 1989). The results showed that over three-quarters of the participants had symptoms indicative of PTSD and almost 30 per cent had experienced an event which met the *DSM-IV-TR* Criterion A requirements. The level of symptoms found in the individuals exposed to severe bullying were found to be significantly higher than those found in people who had been involved in accidents, fire, natural disaster, assault and combat (Foa *et al.*, 1997). Mikkelsen and Einarsen also showed that level of symptoms found in the bullied subjects were affected by the duration of bullying and whether bullying was still taking place. There was also evidence to show that victims of bullying regarded themselves to be less worthy, capable and lucky than their non-bullied colleagues and saw the world as lacking in benevolence, justice and predictability and other people as being unsupportive and uncaring.

Walsh and Clarke (2003)

This study involved workers from a community health trust and was designed to compare the impact of verbal and physical aggression and to identify whether it would make a difference if the employee was alone at the time of the attack or had recognised the possibility of the aggression occurring. The 126 employees who took part in the study had all used the trust's incident report form to notify that they had been exposed to aggression. Most of the participants were female nurses. Each employee was sent a questionnaire which required them to provide details of the incident, their level of training, expectation of the incident and exposure to similar incidents in the past and the Impact of Events Scale-Revised (IES-R; Weiss & Marmer, 1997). The results showed that most of the reported incidents related to physical aggression and in most cases the assailant was a patient. The level of reported symptoms was low but it was found that verbal aggression had higher impact overall and significantly more intrusive symptoms than physical aggression.

Tehrani (2004)

In this study, 165 care professionals were surveyed to establish the level of exposure of bullying as a target and bystander. Unlike the other studies, the participants in this study had not previously identified themselves as victims of bullying. The participants completed the survey whilst attending a training course unrelated to bullying. Demographic information including job status, age, gender and type of exposure to bullying was collected. The survey also included the Impact of Events–Extended (IES-E; Tehrani et al., 2002). The results showed that 36 per cent of men and 42 per cent of women had been bullied and that over 60 per cent had observed bullying taking place. Most of the bullying was psychological with less than 10 per cent involving a physical attack, with men being twice as likely to experience physical violence as women. Nine per cent of the employees were found to be experiencing trauma symptoms indicative of PTSD. However, the relationship between the avoidance, arousal, re-experience had changed when the IES-E data was factor analysed. The arousal and re-experience had formed a single factor which may indicate that the relationship between trauma symptoms in bullying is different to those found in victims of other traumas.

Matthiesen and Einarsen (2004)

In this study 102 participants were recruited from a victim organisation dealing with bullying. Three-quarters of the participants were women and had worked in administration, the health service or teaching. Each was sent a survey with a definition of bullying and asked if they had been exposed to bullying. They also completed the Negative Acts Questionnaire, IES-R, PTSS-10 and Hopkins Symptom Checklist (HSCL; Derogatis *et al.*, 1974). The results showed that between 60 and 70 per cent of the bullied group experienced severe psychological distress and PTSD.

Bond et al. (2010)

This study investigated the relationship between the psychosocial safety climate, bullying and PTSD. Most of the 139 police officers who took part in this study were male. Each officer completed the PSC (Dollard & Bakker, 2010), the NAQ and the Purdue Post-Traumatic Stress Disorder Scale-Revised (PPTSD-R; Lauterbach & Vrana, 1996). The results showed that workplace bullying was significantly related to post-traumatic stress symptoms and that a culture which was conducive to a sense of psychosocial safety could moderate the impact of bullying on post-traumatic stress symptoms.

There are some methodological problems with many of these studies, particularly the fact that most had previously identified themselves as being bullied and the diagnoses were made on the basis of self-report questionnaires, there is also a lack of supporting evidence from formal clinical screening, neuro-endocrinology and neuro-imaging. Nevertheless, the studies provide evidence of a level of avoidance, arousal and re-experience related to their bullying experiences and at the very least warrant further investigation.

Discussion

Diagnosing post-traumatic stress is unusual in that the causal circumstances (Criterion A-1) required to achieve a diagnosis are part of the diagnosis. There is an implied link between Criterion A-1 and the consequent symptoms and in the belief that some events have a unique ability to cause a response which is quantitatively and qualitatively different to other events regardless of other factors. As the diagnostic criterion has gone through various iterations to address the concerns of stakeholders, there have been accusations of causing over-diagnosis as well as failing to recognise the major life traumas. Given that a minority of people exposed to major traumas succumb to PTSD, it would seem reasonable to suggest that other factors have the agency to potentiate or ameliorate the traumatic event and that the assessment of trauma symptoms would be more accurate in determining the presence or absence of the disorder. Suggestions have been made to abolish Criterion A as the gatekeeper to PTSD (Brewin *et al.*, 2009; North *et al.*, 2009) with the diagnosis being based on an assessment of current experiences to the life event, the memory of which causes extreme fear or horror and symptoms of re-experiencing, avoidance and hyperarousal. This change would have the potential for including victims of bullying providing that the range and intensity of their symptoms met the PTSD criteria.

From a practitioner's point of view, the abandonment of Criterion A may not be particularly helpful. However, if it is retained it needs to be more useful in identifying the features of the traumatic experience which need to be considered. Table 3.2 illustrates four types of trauma which may be a helpful starting point of trauma assessment and would allow for bullying to be included within Criterion A and could be diagnosed as causing PTSD providing it met the more stringent symptom, duration and impairment requirements.

Table 3.2 Four types of traumatic exposures

Simple	Trauma related to a physical event, e.g. earthquake, car crash, accidental injury.
Relational	Trauma involving the perceived intentional behaviour of another person(s), e.g. kidnap, rape, bullying, robbery.
Developmental	Trauma which occurred at a time in life when the individual had not achieved the capacity to deal with it, e.g. child bereavement, loss of parent, child accident.
Complex	(a) Trauma related to a combination of two or more of the above, e.g. a car crash where the other driver was drunk, child sex abuse, school bullying.
	(b) A series of traumatic events which are connected by a repetition of one or more traumatic feature.

References

American Psychiatric Association (1980) *Diagnostic and Statistical Manual of Mental Disorders DSM-III*. Washington, DC: American Psychiatric Association.

American Psychiatric Association (2000) *Diagnostic and Statistical Manual of Mental Disorders DSM-IV-TR*. Washington, DC: American Psychiatric Association.

Balducci, C., Alfano, V., & Fraccaroli, F. (2009) Relationships between mobbing at work and MMPI-2 personality profile, posttraumatic stress symptoms and suicidal ideation and behaviour. *Violence and Victims*, 24(1): 52–67.

Beck, A. T., Ward, M., & Mock, E. (1961) An inventory for measuring depression. *Archives of General Psychiatry*, 4: 561–571.

Bond, S. A., Tuckey, M. R., & Dollard, M. F. (2010) Psychosocial safety climate, workplace bullying and symptoms of posttraumatic stress. *Organisational Development Journal*, 28(1): 37–59.

Breslau, N. (1998) Epidemiology of trauma and posttraumatic stress disorder. In R. Yehuda (ed.) *Psychological Trauma*. Washington, DC: American Psychiatric Press.

Breslau, N. (2002) Epidemiologic studies of trauma and posttraumatic stress disorder and other psychiatric disorders. *Canadian Journal of Psychiatry*, 47: 923–929.

Breslau, N. (2009) The epidemiology of trauma and posttraumatic stress disorder and other psychiatric disorders. *Trauma Violence & Abuse,* 10(3): 198–210.

Brewin, C., Lanius, R. A., Novac, A., Schnyder, U., & Galea, S. (2009) Reformulating PTSD for *DSM-V*: life after criterion A. *Journal of Traumatic Stress*, 22(5): 366–373.

Creamer, M. (2000) Posttraumatic stress disorder following violence and aggression. *Aggression and Violent Behaviour*, 5(5): 431–449.

Dahl, S. (1989) Acute respose to rape – a PTSD variant. *Acta Psychiatrica Scandinavia*, 80(355): 56–62.

Derogatis, L. R., Lipman, R. S., Rickels, K., Uhlenhuth, E. H., & Covi, L. (1974) The Hopkins symptom checklist: a self report inventory. *Behavioural Science*, 19: 1–5.

Dollard, M. F., & Bakker, A. B. (2010) Psychosocial safety climate as a precursor to conducive work environments, psychological health problems and employee engagement. *Occupational Psychology*, 83(3): 579–599.

Dorit, R. L. (2007) By any other name. *American Scientist,* 95(2): 118–120.

Einarsen, S., & Mikkelsen, E. G. (2003) Individual effects to exposure to bullying at work. In S. Einarsen, H. Hoel, D. Zapf, & C. L. Cooper (eds) *Bullying and Emotional Abuse in the Workplace: International Perspectives in Research and Practice*. London: CRC Press.

Einarsen, S., & Raknes, B. I. (1997) Harassment in the workplace and the victimisation of men. *Violence & Victims*, 12(3): 247–263.

Einarsen, S., Hoel, H., & Notelaers, G. (2009) Measuring exposure to bullying and harassment at work: validity, factor structure and psychometric properties of the Negative Acts Questionnaire-Revised. *Work & Stress*, 23(1): 24–44.

Etkin, A., & Wager, T. D. (2007) Functional neuroimaging of anxiety: a meta-analysis of emotional processing in PTSD, social anxiety disorder and specific phobia. *American Journal of Psychiatry*, 164: 1476–1488.

First, M. B. (2008) Changes in psychiatric diagnosis. *Psychiatric Times*, 25(13). Available at: http://www.psychiatrictimes.com/display/article/10168/ 1347847?pageNumber=2 (accessed September 10 2010).

Foa, E. B. (1995) *Posttraumatic Stress Diagnostic Manual*. Minneapolis, MN: National Computer Systems.

Foa, E. B., Cashman, L., Jaycox, L., & Perry, K. (1997) The validation of a self report measure of posttraumatic stress disorder: the posttraumatic diagnostic scale. *Psychological Assessment*, 9(4): 445–451.

Gold, S. D., Marx, B. P., Soler-Baillo, J. M., & Salone, D. M. (2005) Is life stress more traumatic than traumatic stress? *Journal of Anxiety Disorders*, 19: 687–698.

Goldberg, D. (1985) Identifying psychiatric illness among general medical patients. *British Medical Journal*, 291: 161–162.

Grob, G. N. (1991) Origins of DSM-I: a study in appearance and reality. *American Journal of Psychiatry*, 148(4): 421–431.

Herman, J. L. (1992) Complex PTSD: a syndrome in survivors of prolonged and repeated trauma. *Journal of Traumatic Stress*, 5(3): 377–391.

Hoel, H., Einarsen, S., & Cooper, C. L. (2003) Organisational effects of bullying. In S. Einarsen, H. Hoel, D. Zapf & C. L. Cooper (eds) *Bullying and Emotional Abuse in the Workplace: International Perspectives in Bullying Research and Practice*. London: CRC Press.

Horowitz, M. J. (1986) *Stress Response Syndromes*. Northville, NJ: Jason Aronson.

Insel, T., Cuthbert, B., Garvey, M., Heinssen, R., Pine, D. S., Quinn, K., Sanislow, C., & Wang, P. (2010) Research Domain Criteria (RDoC): toward a new classification framework for research on mental disorders. *American Journal of Psychiatry*, 167: 748–751.

Janoff-Bulman, R. (1989) Assumptive worlds and the stress of traumatic events: applications of the schema construct. *Social Cognition*, 7(2): 113.

Joseph, S., Mynard, H., & Mayall, M. (2000) Life-events and post-traumatic stress in a sample of English adolescents. *Journal of Community and Applied Social Psychology*, 10: 475–482.

Kamphuis, J. H., Emmelkamp, P. M. G., & Bartak, A. (2003) Individual differences in post-traumatic stress following post-intimate stalking: stalking severity and psychosocial variables. *British Journal of Clinical Psychology*, 42: 145–156.

Kilpatrick, D. G., Resick, H. S., Freedy, J. R., Pelcovitz, D., Resick, P. A., Roth, S., van der Kolk, B., *et al.* (1994) The posttraumatic stress disorder field trial: emphasis on criterion A and overall PTSD diagnosis. In T. A. Widiger,

A. J. Francis, H. A. Pincus, R. Ross, M. B. First, W. Davis, *et al.* (eds) *DSM-IV Sourcebook*. Washington, DC: American Psychiatric Press.

Kilpatrick, D. G., Resick, H. S., Freedy, J. R., Pelcovitz, D., Resick, P. A., Roth, S., *et al.* (2007) Posttraumatic stress disorder field trial: evaluation of the PTSD construct – criteria A through E. In T. A. Widiger, A. J. Francis, H. A. Pincus, R. Ross, M. B. First, W. Davis, *et al.* (eds) *DSM-IV Source Book*. Washington, DC: American Psychiatric Association.

Krishnan, K. R. R. (2005) Psychatric and medical co-morbitities of bipolar disorder. *Psychosomatic Medicine*, 67: 1–8.

Large, M. L., & Nielssen, O. (2010) Improving the reliability of the diagnosis of post-traumatic stress disorder in civil litigation. *Psychiatry and Law*, 17(1): 79–87.

Lauterbach, D., & Vrana, S. (1996) Three studies on the reliability and validity of a self report measure of posttraumatic stress disorder. *Assessment*, 3: 17–25.

Leymann, H. (1990) Mobbing and psychological terror at workplaces. *Violence and Victims*, 5: 119–126.

Leymann, H., & Gustafsson, A. (1996) Mobbing at work and the development of post-traumatic stress disorders. *European Journal of Work and Organizational Psychology*, 5: 119–126.

Lilienfeld, D. E. (2007) Celebration: William Farr (1807–1883) an appreciation on the 200th anniversary of his birth. *International Journal of Epidemiology*, 36(5): 985–987.

Linden, M., Baumann, K., Rotter, M., & Schippan, B. (2007) The psychopathology of posttraumatic embitterment disorders. *Psychopathology*, 40(3): 159–165.

McHugh, P. R. (2010) Psychiatry at stalemate. In D. Gordon (ed.) *Cerebrum 2010*. New York: Dana Press.

McHugh, P. R., & Triesman, G. (2007) PTSD a problematic diagnostic category. *Journal of Anxiety Disorders*: 21: 211–222.

McNally, R. J. (2003) Progress and controversy in the study of posttraumatic stress disorder. *Annual Review of Psychology*, 54: 229–252.

McNally, R. J. (2004) Conceptual problems with DSM-IV criteria for post-traumatic stress disorder. In G. M. Rosen (ed.) *Stress Disorder: Issues and Controversies*. Chichester: Wiley.

McNally, R. J. (2010) Can we salvage the concept of trauma in DSM-V? *The Psychologist*, 23: 386–389.

Malt, U., Karlehagen, J., & Leymann, H. (1993) The effect of major railway accidents on the psychosocial health of train drivers: a longitudinal study of the one year outcome after the accident. *Journal of Psychosomatic Research*, 8(37): 807–817.

March, J. S. (1993) What constitutes a stressor? The criterion A issue. In J. R. T. Davidson & E. B. Foa (eds) *Posttraumatic Stress disorder: DSM-IV and Beyond*. Washington, DC: American Psychiatric Press.

Matthiesen, S. B., & Einarsen, S. (2004) Psychiatric distress and symptoms of PTSD among victims of bullying at work. *British Journal of Guidance & Counselling*, 32(3): 335–356.

Mikkelsen, E. G., & Einarsen, S. (2002) Basic assumptions and symptoms of post-traumatic stress among victims of bullying at work. *European Journal of Work and Organisational Psychology*, 11(1): 87–111.

Mol, S. S. L., Arntz, A., Metsemakers, J. F. M., Dinant, G.-J., Vilters-Van Montfort, A. P., & Knottnerus, A. (2005) Symptoms of post-traumatic stress disorder after non-traumatic events: evidence from an open population study. *British Journal of Psychiatry*, 186: 494–499.

North, C. S., Suris, A. M., Davies, M., & Smith, R. P. (2009) Towards validation of the diagnosis of post traumatic stress disorder. *American Journal of Psychiatry*, 166(1): 34–41.

O'Donnell, S., MacIntosh, J., & Wuest, J. (2010) A theoretical understanding of sickness absence among women who have experienced workplace bullying. *Qualitative Health Research*, 20(4): 439–452.

Ozer, E. J., Best, S. R., Lipsey, T. L., & Weiss, D. S. (2008) Predictors of posttraumatic stress disorder and symptoms in adults: a meta analysis. *Psychological Trauma: Theory, Research, Practice and Policy*, 5(1): 3–36.

Pelcovitz, D., Van der Kolk, B. A., Roth, S., Mandel, F., Kaplan, S., & Resick, P. (1997) Development of criteria set and structured interview for disorders of extreme stress (SIDES). *Journal of Traumatic Stress*, 10(1): 3–16.

Raphael, B., Lundin, T., & Waeiseth, L. (1989) A research method for the study of psychological and psychiatric aspects of disaster. *Acta Psychiatrica Scandinavica, Supplementum,* 353: 1–75.

Ravin, J. M., & Boal, C. K. (1989) Post traumatic stress in the work setting: psychiatric injury, medical diagnosis, treatment and litigation. *American Journal of Forensic Psychiatry*, 10(2): 5–23.

Roberts, G. L. (2000) Evaluating the prevalence and impact of domestic violence. In A. Y. Shalev, R. Yehuda & A. C. McFarlane (eds) *International Handbook of Human Responses to Trauma*: New York: Kluwer.

Robinson, J. S., & Larson, C. (2010) Are traumatic events necessary to elicit symptoms of posttraumatic stress? *Psychological Trauma: Theory, Research Practice & Policy*, 2(2): 71–76.

Roth, S., Newman, E., Pelcovitz, D., Van der Kolk, B. A., & Mandel, F. A. (1997) Complex PTSD in victims exposed to sexual and physical abuse: results from the DSM-IV field trial for posttraumatic stress disorder. *Journal of Traumatic Stress*, 10(4): 539–555.

Scott, M. J., & Stradling, S. C. (2006) *Counselling for Post-Traumatic Stress Disorder*, 3rd edn. London: Sage.

Shalev, A. Y., & Yehuda, R. (1998) Longitudinal development of traumatic stress disorders. In R. Yehuda (ed.) *Psychological Trauma*. Washington, DC: American Psychiatric Press.

Spitzer, R. L., First, M. B., & Wakefield, J. C. (2007) Saving PTSD from itself in DSM-V. *Journal of Anxiety Disorders*, 21: 233–241.

Summerfield, D. (2001) The invention of post-traumatic stress disorder and the social usefulness of a psychiatric category. *British Medical Journal*, 322: 95–98.

Tehrani, N. (2004) Bullying: a source of chronic post traumatic stress? *British Journal of Guidance & Counselling*, 32(3): 357–366.

Tehrani, N., Cox, T., & Cox, S. (2002) Assessing the impact of stressful incidents in organisations: the development of the extended impact of events scale. *Counselling Psychology Quarterly*, 15(2): 191–200.

Turner, S. (2000) Psychiatric help for survivors of torture. *Advances in Psychiatric Treatment*, 6: 295–303.

Van der Kolk, B. A. (2002) Assessment and treatment of complex PTSD. In R. Yehuda (ed.) *Treating Trauma Survivors with PTSD*. Washington, DC: American Psychiatric Association.

Walsh, B. R., & Clarke, E. (2003) Post-trauma symptoms in health workers following physical, verbal aggression. *Work & Stress*, 17(2): 170–181.

Weiss, D. S., & Marmer, C. R. (1997) *The Impact of Event Scale-Revised*. In J. P. Wilson & T. M. Keene (eds) *Assessing Psychological Trauma and PTSD: A Practitioner's Handbook*. New York: Guilford Press.

Woods, R., & Shelton, N. (1997) *An Atlas of Victorian Mortality*. Liverpool: Liverpool University Press.

World Health Organization (1992) *The ICD-10 Classification of Mental and Behavioural Disorders*. Geneva: World Health Organization.

Yehuda, R. (1998) Neuro-endocrinology of trauma and posttraumatic stress disorder. In R. Yehuda (ed.) *Psychological Trauma*. Washington, DC: American Psychiatric Association.

Yehuda, R., & McFarlane, A. (1995) Conflict between current knowledge about posttraumatic stress disorder & its original conceptual basis. *American Journal of Psychiatry*, 152(12): 1705–1713.

Chapter 4

Ya'makasi[1] or the art of displacement in the corporate world

A target's perspective on the impact of workplace bullying

Sarah Vaughan

Introduction

This chapter presents a case narrative of a target of workplace bullying in higher education in France and explores, from an individual perspective, the negative and debilitating impact of the bullying on her physical, social and professional arena. Moral harassment (bullying) is a widespread phenomenon in France (Hirigoyen, 1998) where the proportion of people who become victims of bullying are similar to those found in other countries (Leymann, 1990). Whilst the issue of bullying in the workplace has gained greater recognition in France since it was introduced into labour and civil legislation in 2002, and more recently due to a wave of high profile cases in the automobile and telecommunications industry, it remains difficult to establish or address with the still limited awareness as to its impact and consequences for the targets.

Bullying has serious consequences and devastating effects for physical, mental and social health (Einarsen & Mikkelsen, 2003; Tehrani, 2004) that persist long after the bullying has stopped (Lewis *et al.*, 2002). Targets experience a range of physical and psychological health consequences including sleep disturbances, exhaustion, weight loss, panic attacks, depression and post-traumatic stress. Work is central to our lives and is essential in the building and shaping of our identity and search for daily meaning and recognition. Bullying can be a traumatic and overwhelming experience which violates the target's core values, challenging and impacting on their expectations of the world in general and their professional world in particular. Targets report decreased satisfaction with their work and careers (Tepper, 2000) and find their capacity to return to the hostile work environment or seek other employment undermined and threatened (MacIntosh, 2006). When forced to leave their jobs, their career paths become disrupted and financial burdens increase (Zapf, 1999).

The subject of the case study is a 52-year-old British woman (S) who has lived and worked in France for 30 years. The chapter will explore three phases: the bullying experience and its impact on the target's private and professional life; the rehabilitation plan and return to work; and lastly her post-bullying perspective in terms of the meaning of work, career perspectives and personal outlook on life.

The case

S was a senior management executive for a higher education institution in France where she had worked for 15 years, having occupied a number of senior management positions within the institution and won recognition for her expertise and competence from the different stakeholders (partner institutions, faculty, parents and management). At the time of the conflict (2005) the board made the decision to reorganise one of its departments and to integrate it under S's supervision. Soon after the reorganisation was implemented, S began to experience negative behaviours from a new directly reporting colleague (B) who, whilst remaining pleasant and apparently constructive and collaborative about the change process in public, was circulating rumours and spreading gossip about S behind the scenes. The behaviours intensified as B began to undermine S in meetings and question decisions previously discussed and agreed upon. Over a period of 18 months, the conflictual and aggressive behaviour escalated, becoming more overt, audacious, vindictive and personal in nature. B started to withhold or delay the communication of vital information with the result that all of S's attempts to move the new team forward were being sabotaged. The impact of this behaviour is illustrated in the following testimony written by S during the course of the bullying.

Testimony 1: The origins of the bullying behaviours

At the beginning of the conflict I did not realise what was going on. I had previously had to deal with contexts of change and the resistance of some members of staff to such change. I thought that as time went by things would fit into place. It was so insidious that I did not at first pick up on what was happening nor could I really put my finger on what was going wrong. I just kept on adapting, ignoring or making excuses for B's rude and disruptive behaviour, telling myself I wasn't being clear or supportive enough as a manager or that she was having a bad day. When I first approached the work inspector it was really to get advice on how to deal with B. She (the work inspector) was the first to mention the term workplace harassment: I was surprised and shocked. I had been in the institution for 15 years, was respected by staff, parents and students, had accompanied the organisation through different changes over the years and I was being bullied! I felt guilty and responsible for having caused the behaviour I was being exposed to and ashamed at not being able to do anything to stop B. I also felt weak and inadequate, because the term for me conjured up images of the playground bully, the tough guy, singling out a weaker one as easy prey. In a funny way, I was also relieved because what I was experiencing at last had a name. The problem with the term bullying is that it framed the behaviour as singular – one easily identifiable or single major inappropriate or violent act. But I was describing a string of small and insignificant acts (if taken individually) which I was almost too embarrassed to mention: the pattern and the regularity of the behaviour were only discernable after many months when it was, to all intents and purposes, too late and after the damage was done. As a consequence I struggled to gain recognition of what was happening and did not find the support I had expected from within the organisation.

After three months S officially consulted the work inspector responsible for the enforcement of labour legislation in the workplace. The work inspector made recommendations to the institution to take action in order to bring the behaviour to an end and to provide protection for S from further bullying behaviours. None of the numerous attempts by the business school to deal with the bullying which included mediation, liaison with the work inspector, alerting the work's doctor, written warnings and disciplinary proceedings were successful in bringing an end to B's negative behaviours towards S. The only change in B's behaviour was to become more discreet and avoid putting anything in writing: 'as overtly aggressive behaviour becomes unacceptable in a culture, the manifestations of aggression are transformed from observable behaviour to more subtle, less detectable actions' (Crawford, 1999). As the bullying behaviour escalated it severely undermined S's self-confidence and self-esteem and it became increasingly difficult for her to speak up or take action.

As a result of this bullying behaviour S became emotionally and physically exhausted and by July 2006 she felt totally overcome by the events of the previous two years and had reached the end of her capacity to cope with the continual undermining and bullying. She was forced to go on long-term sick leave from July 2006 to November 2007.

Testimony 2: The impact

For my colleagues my work performance did not appear impaired and I continued to meet challenging deadlines. However, behind the scenes, I was trying to compensate and preserve my self-identity by working harder and longer to meet the performance demands and keep up appearances. I was very quickly trapped in a vicious circle and my health went rapidly downhill: I had no energy, was having difficulty in sleeping, had lost considerable weight due to not being able to eat and in the last three months suffered panic attacks and sickness each time I entered the workplace. I was anxious, depressed and in considerable distress most of the time, exhausted from trying to confront my bully on a day-to-day basis. Each time I was aggressed in meetings, I could not physically leave the room; my legs would not carry me. I felt vulnerable, trapped and isolated, could not see how the bullying was going to end. I was telling colleagues my bully would not stop until she had killed me. For months I went to work in autopilot mode until waking one morning in July 2006 in the knowledge that I would not be able to go to work, not that day nor any other day in the foreseeable future.

The initial therapeutic support sought by S was to help her face the administrative and legal procedures which were involved in taking action to stop the bullying. She was also looking for some ways to bring about some relief from the considerable distress she was suffering on a day-to-day basis. S felt that the events of the previous two years had left her feeling humiliated and ashamed, they had deformed her self-image, crushing her self-belief in her professional context and in her private life. Her social and family life were significantly affected with the formally extroverted and outgoing S gradually withdrawing from all social contact, rarely leaving her home except to meet her basic needs and to pursue the administrative and legal proceedings that were sapping her energy. Her family and friends reacted in one of two ways: either to criticise her for not leaving the organisation, which might have been the most frequent or sensible strategy to adopt (Rayner & Cooper, 1997; Pithers & Soden, 1999) or to wonder why she had not shown the fortitude to stand up to the bully and defend herself. Friends and family gradually began to distance themselves as they grew tired of hearing the same story as S found herself incapable of talking about anything other than the bullying she had and continued to experience.

Testimony 3: Family and friends

I was overwhelmed by the whole process. I didn't understand what was happening to me, living constantly in a climate of fear with intense physical and emotional responses to anything related to my place of work. I suffered panic attacks, felt worthless, couldn't concentrate and started to feel quite paranoid, as each time I went out I would bump into someone connected to the bullying process. I felt constantly judged by others, family, friends and colleagues and withdrew from social contact leaving myself feeling detached from events and people. The sense of isolation I had felt at work extended into my home. For months, work had been the only subject of conversation. However, after some time I began to find it increasingly difficult and distressing to talk about the bully-ing and the subject rapidly became taboo. My husband was overwhelmed by the physical and psychological damage that was happening to me together with his own feelings of helplessness. This situation put considerable strain on what had been until then a supportive marriage; the marriage collapsed a few months later.

Part of the difficulty faced by S was the lack of awareness and familiarity with the impact of bullying on targets and organisations. It is a phenomenon that seriously and negatively affects both individuals and organisations (Hoel & Cooper, 2001), which can be likened to an acute crisis situation that shatters the victim's basic assumptions, threatens their psychological safety and well-being and poses a threat to the functioning and productivity of the organisation (Tehrani, 2004). There is substantive evidence that workplace conflict and bullying culminates in severe workplace injuries which can be identified with the *DSM-IV* criteria for post-traumatic stress disorder (Tehrani, 2004). In practice, the devastating nature of the bullying is difficult for bystanders to apprehend as much of the behaviour is unseen; only the insignificant and inconsequential aspects of the behaviours are perceived which cannot be measured or quantified. As a consequence, organisations and individuals brush off the negative behaviours, with apparent dispassion, as mere personality conflicts or conduct a psychological autopsy of the target in an attempt to explain the decline in physical and psychological health.

Testimony 4: Giving evidence

I felt the need to constantly repeat the details of my ordeal to others which was both traumatic and humiliating. I didn't feel that I was understood or supported by the professionals I met through the administrative and medical processes. It appeared to me that they had little awareness, knowledge or interest in workplace bullying. It did not help that the situation I was describing was one of upward bullying, that is the bullying of a manager by a subordinate, which is less frequent in occurrence and which took place in the cultural context of France where the organisational culture is more hierarchical than in other countries. For the French it is difficult to imagine how a manager could be bullied. Seen through a French lens events were open to interpretation. I was branded as oversensitive or reactive. The work inspector who carried out an enquiry interpreted the conflict as a result of cultural differences and personality clashes. The police, who were also involved in the formal complaint process, found the concept of upward bullying totally outside their frame of reference, a situation which was magnified by the hierarchical structure of the police force. The police officers involved found it difficult to connect the physical and psychological repercussions with the bullying context.

By 2007, S was in a state of despair as she had failed to get the recognition she so desperately needed to allow her to deal with the maelstrom of physical and emotional responses to her situation. Recognition of workplace bullying is still very much in its infancy in France, despite provision in public regulation. Only a few specialists, industrial doctors and mostly associations for the rights and support of victims deal with the subject in France (Hirigoyen, 1998). Whilst awareness has grown, it is treated with 'indifference, trivialization, even mockery' (Bukspan, 2004). S felt that she would need to find somewhere to go to receive the level of recognition and understanding she so sorely needed.

Testimony 5: Where can I find understanding?

I struggled to find help and support from practitioners who had some knowledge or understanding of the phenomenon and its impact on targets but I had no access to specialised support in my area of France. When I described the constant and intrusive thoughts and memories of the bullying, I was encouraged to forget about it or turn the page and move on. Surely I was not still thinking or mulling over such insignificant events! The traumatic nature of the bullying was not recognised and by extension, the haunting aspects of it not understood. Having to constantly describe my experience generated more stress and the subsequent emotional chaos made it difficult to label what had happened and provide an articulate and

coherent discourse. A year later I was still off work and struggling to deal with the effects of the bullying. The bullying had
seriously eroded my self-confidence and identity by taking
away any personal control or power – still being off work a
year later felt much like an extension of this disempowerment.
I was adamant however that I would return to work.

S decided to seek support in the UK because of the lack of provision
or support in her region of France, coupled with a limited understanding
of workplace bullying in general. She also had an intuitive feeling that
rebuilding and reconstructing the destroyed identity would be necessary
via her native language and within her own cultural frame of reference.
During the bullying process, language had been one of the tools and
tactics and during the legal and administrative enquiries her reactions as
an Anglo-Saxon came under close scrutiny and were judged negatively
in comparison with the Latin way.

The results of the initial psychological assessment confirmed S was
suffering from severe levels of anxiety, depression (HADS; Snaith &
Zigmond, 1994) and post-traumatic stress (IES-E; Tehrani *et al.*, 2002).
The process, conducted through weekly phone interviews or by email,
engaged S in a learning process and alliance with her therapist which
enabled her to progressively explore the events and the impact of
the bullying experience. The approach was open and interdisciplinary
(linguistics, psychology, traumatology) grounded in real life experience.

Testimony 6: Glimmers of hope

I can remember leaving the first interview during which the
assessment and structured interview had taken place and
feeling less isolated. Suddenly realising that this had happened
to many others and joining the statistics had a fabulous and
euphoric sense of belonging. I recognised that I wasn't going
mad and that my reactions and symptoms were consistent
with those found in other victims of bullying. As the therapeutic process got underway I discovered the challenges and
opportunities of working in another language to explore and

revisit the bullying process. Whilst I continued to experience considerable difficulty with the re-experiencing of the bullying, the use of English gave me a safe strategic refuge from which to work since it did not trigger the high levels of emotion and distress in the same way as the French narrative. By keeping the emotional intrusions at a distance I found it easier to use my analytical and problem-solving skills to think, plan and implement the rehabilitation plan. Talking about the bullying in English, however, seemed at times very neutral and hollow since it did not convey the kaleidoscopic flux of sensory, perceptual and emotional impressions present in the experience: I was concerned that I was not communicating and conveying to my therapist the intensity of the violence I had experienced.

Language is used to code past experience and personal events and is a primary means through which thoughts and emotions are labelled and later expressed (Altarriba *et al.*, 1999). In the case of a bilingual speaker such as S, more than one language is involved in encoding and processing events and experiences. Each language has distinct verbal and non-verbal characteristics – vocabulary, linguistic patterns, pitch, tone and speed – and S had processed the French language patterns as an integral part of the threatening behaviour. The therapeutic process presented a number of challenges for the monolingual therapist in addressing the specific issues facing S. It required providing a setting and modalities which would enable S to access and express the bullying experience and the associated emotions and physiological responses in a language other than that of the bullying itself.

Testimony 7: Therapeutic processing

The process chosen was holistic, action-focused, and empowering since it encouraged self-management – it gave me tools, techniques and tasks. For the first time in over a year I felt that I was, if not in control, at least a co-pilot in my recovery process. I was convinced I could recover my full health and return to work despite the challenges involved since, with appeals procedures pending, B was still in the workplace. My determination to do so was not always understood by friends and colleagues as many maintained the view that it would have been simpler to have left the organisation. I felt a strong need to return to the work and to disenfranchise myself from the fear and anxiety which hadn't previously dictated my life: 'It is not because things are difficult that we do not dare, it is because we do not dare that they are difficult' (Seneca, 5BC–65AD). I was also convinced that a full recovery entailed reclaiming my dignity in the organisation where I had been abused.

Workplace bullying, as a form of aggression, can be very potent. Beyond the physical and psychological consequences described by targets, the reputational consequences both to the private and professional self were immense. According to evolutionary hypotheses of aggression, a key function of verbal and physical aggression is to inflict cost, primarily on same-sex rivals. Whilst bullies typically select victims who cannot or will not retaliate (Olweus, 1978), if the target does not respond to the aggressive behaviour, this can lead to status loss (Nisbett, 1993). During the therapeutic process S had realised the interactionist nature of the bullying process in which particular features of the perpetrator, target, professional and organisational context had led to aggression as a strategic and evolved solution. Returning to the workplace was perceived by S as a response to the aggressive behaviour and as a way of confronting her aggressor as well as the organisational community. It proved to be an essential step in the healing process and marked a turning point in the integration of the experience, enabling her to reclaim her sense of honour, integrity and reputation.

Testimony 8: Returning to the workplace

My therapist supported me and helped me prepare to return to work: we set a target date and worked on a rehabilitation plan. The tools and techniques helped me at first to control the physical and emotional reactions, journalling and researching helped me to understand and make sense of what was happening and the tasks enabled me to set realistic goals and reach thresholds. Relaxation and visualisation techniques helped me to break the avoidance strategies constructed after the bullying experience and prepare to access the school's facilities, meet people involved in the case and above all overcome the difficulties related to the continued presence of B in the workplace. The therapeutic alliance had enabled me to understand and explore what had happened and the roles people played and why. I gained an understanding of my own role in the process and the impact my behaviour and reactions could have had on my bully. There were cultural issues with the regard to the notion of a rehabilitation plan which was an unfamiliar process for the works doctor. I therefore became the co-ordinator of my own rehabilitation plan, meeting the different parties (employer, work doctor, GP) to explain my needs, to identify the role of each stakeholder in the support process and negotiate the time frame and the conditions required to provide a safe environment to return to work. We agreed that I would return to work on a part-time basis initially and in a new role in the organisation which would not require any interaction with B or other members of my team who had played a role in the bullying process.

The return to work plan was respected, but despite the preparation there were difficulties in areas which S had not considered and as a consequence had not prepared herself to meet. The practical preparation of her workspace had been overlooked; some colleagues were unsure as to how to interact with S and as a result avoided any contact with her. S continued to find her physical and emotional responses being triggered by sensorial stimuli, notably the smell in her office and the sound of B's voice in the corridor. Despite these setbacks, within six months S had largely overcome the difficulties of exposure to these triggers and was successfully delivering projects on time in her new position. Her case was to prove a catalyst to initiate a reflection on the notion of duty of care within the organisation and S played a critical internal role in the process of initiating, constructing and developing the actions adopted in the school: a training programme for the executive board to raise awareness into the issues related to moral harassment and a conference on the theme for the student, academic and local business community.

Testimony 9: The long recovery

I continued to work on a part-time basis for two years, far longer than the initial six-month period of my rehabilitation plan. Some physical symptoms persisted for some time including difficulties in sleeping, digestive problems and fatigue. I continued to get support and advice from my therapist throughout the first year. Professionally I was on a high – all the challenges and objectives set had been met, and I had accomplished a track record I would have been proud of even in the pre-bullying days. It was clear, however, that my career perspectives were being 'capped' in the organisation. Whilst I recognised that with B still in the organisation it was difficult for the institution to find acceptable and appropriate options for me, I was forced to accept that I could never recover the central position I had previously occupied. This became a source of anger and sadness but with time I became resigned to that reality. I had worked hard to overcome the difficulties and consequences of the bullying but the organisational folklore continued to refer to the bullying incident and this polarised the organisation. Despite support from my director, I remained fragile in most people's minds and was often artificially protected by well-meaning colleagues, or exposed to disobliging comments, leaving me feeling disempowered. I had been very focused on the effects of the bullying on my life and that of my family but was shocked to discover at the executive board's strategic seminar how many of my colleagues, including those who had joined the organisation during my sick leave, had been traumatised by the ripple effect of the organisational, legal and social ramifications of my case.

The case polarised the organisation and seriously impacted the workplace climate. Colleagues (on both sides of the case) were traumatised by the 'banality of evil' (Arendt, 1963) they had witnessed, stigmatised by others because they had provided support or witness statements or were tainted by their participation (see Chapter 6, Bloch). As for the target, the events were just as 'undeserved and unjustified' (Keashley & Neuman, 2005). After two years in the workplace and despite the hurdles and difficulties, S believed strongly that she had accomplished her goals and focus on getting back to the future.

> ### Testimony 10: Moving on
>
> My health had improved considerably but I was still conscious of being careful, using relaxation techniques when in meetings with B, but this still took incredible levels of energy. I still continue to suffer from higher levels of anxiety and, whilst considerably alleviated, some of the symptoms of post-traumatic stress persist. However, I had accomplished the goals and objectives I had set for returning to work. I had reclaimed my well-being, dignity and confidence over the two years: now was the time to move on and join another organisation.

Conclusion

Despite growing public awareness and considerable research which has helped to discover and understand workplace bullying and harassment, in practice its nature and impact are still largely misunderstood or unrecognised. From legal, strategic and human relations perspectives, the cost of workplace bullying is far too great. Organisations have a legal and moral responsibility to understand the phenomenon in order to identify training needs and introduce prevention policies which can contribute to radically changing contemporary corporate culture.

The chapter places the reader in the arena of workplace bullying, to discover and understand it through a target's eyes. The destructive process is unwanted and unjustified, progressively entraps the target in a situation where they are unable to react or speak out, exacerbating their sense of humiliation and isolation. Communicating the overwhelming pain and damage it causes is vital: often blamed for the harm they endure, it results for many in suicidal thoughts and suicide. Targets need to feel heard and recognised. Above all the chapter seeks to show that recovery and healing is possible, even if it is a long and uphill process, which implies integration of the experience, integrity and becoming whole again and that the bullying experience can serve as a trigger for personal and professional change and growth.

Testimony 11: Learning

I often used the image at the time of the bullying that my house had been set on fire. Everything I had built, everything I had stood for and the very foundations of my 'self' had been destroyed. And it has taken time and will continue to do so to rebuild. Like the *Ya'makasi* I have developed techniques and endurance, have worked hard to rebuild my strength physically and mentally, thus enabling me to accomplish the acrobatics required in the workplace. I am profoundly different to the person I was before the bullying – not better or worse, just very different. I have undergone a journey of personal growth, have acquired new skills and above all an insight and an outlook which has changed my concept of who I am and of the priorities in my life. Work, for example, occupies a very different and probably more realistic place in my life today where I strive for a better work–life balance. I am more measured in terms of commitment and above all preserve non-negotiable time for myself and the things I love doing outside of work. Trust and safety are both issues which I address differently, being far more wary when entering personal and professional relationships.

I have reclaimed control of my health by becoming far more aware of and respecting my physical and emotional limitations, although I still have difficulty in accepting the invisible scars of the bullying. When tired, I am more reactive to sensorial stimuli, notably sounds, but the effects are less severe and it takes me less time to recover and regain mastery of the situation. When tired I am more likely to be nervous, uptight and panicky for no apparent reason.

The key has been the flexible and constantly adaptive therapeutic process which enabled me to understand and acquire a more constructive view of the bullying experience. Somewhere in that process, my focus on the bully and the need to see her become accountable disappeared and my focus shifted to what I needed. By making sense of it I was able to move beyond the negative effects and identify some positive outcomes.

Note

1 *Ya'makasi* originates from the Congolese Lingala language and loosely means 'strong mind, strong spirit'.

References

Altarriba, J., Bauer, L. M., & Benvenuto, C. (1999) Concreteness, context availability, and imageability ratings and word associations for abstract, concrete, and emotion words. *Behavior Research Methods, Instruments, and Computers*, 31: 578–602.

Arendt, H. (1963) *Eichmann in Jerusalem. A Report on the Banality of Evil*. New York: Penguin.

Bukspan, E. (2004) Bullying at work in France. *British Journal of Guidance & Counselling*, 32(3): 397–406.

Crawford, N. (1999) Conundrums and confusion in organisations: the etymology of the word bully. *International Journal of Manpower*, 20(1/2): 86–94.

Einarsen, S., & Mikkelsen, E. G. (2003) Individual effects of exposure to bullying at work. In S. Einarsen, H. Hoel, D. Zapf, & C. L. Cooper (eds) *Bullying and Emotional Abuse in the Workplace: International Perspectives in Research and Practice*. London: CRC Press.

Hirigoyen, M.-F. (1998) *Stalking the Soul*. New York: Helen Marx Books.

Hoel, H., & Cooper, C. L. (2001) The experience of bullying in Great Britain: the impact of organizational status. *European Journal of Work and Organizational Psychology*, 10(4): 443–465.

Keashley, L., & Neuman, J. H. (2005) Bullying in the workplace: its impact and management. *Employee Rights and Employment Policy Journal*, 8: 335–373.

Lewis, J., Coursol, D., & Wahl, K. (2002) Addressing issues of workplace harassment: counseling the targets. *Journal of Employment Counseling*, 39: 109–116.

Leymann, H. (1990) Mobbing and psychological terror at workplaces. *Violence and Victims*, 5: 119–126.

MacIntosh, J. (2006) Tackling work place bullying. *Issues in Mental Health Nursing*, 27(6): 665–679.

Nisbett, R. E. (1993) Violence and US regional culture. *American Psychologist*, 48: 441–449.

Olweus, D. (1978) *Aggression in Schools*. New York: Wiley.

Pithers, R., & Soden, R. (1999) Person-environment fit and teacher stress. *Educational Research*, 41(1): 51–61.

Rayner, C., & Cooper, C. (1997) Workplace bullying: myth or reality – can we afford to ignore it? *Leadership and Organization Development Journal*, 18: 211–214.

Snaith, R. P., & Zigmond, A. S. (1994) *The Hospital Anxiety Depression Scale Manual*. Windsor: NFER-Nelson.

Tehrani, N. (2004) *Workplace Trauma: Concepts, Assessment and Interventions*. London: Brunner-Routledge.

Tehrani, N., Cox, T., & Cox, S. (2002) Assessing the impact of traumatic incidents, the development of an extended impact of events scale. *Counselling Psychology Quarterly*, 15(2): 191–200.

Tepper, B. J. (2000) Consequences of abusive supervision. *Academy of Management Journal*, 43(2): 178–190.

Zapf, D. (1999) Organizational, work group related and personal causes of mobbing/bullying at work. *International Journal of Manpower*, 20: 70–85.

Chapter 5

When darkness comes

Workplace bullying and suicidal ideation

Angelo Soares

What kind of society is it, indeed, where one finds the profoundest solitude in the midst of millions; where one can be overwhelmed by an irrepressible desire to kill oneself without anybody being aware of it?

(Karl Marx/Jacques Peuchet)

Introduction

Someone once asked Freud during one of his conferences what one needs to be healthy in life. Everyone was expecting a long answer, but Freud simply answered: a healthy life is one of work and love – this, in a display of the centrality and importance of love and work in our lives. In *Civilization and Its Discontents* he wrote: 'The communal life of human beings had, therefore, a two-fold foundation: the compulsion to work, which was created by external necessity and the power of love . . .' (Freud, 1995: 43).

However, the balance between love and work has been difficult to achieve, and transformations of the worlds of the work over the last 30 years have made it more and more difficult. Work organisation and management models are conceived of and created for hypothetical human beings – ideals that exist only in theory which are very far from real daily life. Might one therefore commit irreparable acts because of work?

In several countries, the number of suicides and attempted suicides in the workplace has been increasing dramatically. Several letters left for family members or for union representatives mention 'bullying', 'work overload', 'lack of group cohesion' and 'management through fear' among other organisational reasons. Certainly, suicide is a complex phenomenon, related to a set of complex phenomena that evoke hopelessness and suffering. Work can constitute one of the reasons for suicide, and may in fact be one of its main catalysts. In France, many suicides have been recognised as work accidents. Two experts' reports on workplace suicides in two French organisations identify work organisation as the main reason for suicide. Neo-Taylorism, pressure for performance objectives, overtime, and the loss of the meaning of work, were identified as possible main causes. Workplace suicides may be associated with work organisation transformations which have led to a degradation of 'living together' in contemporary organisations – mainly through an individualisation of performance evaluation and a lack of recognition (Dejours & Bègue, 2009).

Research on suicide and work is still incipient and most research attempts to identify professions where there is a higher prevalence of suicide without analysing the causes that may be at the core of the prevalence. Our research indicates that work organisation may have a preponderant and significant role in suicidal ideation. Our objective will be to analyse two professional groups and the possible relationships between workplace bullying and suicidal ideation.

Bullying and suicide

Bullying is a corrosive organisational disease which degrades work conditions and the mental health of its victims while poisoning social relations at work. While it is not a new organisational phenomenon, it is a problem that is growing in contemporary organisations. Brodsky (1976: 2) defines bullying as being 'the repeated, persistent attempts of an individual to torment, frustrate, or otherwise break the resistance of someone else. It is a treatment that, with persistence, provokes, puts pressure on, scares, intimidates, or inconveniences another individual.' Leymann (1996) defines it as 'a destructive process, characterized by a series of hostile acts which, taken separately, may be seen as inconsequential, but when repeated, may have pernicious effects'. In this definition, it is important to observe a particular aspect of bullying; when one analyses each act separately, one risks trivialising this surreptitious form of violence, since each individual act may seem inoffensive. It is the synergistic and repetitive character of these acts that produce the destructive effects which end up psychologically breaking the target of bullying.

Bullying may be horizontal within the organisation (i.e. perpetrated by a colleague at work), vertically descending (i.e. when it comes down from above in the organisational hierarchy), vertically ascending (i.e. perpetrated by a subordinate), and mixed (i.e. if the bullying comes from two or more sources, such as a superior in association with a colleague). Contrary to other types of violence at work, bullying is a process constituted by different types of acts that develop over time. Since there is a process, it is important to understand how and when it establishes itself, so that we may prevent it or intervene as quickly as possible when it occurs. This is all the more important, for it is precisely at the beginning of the process that preventative measures may be the most efficient.

The individual consequences of bullying are catastrophic: career possibilities are broken and mental health is strongly affected by psychological distress, depression, post-traumatic stress, and even suicide. Indeed, several authors stress that bullying can lead to suicide without, however, having established this empirically (Leymann, 1996; Muller 2000; Bukspan, 2004; White, 2004; Dejours & Bègue, 2009). The question of suicidal ideation associated with bullying has already been studied among Norwegian (Roland, 2002), Canadian (Bonanno & Hymel, 2010) and Finnish students (Kaltiala-Heino *et al.*, 1999) as well as convicts in the Netherlands (Blaauw *et al.*, 2001). In spite of all existing differences between these studies (population, measurements, different methodologies), they signal a correlation between bullying and suicide risk. In the study of bullying among Norwegian students, Roland (2002) indicates that suicidal ideation is not only present among victims, but also among perpetrators.

In the literature on workplace bullying, Leymann (1996) indicates that suicide may be one of the consequences of this form of violence. More recently, in Italy, Pompili *et al.* (2008) indicate that bullied workers have a higher risk of suicide associated to hopelessness, rage and impulsivity provoked by workplace bullying. The authors indicate that victims of workplace bullying should be carefully assessed with a focus on suicide risk.

The media have reported many cases of suicides related to workplace bullying. In France, a case had great repercussions. VB, who was a 43 mother of four and an executive in the HR department of a French company, wrote in her diary the word 'Jump', with an arrow pointing downward. On 25 January, 2003, she jumped off a bridge located 500 metres from her workplace, leaving a letter to her union representative that was subsequently sent to the news media: 'It is not by chance that I make this gesture here, in front of my workplace. If I commit suicide today, it is that, as I frequently said, I cannot support the idea of returning to work in exactly same conditions that made me explode and that I have been suffering since January 2002, sent to coventry, lack of respect, (public) humiliation, moral suffering, no professional recognition' (Henry, 2003).

In Melbourne, Australia, in September 2006, a 19-year-old waitress killed herself after more than a year of abuse: 'She was held down by workmates, had fish oil poured in her bag, was drenched in chocolate sauce and was constantly told she was worthless. She was teased about a previous suicide attempt, and had rat poison left in her pay envelope' (Murphy & Doherty, 2010). Four workmates were convicted and fined over the 'vicious' workplace bullying.

Our objective here will therefore be to investigate the possible relationships between suicidal ideation, hopelessness and workplace bullying.

Methodology

We used a quantitative research strategy centred on the distribution of questionnaires by mail to two union groups representing professional workers in Quebec. The first group, traditionally female, is composed of professionals in the health sector (social psychologists, occupational therapists, dieticians, etc.). The second group, traditionally male, is composed of engineers. We developed a questionnaire using Leymann's Inventory of Psychological Terror (LIPT) for acts of bullying, and various scales relating to mental health, which was sent to both groups of subjects. The response rate for study I was 32 per cent (N = 613) and for study II, 32 per cent (N = 469). Taking into account our subject of research, we sent only one follow-up letter, so as to minimise any possible harassment feeling from the research process itself.

In study I, women constituted 80.8 per cent of the studied population, while in study II, 82 per cent of the studied population was men. It is important to note that no differences of age, gender or ethnic origin and the occupational group could be established in the two studies with regard to the symptoms of mental health. For study I, the average age was 40 years, and this group worked, on average, for nine years in the field, eight years at the current position, and eight years for the same employer. For study II, the average age was 43.5 years, and this group worked, on average, for 19 years in the field, seven years at the current position, and 15 years for the same employer.

Measures

Bullying

We used two methods of identifying individuals affected by bullying. The first measure was based on the Leymann Inventory of Psychological

Terror (LIPT). The second measure was constructed from a definition of bullying[1] elaborated from a question aimed at establishing the type of link between respondents and bullying at work. On the LIPT there are 45 questions related to different acts that may be used in bullying as well as questions to measure the frequency and duration of these acts.

Suicidal ideation

To measure suicidal ideation, we used the Beck Depression Inventory (BDI), where there is a question on thoughts about suicide and the desire to commit suicide. The question offers us the following possible answers: I don't think about committing suicide; I sometimes think about committing suicide, but I would go never through with it; I would like to commit suicide; I would commit suicide if the opportunity presented itself. The BDI is a validated instrument for self-evaluation often used for French-speaking populations to detect the severity of symptoms of general depression (Beck *et al.*, 1996).

Hopelessness

To measure hopelessness we used the Beck Hopelessness Scale (BHS). It is a validated self-evaluation instrument often used for French-speaking populations to evaluate the level of hopelessness of an individual. The BHS is a measure of pessimism and evaluates the individual's suicide risk. More particularly, the scale serves to measure negative images of the future (Beck & Steer, 1988).

Results

We established four groups of workers: those who never experienced bullying (NB); those who currently experience bullying (EB); those who have experienced bullying at work in the last 12 months (AB); and those who were witness to bullying (WB). Table 5.1 indicates the distribution of workers among these four groups. The results showed that between 29 per cent and 38 per cent of the professionals studied were either directly or indirectly affected by bullying. Present for more than six months for 77.2 per cent in Study I and 82.9 per cent for Study II, bullying is just as intense, since approximately 50 per cent of individuals in the two groups experienced it on a weekly basis.

In Study I, bullying was mainly from colleagues (horizontal, 54 per cent), while in Study II the bullying was from a superior (vertical, 50 per cent).

Table 5.1 Levels of workplace bullying found in studies I and II

		Study I (per cent)	Study II (per cent)
I experience bullying	EB	10.5	7.5
I experienced bullying in the last 12 months	AB	12.0	21.5
I witnessed bullying	WB	6.7	9.4
I never experienced nor witnessed bullying	NB	70.8	61.6

However, it should be noted that sometimes bullying was mixed when, for example, a superior associated himself or herself with a colleague of the target when engaging in bullying behaviour (23.7 per cent for Study I and 23.2 per cent for Study II).

In terms of gender, we did not find significant intra-group differences. In both studies, there were no gender differences with regard to the duration and frequency of bullying. Among the acts of bullying experienced in Study I, there were no significant differences between men and women among the ten most frequent episodes of bullying. In Study II, only one form of bullying showed significant differences in terms of gender: women were more likely than men to believe that their performances was being evaluated unfairly or in a negative or destructive way (ANOVA $F(1.461) = 3.88$, $p < 0.05$). There were also no gender differences with respect to the symptoms emerging from the various investigated mental health problems (psychological distress, depression, anxiety and hopelessness). However, differences were found to be significant when comparing the groups which experienced bullying with those that did not experience bullying.

Suicidal ideation

The individual is considered to have suicidal ideation when he or she thinks about committing suicide. Mishara and Tousignant (2004: 39) suggest that 'suicidal ideation is always present before a suicide attempt or a successful suicide'. The results of Table 5.2 reveal a significantly elevated level of suicidal ideation in individuals who experience bullying. The results of the analysis of variance are significant when comparing the NB groups (never bullied) with the two other groups, AB

Table 5.2 Three levels of suicidal ideation found in studies I and II

	Study I (per cent)			Study II (per cent)		
	NB	AB	EB	NB	AB	EB
I don't think about committing suicide	96.4	93.7	77.3	93.6	81.8	71.4
I sometimes think about committing suicide, but I would go never through with it	5.4	6.3	20.5	6.1	16.4	26.5
I would like to commit suicide	0	0	0	0.3	0	2.0
I would commit suicide if the opportunity presented itself	0	0	2.3	0	1.8	0

(bullied in the last twelve months) and EB (experienced bullying at the time of the research). Results for the witness group showed no difference to the results found in the group that had never been bullied. The probability that the differences between the three groups are due to sampling error is ($p < 0.05$).

Using the Scheffé test, multiple comparisons allowed us a more precise analysis. The average differences between the groups were statistically significant when the group that had experienced or was currently experiencing bullying was compared with those that had never experienced bullying. These results show that the average scores obtained by individuals who experience (EB) or that experienced (AB) bullying are significantly higher than the scores of individuals that had never experienced bullying at work (NB).

A positive correlation for the two studies was found between the duration of bullying and suicidal ideation (Study I: $r = 0.13$, significant to $p < 0.0001$, $N = 601$; Study II: $r = 0.19$, significant to $p < 0.0001$, $N = 455$). The same level of correlation has also been established with the frequency of bullying and suicidal ideation (Study I: significant $r = 0.19$ to $p < 0.0001$, $N = 602$; Study II: $r = 0.20$, significant to $p < 0.0001$, $N = 452$). These results indicate that when one experiences bullying, suicidal ideation is more likely to occur than when one has never experienced bullying. Exposure to longer term bullying and higher frequency bullying causes the suicidal ideation to become more intense.

Finally, there is an interaction between suicidal ideation and the perpetrators of bullying. Table 5.3 shows the presence of suicidal ideation according to the instigator of the bullying. For Study I, results of Table 5.3 indicate that when the bullying comes from a hierarchical superior (vertical), or from more than one individual (mixed), suicidal ideation is significantly increased in the bullied targets. The results of the analysis of variance are significant when comparing the groups bullied by a colleague (horizontal) and the two other groups (vertical and mixed). The likelihood of this result being due to a sampling error is very small ($p < 0.05$).

Using the Scheffé test for multiple comparisons, the differences in the averages between the groups are statistically significant when comparing the two groups, i.e. those that experienced horizontal bullying and those that experienced it in a vertical or mixed form. This means that the average scores of individuals who have been bullied by a colleague are significantly less than those of individuals bullied by a hierarchical superior or by several individuals. In Study II, despite similar tendencies, the results were found to be inconclusive.

Hopelessness

Hopelessness occurs when the ability to construct responses and solutions in the face of an event is blocked for the individual. The Beck Hopelessness Scale (BHS) is a measure of pessimism and the value of the individual's suicide risk. More particularly, the scale serves to measure a negative vision of the future.

Table 5.3 Suicidal ideation related to the status of the instigator of the bullying

	Study I (per cent)			Study II (per cent)		
	Horizontal	Vertical	Mixed	Horizontal	Vertical	Mixed
Without suicidal ideation	97.9	89.1	84.7	93.2	78.9	79.5
With suicidal ideation	2.1	10.9	15.3	6.8	21.1	20.5

The results of Table 5.4 indicate that symptoms of hopelessness are significantly more important in individuals who experience bullying. An analysis of variance shows an interaction between bullying and symptoms of hopelessness. For Study I, F = 9.0; p < 0.0001 and for Study II, F = 13.6; p < 0.0001, when one compares the NB group to the AB and EB groups. The results for the witness group are similar to the group that was never bullied. The probability that the differences between the three groups are due to sampling errors is small (p < 0.05).

Using the Scheffé test for the two studies, multiple comparisons allowed us more precise analysis. The differences of averages between the groups are statistically significant when we compared two groups: those that experienced or experience bullying, and those that never experienced bullying. This means that average scores obtained by the individuals who experience (EB) or who have already experienced (AB) bullying are significantly higher than those of individuals that never experienced bullying at work (NB). In the group of individuals that experience bullying in Study II, 14.3 per cent present a severe score of hopelessness and Study I, 6.8 per cent do so.

A positive correlation for the two studies has been found between the duration of bullying and symptoms of hopelessness (Study I: significant r = 0.19 to p < 0.0001, N = 603; Study II: r = 0.27, significant to p < 0.0001, N = 461. The same magnitude of correlation has also been established with frequency of bullying and symptoms of hopelessness (Study I: significant r = 0.22 to p < 0.0001, N = 603; Study II: r = 0.24, significant to p < 0.0001, N = 458).

When we analyse the results of Table 5.5, we find the same tendencies in relation to the type of bullying and suicidal ideation, that is, when the bullying is vertical (hierarchical superior), or mixed (several

Table 5.4 Levels of hopelessness found in the three groups in studies I and II

	Study I (per cent)			Study II (per cent)		
	NB	AB	EB	NB	AB	EB
Asymptomatic	71.9	59.8	36.4	63.3	42.9	36.7
Light	23.5	31.5	50.0	29.1	37.5	30.6
Moderate	4.3	7.1	6.8	5.8	14.3	18.4
Severe	0.3	1.6	6.8	1.8	5.4	14.3

Table 5.5 Levels of hopelessness related to the status of the perpetrator in studies I and II

	Study I (per cent)			Study II (per cent)		
	Type of bullying			Type of bullying		
	Horizontal	Vertical	Mixed	Horizontal	Vertical	Mixed
Asymptomatic	65.3	53.8	51.4	55.9	52.1	33.3
Light	32.6	32.3	37.5	30.5	21.9	42.2
Moderate	1.1	10.8	8.3	11.9	19.2	11.1
Severe	1.1	3.2	2.8	1.7	6.8	13.3

individuals), the symptoms of hopelessness are significantly more elevated in the target of bullying. The results of the analysis of variance are significant when one compares the horizontally bullied groups and the two other groups. The probability that the differences between the three groups are due to sampling errors is small ($p < 0.05$).

Using the Scheffé test for the two studies, multiple comparisons allowed us to note that the differences of the mean scores between the groups are statistically significant when comparing the two groups, i.e. those that experienced horizontal bullying, and those that experienced it in a vertical or mixed form. This shows that the mean scores found in individuals who have been bullied by a colleague are significantly lower than those of individuals that are bullied by a hierarchical superior or by several individuals.

Discussion

Taking the findings from the two studies, it is possible to state that when someone experiences workplace bullying, he or she is likely to have more suicidal ideation. Therefore, there is a link between workplace bullying and suicidal ideations. In both studies, sex and age do not appear to have any significant influence on the results. However, it is important to identify how this link is formed.

When considering the results for severe hopelessness (14.3 per cent in Study I, and 6.8 per cent in Study II), this appears to be an important finding as several studies have shown the predictive value of the Beck Hopelessness Scale in relationship to suicide attempts. Hopelessness appears to be an even more important feature than depression in suicide attempts (Beck *et al.*, 1975; Bouvard *et al.*, 1992).

Among the other factors associated with the incidence of suicidal ideation, the duration and frequency of bullying (even moderate bullying) seems to be influential. Interestingly, when the bullying occurs on a daily basis, suicidal ideation is less frequent. However, further research will be required to establish whether this tendency is statistically significant. Such a link appears possible since the unexpected nature of the bullying experience (sometimes it happens, sometimes it does not), is a characteristic that can destabilise the individual targeted by this pernicious form of violence. Coping strategies seem to be more difficult to deploy when the bullying is unstable.

The source of bullying appears to be important in the appearance of suicidal ideation; the bullying perpetrated by a colleague having less impact than that perpetrated by a hierarchical superior or a group of people. It is important to remember that bullying occurs within an existing power structure and relationships within the organisation and the use of coping or resistance strategies may be more difficult when the violence is coming from different sources or from a hierarchical superior.

An important point, not presented here, in the context of suicidal ideation, is the prevalence of symptoms of post-traumatic stress disorders among the individuals targeted by bullying (see, for example, Leymann & Gustafsson, 1996; Mikkelsen & Einarsen, 2002; Soares, 2002; Matthiesen & Einarsen, 2004; Soares, 2004; Chapter 3, Tehrani). In the two studies presented here, there are correlations between suicidal ideation and hopelessness and the scales used to measure post-traumatic stress are important. However, other studies, not related to bullying also establish a relationship between PTSD and suicide (e.g. Ben-Ya'acov & Amir, 2004; Tarrier & Gregg, 2004; Lebigot *et al.*, 2006; Vaiva *et al.*, 2007).

There are some limits as to the generalisation of the results obtained in these studies. We cannot generalise these results for the whole of the Quebec population, as the studies only examined two populations of professionals. Other research projects are required (and are in progress) to obtain a larger picture of bullying. It will be important to establish whether the results presented here will also be found in a population of blue-collar workers or of technicians. We hope to answer these questions in the future.

It is important to recognise that suicidal ideation does not necessarily lead to the individual committing suicide. There is an important difference between thinking about suicide and acting on those thoughts, although the research shows that suicidal ideation is always present before an attempted or successful suicide. Considerations should also be given to other organisational variables that may exist and their influence on suicidal ideation, for example, work overload, which may have a synergic relationship with bullying in the dynamics of the suicidal ideations. Other research is necessary to analyse those possible interactions.

We should consider how often workplace bullying has destroyed personal lives. Often, the target of workplace bullying ends up separating or divorcing from their spouse and from his or her circle of friends. It is not possible to separate 'to love and to work': suffering resulting from work will echo in personal lives, and vice versa. In this way, important sources of social support coming from outside of the workplace that may lessen suicidal ideation or hopelessness are also weakened and limited. It is important for health professionals, human resources professionals, and others intervening in workplace bullying cases to be aware and conscious of the possibility that targets of workplace bullying may have suicidal ideation, and this risk must be assessed and evaluated to ensure that the individual is not at risk of committing suicide.

We conclude with a metaphor used by Freud when he compared the human being to a crystal glass. As crystal glasses, we have all the same functions and we are similar. However, when we take a closer look we can also see the tensions, fragilities and impurities that lie hidden within. Thus, if we are dropped accidentally, we will each 'break' in our own different and unique ways. However, the pressure felt today from work organisation, management models and bullying is so intense that our crystal glass will inevitably break into thousands of pieces. It is simply a question of time.

One must be aware that the consequences of suicide are devastating at all levels (Kinder & Cooper, 2009). Even bystanders will be affected by bullying. Although they do not present suicidal ideations, they will experience high levels of stress (Soares, 2002; Soares, 2008; Chapter 6, Bloch). Organisations still underestimate the impact of this problem, and it is rare for an organisation to have an action plan on how and what to do in case of a suicide. Denial and individualisation are always the reactions to the problem. The fault is always laid on the individual without accepting at least part of the responsibility in terms of bullying or other organisational dysfunctions. Removing responsibility from the organisation or failing to make an appropriate response can further degrade work conditions, work organisation, work relations and social cohesion, and contribute to more cases of suicide.

Note

1 We used the following definition: 'Bullying at work may be defined as all actions (behaviours, statements, attitudes, etc.) which undermine, by their repetition, the dignity or integrity of a worker. It may be exercised by a colleague or a superior, and may take different forms: insults, humiliation, threats, blackmail, overt and covert accusations, unfounded insinuations, unjustified revenge, and constant criticism against the individual rather than his or her work.'

References

Beck, A. T., & Steer, R. A. (1988) *Beck Hopelessness Scale Manual*. New York: Psychological Corporation.

Beck, A. T., Kovacs, M., & Weissman, A. (1975) Hopelessness and suicidal behavior. *Journal of the American Medical Association*, 234: 1146–1149.

Beck, A. T., Steer, R. A., & Brown, G. K. (1996) *Beck Depression Inventory Manual*, 2nd edn. New York: Psychological Corporation.

Ben-Ya'acov, Y., & Amir, M. (2004) Posttraumatic symptoms and suicide risk. *Personality and Individual Differences*, 36: 1257–1264.

Blaauw, E., Winkel, F. W., & Kerkhof, A. J. F. M. (2001) Bullying and suicidal behavior in jails. *Criminal Justice and Behavior*, 28(3): 279–299.

Bonanno, R. A., & Hymel, S. (2010) Beyond hurt feelings: investigating why some victims of bullying are at greater risk for suicidal ideation. *Merrill-Palmer Quarterly*, 56(3): 420–440.

Bouvard, M., Charles, S., Guérin, J., Aimard, G., & Cottraux, J. (1992) Étude de l'échelle de désespoir de Beck (Hopelessness Scale). *L'Encéphale*, 18: 237–240.

Brodsky, C. M. (1976) *The Harassed Worker*. Lexington, KY: Lexington Books.

Bukspan, E. (2004) Bullying at work in France. *British Journal of Guidance & Counselling*, 32(3): 397–406.

Dejours, C., & Bègue, F. (2009) *Suicide et travail: que faire?* Paris: Presses Universitaires de France.

Freud, S. (1995) *Le malaise dans la culture*. Paris: Presses Universitaires de France.

Henry, M. (2003) L'envers du décor. *Libération*, 31 March: 1–3.

Kaltiala-Heino, R., Rimpelä, M., Marttunen, M., Rimpelä, A., & Rantanen, P. (1999) Bullying, depression, and suicidal ideation in Finnish adolescents: school survey. *British Medical Journal*, 319: 348–351.

Kinder, A., & Cooper, C. L. (2009) The costs of suicide and sudden deaths within an organization, *Death Studies*, 33(5): 411–419.

Lebigot, F., Nicolas, J.-D., & Hariki, S. (2006) Les tentations suicidaires du traumatisé psychique. *Revue Francophone du Stress et du Trauma*, 6(4): 207–212.

Leymann, H. (1996) *Mobbing – la persécution au travail*. Paris: Seuil.

Leymann, H., & Gustafsson, A. (1996) Mobbing at work and the development of post-traumatic stress disorders. *European Journal of Work and Organizational Psychology*, 5(2): 251–275.

Matthiesen, S. B., & Einarsen, S. (2004) Psychiatric distress and symptoms of PTSD among victims of bullying at work. *British Journal of Guidance & Counselling*, 32(3): 335–356.

Mikkelsen, E. G., & Einarsen, S. (2002) Basic assumptions and symptoms of post-traumatic stress among victims of bullying at work. *European Journal of Work and Organizational Psychology*, 11(1): 87–111.

Mishara, B. L., & Tousignant, M. (2004) *Comprendre le suicide*. Montréal: Les Presses de l'Université de Montréal.

Muller, M. (2000) Quand le management tue. *Le Nouvel Observateur*, 1842: 9–10.

Murphy, P., & Doherty, E. (2010) And they still won't say they're sorry. *Herald Sun*, 9 February: 1.

Pompili, M., Lester, D., Innamorati, M., De Pisa, E., Iliceto, P., Puccinno, M., *et al.* (2008) Suicide risk and exposure to mobbing. *Work: A Journal of Prevention, Assessment and Rehabilitation*, 31(2): 237–243.

Roland, E. (2002) Bullying, depressive symptoms and suicidal ideation. *Educational Research*, 44(1): 55–67.

Soares, A. (2002) Quand le travail devient indécent: le harcèlement psychologique au travail. *Performances*, 3: 16–26.

Soares, A. (2004) Comme 2 + 2 = 5 – Le harcèlement psychologique chez les ingénieurs d'Hydro-Québec: les conséquences. *Performances*, 18: 30–38.

Soares, A. (2008) Assédio moral: o stresse das vítimas e das testemunhas. *Segurança*, 184: 27–29.

Tarrier, N., & Gregg, L. (2004) Suicide risk in civilian PTSD patients. *Social Psychiatry Epidemiology*, 39: 655–661.

Vaiva, G., Ducrocq, F., Jehel, L., Genest, P., Duchet, C., Omnes, C., *et al.* (2007) Psychotraumatismes et risque suicidaire en France. *Revue Francophone du Stress et du Trauma*, 7(2): 69–77.

White, S. (2004) A psychodynamic perspective of workplace bullying: containment, boundaries and a futile search for recognition. *British Journal of Guidance & Counselling*, 32(3): 269–280.

Chapter 6

How witnesses contribute to bullying in the workplace

Charlotte Bloch

Introduction

Workplace bullying has been attracting an increasing level of attention in recent years. Research on workplace bullying has primarily been quantitative and focused on the links between organisational features and individual effects. In addition, both quantitative and qualitative research has concentrated on victims and perpetrators of bullying. Research into witnesses of bullying in the workplace has been limited (Agevall, 2007). In some of the original research into bullying (Heinemann, 1972; Olweus, 1973; Leymann, 1986; Adams, 1992) witnesses were not even mentioned, whilst in more recent research witnesses are rarely mentioned, and then only in terms of the experience of the victims (Hallberg & Strandmark, 2004) or the effect that bullying has had on witnesses such as reduced job satisfaction and productivity, increased stress and impaired well-being (Einarsen *et al.*, 2003), depression (Vartia, 2001; Lutgen-Sandvik, 2006; Niedhammer & Degioanni, 2006) or intentions to resign (Rayner, 1999). Whilst these studies show that witnesses to workplace bullying are influenced by the bullying process, little has been said on how witnesses become involved in the process. Workplace surveys show that witnesses are by far the largest group affected by bullying, with 35 per cent of respondents in a Danish survey (Hogh *et al.*, 2009) indicating that they had witnessed bullying. Other surveys show substantially higher levels of witnessing with Lutgen-Sandvik (2006) identifying that more than 80 per cent of employees had witnessed workplace bullying. Generally (Einarsen *et al.*, 2003), most employees report that they would support a victim of bullying, yet many victims of bullying indicate that they received little support from witnesses. Rayner (1999) found that although a third of witnesses said they wanted to help victims, they did not do so due to fear.

These results illustrate the complex relationship formed between witnesses, victims and perpetrators.

The aim of this chapter is to give voice to the witnesses and to examine the ways in which witnesses of bullying at the workplace participate in the bullying process. To this purpose I have conducted a qualitative study.

The study[1]

The study described in this chapter involved qualitative interviews with 40 employees and an in-depth analysis of 17 interviews undertaken with witnesses to bullying. In research a distinction was made between horizontal and vertical bullying. This study involves bullying among work colleagues. The analysis of the interviews was inspired by a number of micro sociological theories:

- *Clark's theory* (1990, 1997, 2004) which looks at how we interpret, feel and act towards people in trouble
- *interactional theory* (Goffman, 1967) which regards bullying as an insulting behaviour that affects not only the victim, but also the other players involved in the social order
- *deviance theory* (Becher, 1963) which asserts that the labelling of a person as deviant is not determined by their actions but rather by the assessment of what is acceptable and normal in the opinion of observers. Becher's theory provides an explanation of how witnesses identify and influence what is regarded as normal behaviour within the workplace.

The results of the study of witnesses to bullying among colleagues has been summarised in five analytical themes: interpretative schemas of who to blame; witnesses' emotions; micro-political actions and social place; sympathy etiquette, and denial.

Interpretative schema of who to blame

Bullying is a disturbance in social interaction, in which there needs to be an understanding of what really happens as well as what other people present believe has happened. The witnesses described how, through interpretation and classification, they constructed a moral schema with which to interpret who is to blame. These interpretations and classifications are not only a cognitive process, but also are connected to spontaneous emotions such as anger, indignation and irritation. A distinction can be made between three forms of moral blame:

1   Normalisation of the victim, i.e. an assessment that the victim's actions and behaviour were within the social norms of the workplace (*defender schema*).
2   Viewing the victim as a deviant in terms of the norms of the workplace (*prosecutor schema*).
3   Switching between views of the victim as a deviant and normal (*commuter schema*).

The way that witnesses used these interpretive schemas as a basis for negotiating normality and deviance at the workplace is now illustrated:

Normalisation of the victim (defender schema)

This mental schema places a positive emphasis on the victim as a person, emphasising the victim's normalcy, by using empathic descriptions of the victim and in the interpretations of the events that support this mental outline. The following is an example of this schema.

A witness talks about an incident involving a colleague. The colleague is a recent employee in a different department to the witness; it becomes apparent from the witness's story that the victim has used the witness as a confidante. It also emerges that the victim is aware that colleagues are talking about her and that she feels excluded from the group. Through the witness's narrative, the victim is construed as someone with socially positive characteristics. The witness emphasises that: 'she [the victim] had a really good education' and 'she really took her work function seriously'.

It can also be construed that the victim's colleagues have complained about the victim interfering with their work. In the witness's story, this behaviour is paraphrased as: 'If one of the others came and asked about something, or if she heard something wrong being said, she was quick to say, "Sorry, may I break in because I've just read the new rules in the area and I know that changes have been made".'

In the witness's story the behaviour of the victim which colleagues experience as meddling have been transformed into a description of the victim being polite, helpful and technically up to date. The witness construes the victim as behaving within a normal range and rejects the colleagues' definition of her as a social deviant. When the interviewer asked whether the victim deviated from the norms of the department, the witness responded: 'Well, she did a little, she was the one who often said things ... there are some people who like calling a spade a spade.' This quote indicates that the witness's view of the victim's behaviour, whilst deviating from the norms of the perpetrators, was still positive.

Witnesses who unequivocally categorised victims as normal often described themselves as having experienced bullying and that this influenced their interpretation of the behaviour. These witnesses characterised the victims as having positive social and work-related characteristics, whilst perpetrators were regarded as demonstrating negative social and occupational behaviours.

The victim as a deviant (prosecutor schema)

This schema is expressed through a neutral presentation of the perpetrators and a characterisation of the victims as moral and occupational deviants. This schema is similar to the perpetrator's interpretation. Witnesses with this mental schema reject bullying as a sanction whilst maintaining that the victim's behaviour is deviant. The following is an example of this schema.

A witness describes the bullying of some colleagues as follows: 'Well, I have seen some employees [perpetrators] who are more insistent than others because they don't feel that the employees [they criticise] are such good workers, so they let them know it through vague remarks.' This neutral description is rejected when the victims are described as 'some people who may not be as enthusiastic about their work as their colleagues are'; 'who take things a bit more easily'; 'who may have been at the workplace for a long time and have slackened a little'; 'who are slapdash and try to cheat others'; and 'whose professional standards are not in order and who are not interested in them either'. The witness then gathers the negative descriptions into the following stigmatisation: 'I would say that the group we've been talking about all the time, purely socially they probably belong to a group that are lacking in terms of – now we're talking about on the home front too – but also purely, it's so difficult to say again, intellectually, you know.'

The witnesses who made use of the prosecutor schema did not spend much time empathising with the victims; rather they classified the victims as deviants and the cause of their own difficulties.

The victim as both victim and deviant (commuter schema)

This mental schema is demonstrated in an expression of ambivalence and doubt, where the witness fluctuates between viewing the victim as normal and then as deviant. The following is an example of this mental schema:

A witness describes an episode during which the employee has been exposed to bullying. It takes place at an organisation dealing with freight transport. The witness describes the victim initially in positive social terms: 'He [the victim] was actually highly educated too, he was an engineer actually, but he was different from the rest, had no time for that macho jargon.' The victim is described in terms of his positive characteristics, but as a deviant in terms of the prevalent culture. However, the witness also distances himself from this culture by his use of the negative expression 'macho jargon'. The witness is ambivalent in relationship to the victim: 'Well it was the way he acted, if you can put it that way, his hands were put on the wrong way and he was very unfortunate and awkward all the time and destroyed things, which wasn't so funny for the person with whom he worked.'

The witness is uncertain as to whether the victim is completely unable to do his job, unfortunate and awkward, or whether the problem was in the workplace. According to the witness's description, the victim does silly things that have negative consequences and which leave him open to teasing and banter. The witness expresses his doubts in the following quote: 'Sometimes I suspected him of doing some things deliberately, maybe to get attention.' And 'He always grinned and smiled, but it seemed to be a mask.' This witness is uncertain of the extent to which the victim's behaviour should be interpreted as an attempt to gain attention, or an attempt to survive in the culture by playing the fool. The witness reports having taken part in the bullying, but also wishes to be dissociated from the main perpetrator, whom he described as having negative attributes, such as being 'narrow-minded, aggressive, and muscle bound'.

Witnesses who presented the commuting schema blame the victim and the perpetrator in turn. While the witnesses tried to understand and empathise with the victims, they also supported the perpetrators' interpretation of the victim as deviant.

Examination of the 17 witness stories showed that ten witnesses presented variants of the commuter schema, four of the defender schema and three of the prosecutor schema in their interpretation of the bullying observed.

Witnesses' emotions

Emotions connect and separate us from each other. Respect, sympathy, admiration and love connect whilst disrespect, contempt, gloating, hostility and irritation separate. Victims of bullying are in a vulnerable position; sympathy or pity will connect and create social bonds, whilst gloating and irritation will break the bonds causing separation. Clark's theory of empathy and sympathy is useful in understanding the bonding between the victims and witnesses. In the following accounts the witnesses' feelings are analysed from this perspective.

Separating emotions

Witnesses who categorised victims as deviants (the prosecutor schema) expressed emotions of dissociation from the victim. They described being irritated with people who 'did not pull themselves together', and gloated when the victims were exposed to negative acts, in statements such as: 'But deep down I'm thinking that you also deserved that [negative action].' They were contemptuous in their condescending descriptions of the victims, expressing patronising sympathy such as: 'They're only shooting themselves in the foot', and righteous indignation that the victims through their own actions had deserved the negative acts.

On the other hand, witnesses employing the defender and the commuter schema expressed empathy and emotions that allowed for the formation of social bonds with the victim.

Empathy

Clark (1997) distinguishes between cognitive and emotional empathy. The following witness stories illustrate the different forms of empathy they experience with victims. Some described cognitive forms of empathy: 'But I talked to him [the victim] several times. After all, I was curious and irritated at the same time [about the victim's norm-breaking behaviour], and I wanted to know how he felt.' This quote shows that the witness does not understand the behaviour of the victim, but rather than categorising him as a deviant, tries to understand how the victim thinks and feels. Another witness described emotional empathy with the victim's feelings like this: 'I can read quickly as lightning how he [the victim] is upset, how upset he can be . . . He [the victim] is hurt every time. They [the perpetrators] stab one's heart and smash the person's soul for ever.'

According to Clark, it is emotional empathy that paves the way for sympathy (Clark, 1997).

Sympathy emotions

Sympathy emotions link us to the vulnerable person or victim. These emotions are a response to the emotions which are perceived as being experienced by the other person. These emotions can be simple, such as concern for another person, or complex, encompassing a number of emotions such as pity, sorrow and frustration. Witnesses describe various emotions. However, one of the main emotions was of pity for the victim. This emotion was expressed in statements such as: 'I felt sorry for her' and 'I thought it was a pity for her'.

Indignation and anger formed another group of emotions. Whilst pity is normally directed towards the victim, indignation and anger become directed towards the situation or organisation. The following quote illustrates this situation. A witness said: 'Well, then she [the victim] started to come more and more frequently, and when she came several times a week and sat crying over a cup of coffee – well then I thought that it simply cannot be right that going to work should be so hard. We just don't get paid enough for it to be so hard, and we should by no means – there should be orderly conditions, and in a public place like this one expects things to be in order. And I remember that I just got so angry. Right after that I was in the elevator with my boss and I was so mad at her.' In this quote the witness first expresses indignation at the workplace, and then the indignation is transformed into anger directed at the manager.

Pity, anger and indignation are externally or other-targeted emotions. Besides these emotions witnesses also described self-targeted emotions such as shame, guilt and frustration, powerlessness. These emotions were expressed in statements such as: 'Well, maybe I felt it a bit [guilt] sometimes, that is why I didn't go straight to him and ask more about it, that is "What's going on here, is it something you do deliberately, or is it something we can help you with?", Yes, of course I felt a bit guilty.' Others described their moral discomfort as witnesses. As one witness puts it: 'I feel I have to do something, I can't just go on, I can't just stand and look at my colleagues teasing and belittling a grown man, I won't put up with that.'

These descriptions of the feelings triggered in relation to the victims are woven into the interpretative schemas. Most frequently it was the defender and the commuter who expressed empathy and sympathy. The misfortune of others can, however, also cause ambivalence expressed in mixed feelings. Some witnesses failed to experience any empathy and sympathy, and instead found themselves becoming irritated and contemptuous of the victim as a deviant and in a situation which was their own fault.

Micro-politics and social place

Feeling must be expressed in social behaviours in order to achieve social significance. The aim of bullying is to denigrate or exclude victims. In order to understand our positions within the informal hierarchies of everyday life, Clark introduced the concept of social place; this concept is to the level of interaction, what position is to social structure. The difference is that where positions are stable because they are based on formal rights, social place is a less well-defined, momentary and situation-dependent placing. Social place refers to one's sense of relative standing to others in terms of esteem and rights of interaction. Social place is experienced as a feeling and therefore by showing and provoking feelings in the other we can increase or reduce our social place or the social place of others. Within this concept, offensive actions can be interpreted as actions by which perpetrators evoke feelings in the victim that indicate a loss of the victim's social place. On the other hand, expressing sympathy can increase social place to someone experiencing difficulties. Clark's theory indicates the existence of dynamic relationships between the witness's emotions and actions in terms of their consequences on the social place of the victims. Clark terms these place-negotiating actions as emotional micro-politics. The following provides examples of place-taking and place-giving actions.

Negative actions

Witnesses who categorised the victims as deviants (the prosecutor schema) transformed their separating feelings into actions by emphasising the victim's low social place. They dissociated themselves from bullying in principle, but their descriptions show how they made use of more subtle forms of bullying, by ignoring, gossiping about or slandering the victims (Bloch, 2009, 2010). A witness said: 'Well, I just avoid sitting at a table where [the victim] is sitting – I simply don't feel inclined to.' To this is added gossip with colleagues and the shop steward about the victim's poor performance and poor work ethic, because, as one witness says: 'It could be catching.'

Witnesses who sympathise with victims describe different types of micro-political actions designed to give social place to the victim. However, these actions were interpreted within the norms of the working community and could have different and unintended effects on social standing and the witness's social place. These actions and their significance for social place relations are illustrated in the following witness stories.

Listening

A discreet way of expressing sympathy is through 'bonding' with the victim by talking, providing advice or listening to the victim. This action was expressed in statements such as: 'It was just that she [the victim] could come in and let off some steam if she wanted to – "Just come in and get a cup of coffee", and we chatted a little, you know. We had a cosy chat and things like that . . . I sort of tried to solve it when she was there – we talked about it and then she took her cup and left again.' And another witness: 'I have talked with him a lot . . . Listen here, you have to learn to stand up for your rights, and when people say things like that to you, it isn't humour, it's not funny either, as I know myself.' The witnesses showed some interest in the victims, validating them as a person, and through this provided the victim a social place within their relationship.

The protective intervention

Social place can be provided where witnesses intervene in a protective way during the bullying process. This action was expressed in statements like: 'I sometimes also defend some people, among others the victim. I say, "Hey, stop that. It's not funny anymore." ' And: 'I was also one of the few to open my mouth and say "stop that! I don't want to listen to that".' And: 'Yes, I did that [intervened and said stop], because I thought, now we're there again and we have to stop, because I know that it won't end well because one of them is stronger than the other in some way.'

However, these protective interventions may also have unintended consequences for the victim's social place. As one witness says: 'But when I intervene in things like that [teasing, bullying, etc.], then I sort of feel I have made things even worse, because [my intervention shows] that he cannot [lacks the ability to] defend himself and I have confirmed that he cannot, and that hurts even more. But what am I to do?' Another witness expresses it like this: 'It's difficult to find out how to provide help and support and what one can do. Because one is worried that one is exposing them more than one wants to, so how does one tackle it and how does one discuss things?' In other words, the protective intervention can not only make it more visible that the victim is experiencing difficulties, but may also show that the victim is unable to defend themselves, indicating that they are weak and causing them to lose even more social place.

Intervening can also put the witness at risk in the conflict, as a witness put it, 'getting a punch on the nose himself or herself'. The protective intervention by witnesses publicly challenges the perpetrators' construction of the victim as a deviant. This runs the risk of the witness being exposed to negative actions against himself or herself including losing social place and rights as a negotiator of what is normal and deviant.

The protective intervention could also take the form of mediation between the parties. A middle manager describes how a victim approached him because he was being bullied, he said: 'I thought it was a pity for him if he experienced it like that, I called a personnel meeting to get people together to talk. And I was allowed to say it all as he had said it to me. But it turned out that people had misunderstood some things, so the whole thing was solved by us talking about it.'

The middle manager, by virtue of his position, had an established social place. In the interview he expresses empathy with the perpetrators and the victim. The space for normalcy can be expanded through mediation in which the victim is given social space and is included in the working community. There were, however, very few examples of this type of success story.

Whistleblowing

Several of the witnesses described whistleblowing as a protective action in relation to the victim. In whistleblowing the witness addresses a higher authority. In many workplaces whistleblowing is regarded as a breach of the collegial code of practice and an infringement of the norm of confidentiality. When the witness approaches the management, information is passed on which the victim may regard as confidential, and at the same time, through the approach, the witness contributes to the notion of the vulnerability of the victim. As a witness states: 'She, the colleague [the victim] gets so upset that someone has gone behind her back.' Whistleblowing can result in exposing colleagues and a breach of solidarity. Interviewed witnesses who had blown the whistle showed signs of being uncomfortable in describing what they had done. The whistleblower is viewed as a 'tell-tale'. Similarly, witnesses emphasised how they tried to avoid reporting perpetrators and victims by 'not focusing on the other and saying that she said something or other, but saying on my own behalf that I perhaps think it was too much'.

Several witnesses expressed reluctance to involve the management because when transferred to management the problem was treated as a bullying problem and further influence taken out of their hands. As one witness said: 'We don't use the word bullying, because if that word is used then it disappears [out of our hands] and becomes a work issue, and then it ends in disaster.'

Bullying is a disturbance of the existing social micro-hierarchies where the victim is exposed to negative actions and through this to loss of social place. The witnesses can join in with the perpetrators' definition of the vulnerable person as a deviant and express feelings that confirm the victim's loss of social place. They can, however, also express sympathy aimed at giving the victim a social place. These micro-political initiatives are interpreted through the lenses of the work culture, and this study shows here that actions which originate in sympathy can have a negative impact on the victim's social place and be interpreted as a breach of what is acceptable, putting pressure on the witness's social place.

Sympathy etiquette

Sympathy is not an unlimited resource. According to Clark, sympathy may be regarded as a gift that should involve the principle of reciprocity with limits to the amount of sympathy which can be offered. Clark identified rules for the receipt of sympathy, which are summed up in the concept of sympathy etiquette. The following examples illustrate the way in which the witnesses view the victims' compliance with sympathy etiquette.

Being worthy of sympathy

One must show that one is worthy of receiving sympathy. Many of the witnesses expressed sympathy, but they also said that the victims themselves should do something to resolve their situation. As one witness says: 'He (the victim] gets very upset, but he doesn't say anything and he doesn't do anything'; and 'You [the victim] get hurt every time and you still do it. When are you going to do something about it?' Several of the witnesses expressed both disappointment and irritation at the victims not doing anything, raising the question of whether the victims were actually worthy of their sympathy.

Do not demand too much sympathy

This principle was expressed indirectly in statements where the witnesses marked the limits of their empathy and sympathy. This demarcation was expressed in statements such as: 'Well, I told her about [institution x]. I didn't contact them myself, but now I had told her, and it was up to her, but she didn't do anything.' And: 'Now that she was there and we were sitting chatting, we talked about it and then she left again with her cup, and so I thought now I have listened to her and done what I could.'

Repayment of sympathy

Bullying is a complex and sometimes obscure process. Several of the witnesses mentioned examples of how their protective intervention was rejected by the victim. One witness said: 'I can see that it is starting and that it isn't fair, but when I then intervene, I risk getting slapped myself [by the victim].' This witness feels sympathy for the victim, but also feels that the victim is breaking the sympathy etiquette.

Clark suggests that everyone has a sympathy account, which refers to how deserving we are of the sympathy of others. This account is constantly changing as we give sympathy and receive sympathy. However, it is possible to overdraw our sympathy account through excessive needs and it is here that the sympathy etiquette determines the conditions for the continued receipt of sympathy. Bullying is a lengthy process and constantly appealing for sympathy eats into the victim's sympathy account. Moreover, in many cases the victims are unable to fulfil the reciprocal requirements of the etiquette. Many of the witnesses express sympathy for the victims but there is a gradual wearing down of witnesses' sympathy reserves and the victim's perceived deserving of sympathy.

Denial

The majority of witnesses felt for the victims and tried to include them through the use of micro-politics. These were not, however, the only actions. The so-called commuters fluctuated between normalising and sympathising with the victims and conformity with the assessment of the victims as deviants. This commuting is likely to be motivated through the discomfort of feeling at odds with the culture and risking the possibility of being excluded oneself. As a witness puts it: 'Well, I'm no saint either. I was part of it myself. Made sarcastic remarks. For my own sake, not to be out of line with the others.'

The commuting could, however, also be motivated by a contradiction between sympathy for the victim and genuine solidarity with the work culture. Handling contradictions and the cost of showing sympathy caused several of the witnesses to describe their mental and emotional withdrawal from the victim causing the witness to stop engaging or acting in support of the victim. Cohen interprets this withdrawal as denial which is used as a defence mechanism in which we know and do not know what is happening at the same time. Cohen (2001) states that denial of responsibility is the most frequently used defence strategy of remaining passive. Witnesses deny their responsibility by projecting it on to other involved actors including the victim, as in the following quote where a witness makes the victim an accomplice: 'But when he [the victim] himself was smiling and laughing, then I myself could make some sarcastic remarks about him.' Or the perpetrators, as another witness puts it: 'I've also reached the conclusion that I can't change people [the perpetrators], I can't fix everything, and I can't be pedagogical with everybody either. I just can't. So, no, it's not my problem. It's their problem.' The witness has given up and he legitimised his passivity by emphasising that the perpetrators were responsible.

Another witness said: 'And then it didn't affect me, and so I thought – well, if they want to do that themselves, they can just do it, because I don't have to interfere and feel that I have to save them or solve the problem or talk to them about that or something or other.' Here the witness disclaims responsibility by placing the blame on others. Finally, management was held responsible, as a witness says: 'Now I've done what I can and management must take over. It is basically their responsibility.'

From the perspective of interaction theory, all the actors contributed to bullying as a process. Whilst legally witnesses are 'not guilty', morally they are involved. The witnesses described tried to handle moral guilt by projecting their responsibility on to other actors. In addition to the disclaiming of responsibility, getting used to things or habituation to negative behaviours also occurred with the normalisation of the bullying, with a witness relating how she was shocked by the atmosphere when she started her job, but as she says: 'I've grown accustomed to it now, and I would never have thought I would. Now that's just what it is, and we continue regardless, don't we?' Witnesses are involved and active in the bullying process and withdrawal from the process is a denial of their moral responsibility together with the placing of responsibility on to the shoulders of others.

Conclusions

The aim of the chapter has been to give voice to the witnesses by analysing the way in which they participate in the workplace bullying process. The analysis shows that the witnesses are actors through the act of interpreting who to blame, forming solidarity with the victim to solidarity with the perpetrators. The analysis also shows how the witnesses become emotionally involved and through the use of negative and sympathy actions give or take social place from the victims. These witness actions contribute to either the integration or the social exclusion of the victims.

The analysis also shows that sympathy actions may conflict with the informal work culture causing the witnesses' sympathy actions unintentionally to contribute to the further exclusion of the victim. Witnesses' sympathy actions can be interpreted as a breach of norms causing the witness to lose their social place and increase the conflict. Cultural rules for sympathy set limits to the availability of sympathy with witnesses suffering from sympathy fatigue for the victims. The present analysis shows that the witnesses manoeuvre within a complex and contradictory social universe, which paves the way for moral dilemmas handled through denial and disclaiming responsibility. Bullying is a morally loaded concept which may cast a shadow over our understanding of mobbing as a social phenomena. As witnesses constitute the largest group in the bullying process, they play a key role in the fight against bullying and in the struggle for an open workplace. This not only requires an appeal to the individual's moral responsibility for action against bullying, but also additional insight into the social and cultural mechanisms in which the witness navigates and acts.

Note

1 The study was conducted as part of a larger investigation of bullying in Danish workplaces (Hogh *et al.*, 2009). The investigation was supported by the Danish Working Environment Research Fund.

References

Adams, A. (1992) *Bullying at work: How to Confront It and Overcome It*. London: Virago.

Agevall, O. (2007) *The Career of Mobbing: Emergence, Transformation, and Utilisation of a New Concept*. Växjö: Växjö Universitet.

Becher, H. S. (1963) *Outsiders: Studies in Sociology of Deviance*. Glencoe, IL: Free Press of Glencoe.

Bloch, C. (2009) Sociale interaktioner, følelser og mobning. In A. Hogh *et al. Mobning og negativ adfærd på arbejdspladsen*. København: NFA.

Bloch, C. (2010) Negative acts and bullying: face-threatening acts, social bonds and social place. In B. Sieben & Å. Wettergren (eds) *Emotionalizing Organizations and Organizing Emotions*. Basingstoke: Palgrave Macmillan.

Clark, C. (1990) Emotions and Micro-politics in everyday life: some patterns and paradoxes of place. In T. D. Kemper (ed.) *Research Agendas in the Sociology of Emotions*. New York: Wiley.

Clark, C. (1997) *Misery and Company*. London: University of Chicago Press.

Clark, C. (2004) Emotional gifts and 'you first' Micro-politics: niceness in the socio-emotional economy. In A. S. R. Manstead, N. H. Frijda & A. Fischer (eds) *Feelings and Emotions*. Cambridge: Cambridge University Press.

Cohen, S. (2001) *States of Denial. Knowing about Atrocities and Suffering*. Oxford: Blackwell.

Einarsen, S., Hoel, H., Zapf, D., & Cooper, C. L. (2003) *Bullying and Emotional Abuse in the Workplace: International Perspectives in Research and Practice*. London: CRC Press.

Goffman, E. (1967) *Interaction Ritual. Essays on Face-to-Face Behaviour*. London: Penguin.

Hallberg, L. R. M., & Strandmark, M. (2004) *Vuxenmobbning*. Lund: Studenterlitteratur.

Heinemann, P. P. (1972) *Mobbning: gruppvold blandt barn och vuxna*. Stockholm: Natur och kultur.

Hogh, A., Bloch, C., Gemzøe, E., Mikkelsen, E., Maier, C. M. Persson, R., *et al.* (2009) *Mobning og negativ adfærd på arbejdspladsen*. København: NFA.

Leymann, H. (1986) *Voksen mobning*. Lund: Studenterlitteratur.

Lutgen-Sandvik, P. (2006) Take this job and . . .: quitting and other forms of resistance to workplace bullying. *Communication Monographs*, 73(4): 406–433.

Niedhammer, I. D., & Degioanni, S. (2006) Association between workplace bullying and depressive symptoms in the French working population. *Journal of Psychosomatic Research*, 61(2): 251–259.

Olweus, D. (1973) *Hackkycklingar och översittare: Forskning om skolmobning*. Stockholm: Almquist & Wiksell.

Rayner, C. (1999) *Workplace bullying*. PhD thesis, UMIST.

Vartia, M. A. (2001) Consequences of workplace bullying with respect to the well-being of its targets and the observers of bullying. *Scandanavian Journal of Work Environmental Health*, 27(1): 63–69.

Chapter 7

Compassion fatigue in human resource professionals

Noreen Tehrani and Joan Popovic

Introduction

Being closely involved in investigating, supporting, counselling or advising employees involved in workplace bullying can be exhausting. Whilst human resource professionals (HRP) will do their best to deal with situations sensitively, speedily and within the organisational and legal frameworks, employees may have unrealistic expectations of what can be gained from initiating the informal or formal grievance procedures. For the HRP, the cost of engaging with workplace bullying and abuse stories can result in them becoming overinvolved in their cases and experiencing feelings of inadequacy, resentment and distress similar to those of the employees they are trying to assist. In this chapter we will be using a number of anonomised case histories to explore some of the issues faced by the HRP when dealing with particularly demanding or difficult cases. Evidence is presented to show that dealing with workplace bullying can increase levels of stress, burn-out and compassion fatigue. Signs showing that personal resilience is failing are described, as is the need for pre-deployment screening and training for HRPs and others involved in dealing with bullying and harassment. The minimum levels of support and personal supervision for HRPs and others involved are discussed and a model of support described.

Difficulties faced by human resource professionals dealing with bullying and harassment

A survey of human resource professionals (CIPD, 2003) provides an indication of the roles and skills required if the HR function is to meet the needs of organisations. The survey shows that there is an increasing emphasis on the achievement of the business strategic goals through proactive, tailored and business-driven solutions. HRP's role is becoming wider and more complex needing to understand and take account of business pressures as well as dealing with basic human emotions. This dichotomy of pressures is particularly evident for those HRPs who are dealing with employee conflict, bullying and harassment where there is a need to be able to do the following:

1   Act as a balance between the needs of the workers and the needs of the organisation.
2   Be the bearer of bad news.
3   Take the role of honest broker between employees in conflict.
4   Be the sympathetic ear for distressed employees.
5   Provide a professional and confidential service.
6   Advise, organise, undertake and be responsible for formulating, administering and being legally accountable for the organisation's bullying policies and procedures.

HRPs are constantly confronted by the challenge of attempting to reconcile the needs of their organisation with the needs of the individual employee (Andrews, 2003). The psychological impact of work and personal stressors is well documented (Cox, 1993; Tasho et al., 2005). Despite the evidence of work-related harm, HRPs are not the easiest group to persuade that they should take care of their health and well-being. Often HRPs are so busy looking after others that there is no time to reflect on their own needs and they may even experience feelings of guilt or embarrassment when asking for time for self-care. However, there is a cost to engaging with distressed employees in what is already a pressurised environment which may lead to the HRP finding they are experiencing similar feelings to those described by the bullied employees. This 'shared' experience is disconcerting, particularly when it includes intrusive thoughts, images and emotions relating to a bullied employee's story rather than to current events in their own life. This phenomenon, known as emotional transference, is well recognised in psychology and can be found when two or more people have emotionally engaged with one another causing the strong emotions experienced by one to be transferred and absorbed by the other. The effect of these processes may also be played out in other situations (parallel process) or as an unconscious response (countertransference) with the possible additional involvement of unresolved events and emotions from the HRP's past (Wilson & Thomas, 2004). This process, which affects counsellors, human resources, lawyers, nurses, police officers, social workers and others, is known as compassion fatigue (Figley,

2002) – a natural consequence of helping or wanting to help distressed people. For HRPs a continual exposure to employees experiencing the anger, fear, distrust and anxiety of bullying may result in some of the feelings, attitudes and beliefs of those involved affecting the way in which they view the world. Where a distressed employee's recounted experience is particularly intense or has a resonance in the life of the HRP the disruption to the HRP, may be sudden and dramatic (Janoff-Bulman, 1992).

Case studies

The following case studies illustrate some of the demands and complexities of the work of HRPs involved in dealing with bullying and harassment cases. Whilst the case studies are based on real cases and events, they have been anonomised to protect the confidentiality of all those concerned. As soon as a bullying complaint becomes formal, the HRP knows that they will have to interview potential witnesses and the person accused of bullying. The accused person may express shock when they are approached as they may not be aware that a complaint had been made against them. The HRP also has to decide whether there is a possibility of retribution or other risk to the complainant in order to make the necessary arrangement for the alleged bully to be moved to another location or role. As soon as the HRP becomes involved and interviews begin, the atmosphere within the team is likely to change and despite confidentially being emphasised to everyone involved the HR presence in a unit or section makes it impossible to prevent gossip and speculation. It is for this and other reasons that organisations like bullying investigation to be undertaken swiftly as delay can lead to a reduction in morale, motivation and productivity. The HRP may be placed under extreme pressure to undertake a large number of emotionally difficult and challenging interviews and to write reports within a short timescale.

> I would never have believed how quickly the grapevine got into action. What seemed to be a reasonably easy task suddenly became much more difficult with people approaching me to ask what was happening. The pressure to complete the interviews quickly was enormous. I ended up working 14-hour days to complete on time. At the end I felt that my needs had not been recognised.

HRPs are aware of the need to be sensitive to equal opportunities and recognise that cultural differences, be they regional, national, ethnic or religious, can affect behaviours. What may be accepted in one culture may not be acceptable in another. Where an employee does not accept that the organisation's procedures for dealing with bullying and harassment are adequate for dealing with diversity issues, this can make it difficult for the HRP to handle cases, particularly if they are labelled as being racist or prejudiced when an employee does not get the outcome they expected. In the following case an Asian employee complained of being racially harassed by a white male colleague within his team. The complaint involved a comment being made about his name being similar to that of a notorious terrorist. The complainant was not prepared to have informal discussions and requested an immediate formal investigation. The female HRP investigator, conscious of the cultural issues, explained the investigation process and offered a male HRP, but this was turned down as the complainant said he wished to continue with the female investigator. During the interview inconsistencies began to appear in his account. When the HRP asked for clarification she found the complainant was changing his attitude towards her and became rude, arrogant and dismissive. The HRP was upset but tried to remain calm whilst reiterating the need for accuracy as the investigation might have serious consequences on those he had accused. When the HRP interviewed the complainant's colleagues, they provided objective evidence that the complainant was in the habit of sharing online jokes and caricatures demeaning other ethnic groups and women.

This was one of the most difficult investigations that I had ever undertaken, I felt totally disempowered in my role of investigator. The complainant began by being really pleasant to me but as soon as I started to identify gaps in his story the whole atmosphere changed. He became rude, dismissive and abusive towards me. I kept my cool; in other circumstances I would have made a complaint against him myself. What really irritated me was that he went to the national press and retold his story which I knew was totally untrue. It seemed to me that all he wanted was to get as much money as he could out of the company before he moved on to somewhere new. I guess this is part of the job but I don't see why I should have to put up with this kind of abuse.

The abuse of power is central to bullying; sometimes the abuse is mirrored in the organisation and the investigation (see Chapter 17, Bloom). The next case study examines how an organisation colluded with a union when one of the union's executive members (EM) was accused of bullying by two union representatives. The representatives approached the HRP to request mediation as they were aware of the sensitivity of the situation and their desire not to cause embarrassment to the union. However, the EM would not engage with mediation and asked for the case to be handled informally. When the EM was told that the representatives were taking out a formal grievance he asked for representation from another union. The HRP met the representative and was put under extreme pressure to drop the case. The HRP reminded the EM and external representative that the union had been involved in the development of the policy and that it was this policy which was being carried out. Nevertheless, throughout the investigation there was continual pressure on the HRP to stop the investigation. Eventually the EM agreed to be interviewed with the interview taking many hours as each aspect of the complaint was challenged. Despite the overwhelming evidence that showed that the EM had bullied the representatives, the HRP learnt that the company had decided not to take any action against the EM. The HRP had to convey this decision to the complainants, who were so upset that both left the organisation believing that they had been let down by the union and the company.

> How can I come to terms with these double standards? I am a member of the same union. I feel ashamed that the union, which has a duty to support the rights of its members, abuses this power when it comes to protecting their own. I even felt that my own standards were being challenged by the coercion and pressure I was put under to drop what was a justified complaint. I was left feeling that all my efforts for the complainants were wasted, when my HR director succumbed to union pressure to drop the complaint in order to maintain cordial relationships. I felt that I and my role had been abused.

Sometimes HRPs face having to deal with a lack of objective evidence which means that it is difficult to take cases forward. On occasions the HRP will have to ask the employee to remain in a bullying situation in order to gather the information that they will need in the grievance hearing. In this case a manager had an issue with control; he found it difficult to allow his team to do their work without continually checking on them. He was well respected by the organisation as a troubleshooter as he could be decisive and effective in complex situations. All the supervisors working for him had been hand-picked and always supported his decisions. One of his team had some health problems leading to a number of sickness absences. The manager began to criticise and undermine her, resulting in her becoming isolated and excluded and regarded as a poor performer. Eventually, the targeted worker made a complaint which was investigated by the HRP.

The target found it difficult to provide evidence of actual bullying behaviours as many were subtle, such as being left out and excluded rather than any more active forms of bullying. When she took the grievance against the manager she was accused of using the process to avoid being disciplined for her attendance. When the HRP interviewed the team members no one was prepared to give a statement although some said, off the record, that the manager's behaviour had been aggressive and undermining, but that they were not prepared to do anything about it for fear of it happening to them.

> I often feel there is injustice where cases are not resolved sufficiently due to lack of evidence and the complainant has gone through a very traumatic process with nothing to show for it. I am now much more reluctant to suggest that employees take action against bullies, particularly the ones with friends in high places. I really wonder if my role makes matters worse in giving hope just to have it dashed later.

At times the HRP may feel that they are being bullied by the so-called victims of bullying. It can begin to feel that whilst an employee may have a justifiable complaint, the way that they go about proceeding with their grievance demonstrates that they are not the innocent victim they claim to be (see Chapter 16, Tehrani). In the following case the HRP felt trapped and harassed by the complainant who appeared obsessed with destroying the person he perceived as a bully together with anyone that stood in the way of him achieving that objective. The complainant had been in his job for ten years and had been underperforming for some time. He was invited to a performance management meeting during which he claimed he had been bullied by his manager, and asked to speak to an HRP under the organisation's bullying and harassment policy.

When HRP contacted the complainant he was told that the initial meeting would hear his concerns and look at the options for resolution. When the complainant arrived for the meeting he had five lever arch folders full of documents. It transpired that the complainant had followed up every conversation with his manager with an email with his own interpretation of the discussion. The documents went back four years. When the complainant was asked why he had kept so much information, he said that it was the way he liked to keep track of things. The HRP became even more concerned when she found that the complainant was beginning to keep similar records of every contact that he had with her and made it clear that he knew his legal rights and that he had contacts that would help him sue the organisation if he did not get the outcome he desired.

> I did not feel that I was dealing with a normal person. He moved from issue to issue and just when I thought that we had resolved one area he would jump to something else, then back again to the first thing. I felt that I would have to cover my back and became very nervous whenever I saw an email from him. By the end of this case I had dozens of emails from him and felt that it was me who was being harassed. I am not at all sure that I am qualified to deal with people who are mentally sick.

When talking to HRPs involved in dealing with bullying and harassment cases it is not unusual to come away feeling that their role is one of the most difficult aspects of people management and that the time and energy required in dealing with bullying cases, personally and professionally, is not adequately recognised by the human resource profession.

Vulnerability

Although it is unlikely that anyone working with bullied or harassed employees will be totally unaffected, there are some HRPs who have an increased vulnerability. It has been shown that those professionals who demonstrate the greatest capacity for feeling and expressing empathy (Figley, 1995) are more likely to absorb the symptoms of troubled employees. In addition, where an HRP is experiencing personal or role-related difficulties or challenges this may affect their physical and psychological functioning, with the added problem that there will be little or no time or energy to take care of themselves, their partners or families. A lack of self-care can also result in an increasingly cynical attitude to life, feelings of isolation, intense sadness and incompetence. Some HRPs may find that they begin to experience heightened emotions and become hypersensitive to anything that reactivates their feelings of being helpless or vulnerable in their attempts to deal with these highly emotionally charged employees (Pearlman, 1999). In order to deal with the impact of listening to bullying stories from employees, HRPs may defend themselves by becoming distant or dissociated from their work or by questioning the truth and reliability of the complainant (Danielli, 1996). If the complainant's story touches upon an incident that has affected the HRP's own life, there may be a numbing or an inability to listen to the employee. In studies looking at caring professions it has been shown that up to 50 per cent were vulnerable to experiencing compassion fatigue (Steed & Bicknell, 2001) and significantly lower levels of personal growth and feelings of achievement than other caring groups (Tehrani, 2010).

Selecting, training and supporting the HRPs

Not everyone is suited to working in the murky area of bullying and even for those who choose this work there need to be opportunities to opt out should it become too exhausting or personally demanding.

Selection

Some HRPs choose to be involved in dealing with bullying because they have experienced it themselves and believe that this makes it easier for them to understand how it feels; other HRPs like the idea of helping people. Although people with a disrupted childhood are more vulnerable to psychological difficulties, they appear to be attracted to this kind of work (see Chapter 17, Bloom) which is concerning.

The first safeguard in protecting HRPs is to have open, fair and effective selection processes which include a role profile, key competencies and capabilities for dealing with the work. Table 7.1 provides a sample

Table 7.1 Role profile for a HRP involved in dealing with bullying and harassment at work

Role title	*Human resource professional – Dignity at Work (DAW)*
Aim of the role:	To support the organisation's Dignity at Work programme by supporting the effective implementation of the Dignity at Work policy and procedures throughout the business. Guiding, supporting and monitoring the Dignity at Work supporters in providing information and support to employees affected by bullying and harassment.

I Key responsibilities/accountabilities

(a) General

- Identify opportunities to enhance and promote the Dignity at Work policy and procedures to leaders.
- Identify improvements to the DAW policy and procedures.
- Undertake investigations and provide accurate and appropriate written reports.
- Be a source of information and advice to HR and management on DAW issues.
- Keep abreast of legislation and new developments in Dignity at Work.
- Keep records of the number and nature of cases handled.

(b) DAW supporters

- Manage the selection, training and support for DAW supporters.
- Provide personal support and guidance to DAW supporters.
- Maintain a register of DAW supporters and identify where additional advisors are required.
- Monitor the performance of the DAW supporters.

2 Behavioural competencies

The job holder must be able to:
- undertake formal investigations
- manage difficult and demanding relationships
- write accurate and effective investigation reports
- interpret and apply legislation and guidance on bullying and harassment
- represent the organisation in employment tribunals involving bullying and harassment
- liaise with the organisation's legal representatives
- undertake mediation
- use coaching and training skills to support DAW supporters
- create and maintain databases to monitor the levels of bullying and harassment in the organisation.

(Continued overleaf)

Table 7.1 Continued

Role title	Human resource professional – Dignity at Work (DAW)

3   Personal skills

Is able to:
- maintain confidentiality
- challenge unacceptable practice, process and behaviours
- use verbal and written communication effectively
- demonstrate objectivity and fairness
- be accurate and systematic in case handling
- accurately listen and respond
- adopt a creative approach to problem solving

- treat all employees with respect
- demonstrate empathy and sympathy
- be resilient and energetic
- use effective influencing styles
- deal with distressed employees
- manage own emotions and behaviours under pressure
- support and encourage DAW supporters
- provide training and support for DAW supporters
- recognise own needs for support.

4   Other requirements

The job holder is required to:
- undergo a selection process which includes psychometric testing to assess suitability for the role
- attend regular personal supervision and/or counselling sessions
- report if they become unable to undertake their role due to a conflict of interests or emotional fatigue.

job description for an HRP working with bullying. Technical knowledge such as understanding the legislation and company policies, differentiating between bullying, harassment and victimisation and knowing where to refer employees for therapy can be learnt and assessed. Less easy is the assessment of the essential critical thinking skills, including the ability to recognise where people are making assumptions and to evaluate the arguments presented without introducing bias or prejudicial thinking that is essential to undertaking interviews and writing reports. It is possible to test critical thinking skills using critical thinking appraisal testing (Watson Glaser, 2002). Perhaps the most difficult competence to establish relates to the HRP's emotional resilience, self-awareness, integrity and ability to reflect, particularly when faced with disturbed and distressed employees, or organisational pressure. Emotional intelligence tests (e.g. Dulewicz & Higgs, 1999) and burn-out questionnaires (e.g. Maslach & Jackson, 1986) can provide useful assessments of these important personal abilities. The selection process should include all of the following elements:

Initial screening (one day)

- *Screening the applications*: making sure that their skills and experience are in line with the job description.
- *Behavioural interviewing*: seeking examples of behaviour which demonstrate knowledge, skills and experiences of bullying and conflict, how they have handled conflict and their motivation for applying for the role.
- *Psychometric testing*: emotional well-being, critical thinking skills and emotional intelligence.

Induction training and assessment (2–3 days)

- *Role plays*: realistic role plays which test the applicants' listening and responding skills, including their confidence in dealing with strong emotions and challenges.
- *Writing tests*: testing written skills and ability to convey information accurately and appropriately.
- *Written examination*: testing candidates' knowledge of legislation and company policies and procedures relating to bullying and harassment.

The initial screening should be organised in such a way that the applicants have a clear idea of what is involved in the role. For some applicants this provides an opportunity to withdraw their application and for those found not to be competent time to discuss the areas they should develop if they wish to apply again. The induction training and assessment provide an opportunity to convey the important information and to develop personal skills and awareness. There need to be assessments of each of the elements of the induction training. However, the real test of competence cannot be fully established when the recruit is faced with a 'live' case. It is important that new recruits are assisted in dealing with their first cases by a more experienced HR mentor.

Update training

Update training and support needs to be provided on a regular basis. An annual training day or attending conferences dealing with bullying helps to maintain knowledge and technical competence and reduces the likelihood of burn-out. Where there are a number of HRPs involved in this work, meeting as a group provides not only the opportunity to share views and experiences in a confidential environment, but also builds in interpersonal support and feelings of being part of a collegiate group. It is helpful to invite speakers from other organisations to describe their programmes or researchers to present their work on recognising and responding to workplace bullying and harassment. There may also be opportunities to undertake skills training and to review new legislation, case law or company policies. Finally, there should be a review of the use of the programme, feedback from users and staff surveys. Ideally, this should be used proactively with interventions introduced to deal with issues through training or emphasising the organisation's commitment to dignity at work. Monitoring activity across the organisation can also identify trends or pockets of activity. This may be due to the organisation going through rapid change or where a particular manager, worker or group is causing conflict. This approach provides the organisation with information on where particular business sections or geographical area require some attention in terms of reinforcing policy and procedure, skills training or employee education sessions.

Consultative support for HRPs

The incidence of secondary trauma and compassion can be reduced when the HRPs have access to supervision or consultative support (Salston & Figley, 2003). The importance of regular supervision has been identified as essential (McCann & Pearlman, 1990; Cerney, 1995) with many caring professions regarding supervision or consultative support as a professional requirement (BACP, 2002; BPS, 2007). The aim of the supervision is to enable the professional carer to process the painful or confusing material, as well as explore and reduce the impact of the material on their thinking and emotions. While personal supervision for some caring professional groups is less common, it is a growing phenomenon with many occupational nurses (Faculty of Occupational Medicine, 2010) and social workers (Beddow, 2010) benefiting from regular supervision or consultative support. Indeed, the emerging discipline of coaching is moving towards a position where supervision is becoming a requirement for practice (Lee, 2006). Supervision and consultative support come in a number of forms and may be provided by a manager, clinical supervisor or peer, it can be face to face, by telephone or email, one to one or in a group. There are a number of approaches to supervision (Scaife, 2001). However, most models accept that to be successful, supervision needs to meet three needs (Inskipp & Proctor, 1995):

- *normative needs* to deal with managerial and ethical issues
- *formative needs* for education, learning and development
- *restorative needs* which acknowledge the emotional impact of the work and help the carer regain their sense of psychological, physical, social and spiritual well-being.

However, the needs of the HRP may change over time and a development approach to supervision recognises the changing needs as the carer moves from inexperienced to experienced practitioner status (Stoltenberg *et al.*, 1998). To protect themselves from compassion fatigue, HRPs should aim to have a balanced life in which their own needs are taken into account alongside the needs of work, home, family and friends (Stamm, 1995).

Resilience building teams – a model of support

It has been found that facilitated peer support has almost the same level of benefit as clinical supervision (Tehrani, 2010). It also has the benefit of developing additional skills and confidence within the team. Organising opportunities for people involved in dealing with bullying in a safe and supportive environment with a trained facilitator provides an opportunity for the group to talk in a way that makes them more resilient and able to learn from each other (White & Epston, 1999). This model of support has been used to support a wide range of professionals, including police officers, nurses, investigators and human resources, and involves a facilitated group in which the facilitator helps individual team members to explore their difficulties in an environment which clearly separates the issue from the individual, using skills which are similar to those found in appreciative enquiry (Whitney & Trosten-Bloom, 2003).

Growth from adversity

Given the inherent dangers for an HRP working with bullying, one might wonder why anyone would willingly put themselves at risk of psychological pain and injury by working with bullying. While it is clear that there is a risk of secondary trauma and compassion fatigue from this work, this is not the only outcome. An emerging body of evidence is showing that where an HRP has been able to understand and make sense of their role and has an ability to create meaning out of the chaos of distress, personal growth is possible (Tedeschi & Calhoun, 2003). It has even been suggested (Janoff-Bulman, 1992) that the more extreme the exposure to distressing events the more positive the potential growth. The qualities of the HRPs who are able to transform the negative effects of exposure to bullying to well-being include an ability: (a) to create positive emotional states in order to challenge the negative psychobiological effects of the traumatic exposure; (b) to generate high levels of physical and mental energy; (c) to create meaning and to live life for the moment; (d) to feel connected to and behave altruistically towards others (Wilson, 2006). These health-enhancing effects of understanding and making sense of a distressing event can be facilitated by a range of personal and professional activities (Figley, 1995):

- maintaining physical health and fitness
- enjoying a well-balanced work/life balance
- using reflection, meditation or other form of spiritual practice
- the availability and use of social support
- clearly defined professional boundaries and limits
- the use of professional supervision or consultative support.

Conclusions

The suggestion that anyone can deal with cases of bullying underestimates the true nature of the role. Whilst many of the tasks involved may be administrative, the nature of working with bullying can have a profound impact on everyone involved. A key role for the HRP is to act as an honest broker balancing the needs of all parties. However, taking this role when dealing with cases of bullying may put the HR practitioner in a position which requires them to manage competing interests. This is particularly true when the bullying issues are complex or where double standards may occur: for example, where a senior manager accused of bullying is given more support or opportunities to defend himself or herself than someone lower in the organisational hierarchy. Whether the HRP wishes to take on the role of moral standard bearer or not, they will need to deal with a wide range of moral, ethical and personal dilemmas and this should be recognised by their organisation through the support they provide and their willingness to acknowledge that there may be a times when the HRP needs a break from the work.

References

Andrews, L. W. (2003) Avoiding HR burnout: dealing with the human side of business. *HR Magazine*, 48(7): 1–2.

BACP (2002) *Ethical Framework for Good Practice in Counselling and Psychotherapy*. Rugby: British Association for Counselling and Psychotherapy.

Beddow, L. (2010) Surveillance or refection: professional supervision in the risk society. *British Journal of Social Work*, 40(4): 1279–1296.

BPS (2007) *Guidelines for Supervision*. Leicester: British Psychological Society.

Cerney, M. S. (1995) Treating the 'heroic treaters'. In C. R. Figley (ed.) *Compassion Fatigue*. New York: Brunner/Mazel.

CIPD (2003) *HR Survey: Where We Are, Where We Are Heading*. Wimbledon: CIPD.

Cox, T. (1993) *Stress Research and Stress Management: Putting Theory into Practice*. Sudbury: HSE Books.

Danielli, Y. (1996) Who takes care of the caretakers: the emotional consequences of working with children traumatized by war and communal violence. In R. J. Apfel & B. Simon (eds) *Minefields in their Hearts*. New Haven, CT: Yale University Press.

Dulewicz, V., & Higgs, M. (1999) *Emotional Intelligence Questionaire*. Windsor: NFER-Nelson.

Faculty of Occupational Medicine (2010) *Occupational Health Service Standards for Accreditation*. London: Faculty of Occupational Medicine.

Figley, C. R. (1995) *Compassion Fatigue – Coping with Secondary Traumatic Stress Disorder in Those Who Treat the Traumatised*. New York: Brunner/Mazel.

Figley, C. R. (2002) *Treating Compassion Fatigue*. Hove, UK: Brunner-Routledge.

Inskipp, F., & Proctor, B. (1995) *The Art, Craft and Tasks of Counselling Supervision: Part 2 Becoming a Supervisor*. Twickenham: Cascade Publications.

Janoff-Bulman, R. (1992) *Shattered Assumptions*. New York: Free Press.

Lee, G. (2006) The psychology of coaching supervision. *Coaching at Work*, 1(3): 26.

McCann, I. L., & Pearlman, L. A. (1990) *Psychological Trauma and the Adult Survivor – Theory, Therapy and Transformation*. New York: Brunner/Mazel.

Maslach, C., & Jackson, S. E. (1986) *MBI Maslach Burnout Inventory Manual*. Palo Alto, CA: Consulting Psychology Press.

Pearlman, L. A. (1999) Self care for trauma therapists. In B. H. Stamm (ed.) *Secondary Traumatic Stress – Self-Care Issues for Clinicians, Researchers and Educators*. Lutherville, MD: Sidran Press.

Salston, M. D., & Figley, C. R. (2003) Secondary traumatic stress effects of working with survivors of criminal victimisation. *Journal of Traumatic Stress*, 16(2): 167–174.

Scaife, J. (2001) *Supervision in the Mental Health Professions*. Hove, UK: Brunner-Routledge.

Stamm, B. H. (1995) *Work-Related Secondary Traumatic Stress – Self-Care Issues for Clinicians, Researchers and Educators*. Lutherville, MD: Sidran Press.

Steed, L., & Bicknell, J. (2001) Trauma and the therapist: the experience of therapists working with perpetrators of sexual abuse. *Australian Journal of Disaster and Trauma Studies*, 1: 1–9.

Stoltenberg, C. D., McNeil, B., & Delworth, U. (1998) IDM *Supervision: An Integrated Development Model for Supervising Counsellors and Therapists*. San Francisco: Jossey-Bass.

Tasho, W., Jordan, J., & Robinson, I. (2005) *Case Study: Establishing the Business Case for Investing in Stress Prevention Activities and Evaluating their Impact on Sickness Absence Levels*. Norwich: HMSO.

Tedeschi, R. G., & Calhoun, L. G. (2003) Routes to posttraumatic growth through cognitive processing. In D. Paton, J. M. Violanti, & L. M. Smith (eds) *Promoting Capabilities to Manage Posttraumatic Stress – Perspectives on Resilience*. Springfield, IL: Charles C. Thomas.

Tehrani, N. (2010) Compassion fatigue: experiences in occupational health, human resources, counselling and police. *Occupational Medicine*, 60(2): 133–138.

Watson, G., & Glaser, E. M. (2002) *Watson-Glaser Critical Thinking Appraisal*. London: Psychological Corporation.

White, M., & Epston, D. (1999) *Narrative Means to Therapeutic Ends*. London: Norton.

Whitney, D., & Trosten-Bloom, A. (2003) *The Power of Appreciative Inquiry – A Practical Guide to Positive Change*. San Francisco: Berrett-Koehler.

Wilson, J. P. (2006) *The Posttraumatic Self-Restoring Meaning and Wholeness to Personality*. London and New York: Routledge.

Wilson, J. P., & Thomas, R. B. (2004) *Empathy in the Treatment of Trauma*. New York: Brunner-Routledge.

Part II

Individual interventions

Chapter 8

Narrative approaches or the alternative story

Debbie Dunn

I have worked with workplace bullying over the last 15 years and this relationship continues today. My work started with the Bullied Workers Support Action Network (BWSAN) in Adelaide, Australia, and has continued in my work as a mediator, therapist and human relationships manager in Adelaide and Hobart. This chapter is based on my experiences as a practising narrative mediator.

Introduction

Contemporary writings in workplace bullying remain embedded in the same set of ideas which have dominated the literature for the last 20 years. These ideas construct a 'target', singled out by a 'bully', who is subjected to a systematic process of intimidation with the intention of causing harm. This view has almost exclusively been informed by the voices of those who claim to have experienced the effects of workplace bullying; effects which have been described as devastating with negative impacts on lives and relationships (Namie & Namie, 2009). This impact has been so great in many instances that the bullying has been classified as a workplace injury and the victims compensated accordingly. In this dominant discourse, the voices of the bullies remain silent. They are not consulted or invited to contribute to the debate. As a result the legislation, policies and processes developed to deal with workplace bullying have only been informed by the alleged victims. The 'bullies' are subsequently pathologised and typically demonised in the literature (Clarke, 2005).

Typically, formal investigations are the preferred option for determining whether or not allegations are upheld, often with little effort to assess the merits of the allegations. There is an assumption that 'one truth' exists and this can be determined through an essentially adversarial process which will result in the 'guilty' party being exposed and punished. Such an approach ignores the existence of competing truths. It denies how power, hierarchy and claims to entitlement shape different understandings of what constitutes bullying practice in the workplace. Further, pathologising the bully has resulted in a resistance to the use of mediation as a suitable intervention. This resistance is based on ideas that mediation denies the 'power imbalance' between alleged perpetrator and target and somehow precludes the possibility of the perpetrator taking responsibility for their actions and subsequent impacts of the bullying practices (de Guzman, 2010).

The practice of mediation teaches many things, including that there are at least two sides to any story. Where bullying has been named as the problem, mediation offers an opportunity to hear the other side of the story, to hear the voice of the alleged bully. Narrative therapy, which underpins the mediation practices described in this chapter, emerges from a post-structural[1] tradition which recognises the possibility of multiple truths. This approach offers participants in the mediation an opportunity to arrive at different understandings on the nature of 'workplace bullying'.

The purpose in this chapter is to examine the practices of narrative mediation in a workplace where there have been claims of 'workplace bullying'. It aims to demonstrate how narrative mediation can be used to bring about a different understanding to those making the claim of 'bullying' and the consequences for workplace relationships. It shows how collaboration against the behaviours named as bullying leads to a better understanding of the nature of 'workplace bullying', by offering an alternative story. This alternative story draws on evidence from 200 mediations where bullying was, in the first instance, named as the problem story.

Narrative mediation

Narrative mediation brings to mediation the practices of narrative therapy. These practices were developed by White and Epston (1990) and elaborated on by White (2005, 2007) and Winslade and Monk (2000, 2008). Central to narrative therapy is the belief that identity is socially constructed. In other words, the meaning we give to our experiences, to the stories of our lives, shapes who we are, our sense of identity and well-being. These stories are themselves informed by a broader social construct whose origins are embedded in our culture and history. Particular dominant social constructs or discourses emerge in society and these stories shape how we believe we should be in life, how we should look and what it means to be successful. Dominant discourses are also evident in workplaces. They shape the workplace culture and provide the norms for how people behave in the workplace. Carey (2003) described dominant discourses as 'ideas and beliefs that masquerade as truths and that tell us how we should be in the world'. For example, the dominant contemporary discourse on body image normalises thinness in women. This has resulted in a significant increase in anorexia and bulimia as some women strive to achieve this dominant image (Hargreaves & Tiggemann, 2004).

A post-structuralist approach offers different ways of understanding conflict. It recognises that conflict is itself socially constructed and is a contest over entitlement which is often exaggerated. It also recognises that the operation of power in the workplace is socially constructed and is informed by the dominant discourse in that workplace. The goal or intention of narrative mediation is 'to enable a relational story to go on and to develop a relational narrative that is incompatible with the conflict story. Agreement may be part of this' (Winslade, 2003).

The stages

The practices of narrative facilitate a shift away from 'adversary' towards 'collaboration' in circumstances where 'bullying' has initially been named as the problem by both the organisation and the complainant. Narrative mediation is best understood as occurring in a number of stages. This stages framework is also useful for informing participants of how the narrative mediation process works.

Stage one: individual meetings

In stage one each participant meets the mediator separately. This session normally takes one and a half hours and if more time is required another session is arranged. In this initial meeting, each participant can tell their story of the problem. This allows them to locate the problem and to objectify it through externalising conversations. Externalising invites participants to the mediation to see the conflict or the problem as a third party. By objectifying the problem the person is no longer seen as the problem but rather the problem is the issue. This makes it possible for each person to notice and describe the effects that the problem has brought to their relationship, with the other person and to their lives. A space is then created for the emergence of a different, alternative and more preferred story of the relationship to emerge.

In this process, the dominant discourses supporting the problem are identified and exposed and an alternative or preferred relationship between the antagonists can be storied. The participant can voice the hopes held for the relationship with the other person. They are also given an opportunity to explore what it would be like to sit in a room with the other person and how to signal to the mediator if the situation has become too difficult and the participant wishes the mediation to stop. The role of the mediator is explained to the participant. Furthermore they are invited to bring along a support person if they desire and the role of the support person is explained.

Stage two: joint meeting

The joint meeting is scheduled for three hours with the clear under-standing that either participant can stop the mediation at any time and that another meeting can be scheduled if required. At the joint meeting each participant speaks of their hopes for the mediation and for their future relationship. The mediator explores the importance of these hopes with the participants and together they identify any obstacles that are preventing these hopes from being realised.

This presents the opportunity to locate the problem and to objectify it again through externalising conversations. Participants are then invited to speak about the plans and the influence the problem has had on them and their relationship with the other person. Again the dominant discourses that have supported the problem are identified and exposed. By tracing the history of the problem and when it initially began to impact on their relationship, the possibility for reconstructing the problem is presented. This offers the possibility of a different problem description, one that is shared. The mediator then returns to the hopes that each participant holds and what can be put in place to keep the problem out of their relationship.

Narrative mediation in practice

The following case study looks at narrative mediation in practice using a set of conversations between Lori and Milly (not their real names). It looks at particular practices of narrative mediation and not the whole mediation. It demonstrates how the problem story changes and how together the participants collaborate against the problem.

Lori and Milly's story

Lori and Milly worked together in the same team for just over two years. In the first year they both worked as clinical nurse educators (CNE), but when the then clinical nurse manager (CNM), went on maternity leave Milly was appointed to acting CNM. Lori had submitted a formal complaint to Milly's manager claiming that she was being bullied by Milly. Lori elected to deal with the grievance through mediation with the proviso that if the mediation did not work then the complaint would be formally investigated. Lori and Milly were contacted, the mediation process explained and an individual meeting with each was scheduled.

Individual meetings

Lori

Lori was asked how long she had been a nurse and what it was about nursing that attracted her. She was asked what had brought her to mediation with the intention of hearing her story and working with her to 'name' the problem and to engage in an externalising conversation with the intention of locating the problem and objectifying it.

Mediator: Lori you said that you are here today because you have been bullied by your manager Milly. Are you okay to tell me about what happened that got you naming it as bullying?

Lori: Yes of course. I have been in Milly's team for two years and over time I could feel myself withdrawing as I was scared to contribute in case I got on the wrong side of her. She asks for ideas on things and then I would find out she had already made the decision. She gets defensive when you disagree with her. I felt like I was being victimised and isolated by her. Then a few weeks ago she let rip at me at a team meeting. I always thought of myself as being a strong character, now I don't know any more.

Mediator: So has this been going on for two years?

Lori: Oh no, it started when she got the acting CNM role.

Mediator: I'd like to come back to that but first are you okay to tell me more about the let rip event? What happened?

Lori: Well, I was developing a leaflet to give to the parents of our sick kids and was running way behind schedule. When I reported this at our team meeting, Milly screamed at me

| | saying that she wanted it by the end of the month. I was stunned and humiliated. This was the last straw. |

Mediator: So what happened after the meeting?

Lori: The next day there was note from Milly saying she was sorry and asking me to meet her for coffee. But I didn't believe her. You never knew where you stood; one day she seemed okay and the next day she wasn't. She was never consistent with anything. Team meetings would be postponed at the last minute and for me they are really important. Anyway I reported her to the director of nursing [DON], her manager.

Mediator: There are a number of things I heard there that I would like to come back to if that's okay? I heard you say you never knew where you stood, that Milly was never consistent and I was curious about this and if this speaks to the problem?

Lori: Well yes, that's it, if I knew where I stood, if she was consistent that would be better.

Mediator: So if you had to name the problem now would something like 'The Inconsistency' fit for you?

Lori: Yes that does fit.

Working with Lori, the mediator traced the history of 'The Inconsistency', how long it had been around and how it had impacted on her and her relationship with Milly.

Mediator: Tell me what plans 'The Inconsistency' has had for you and your relationship with Milly?

Lori: Well it's been awful. As I said before I have withdrawn and I felt victimised and isolated. I have had more sick days than normal as some days I just can't face coming to work. It has certainly destroyed the relationship I had with Milly.

Mediator: So are you saying that it was 'The Inconsistency' that perhaps had plans to make you feel victimised and isolated?

Lori: Yes, I think I am. That seems to make more sense now. I am now also thinking about Milly and why she has changed in the last 12 months, since she got the acting job.

Mediator: I was going to ask you what it was like when you first started working together, you said that she has changed, what has she changed from?

This question presents the opportunity to hear about the history of relationship, what it was like before the problem took over, and to then, if appropriate, to ask questions that offer the possibility to expose the discourse that supports the problem.

Lori: It was great; she seemed to really appreciate me, my input. I would say we worked well together. It felt like a real team.

Mediator: If you were to take a guess what do you think brought the change?

Lori: I don't know, maybe it was something to do with getting the CNM role.

Mediator: What do you mean by that?

Lori: Well it's a very senior position, with a lot of responsibility. There's a lot of expectations that go with the job.

Mediator: Where do these expectations come from?

Lori: Let me think. Well it comes from the whole nursing culture.

Mediator: So is it possible that acting differently also comes from that nursing culture?

Lori: I suppose it might.

Mediator: When we get together with Milly is that something you would be interested in finding out more about? About what has brought the change?

Lori: Yes that would be really important.

The mediator continued discussing the first 12 months of Lori working with Milly before moving on to the hopes that Lori held for relationship and what she wanted to take away from the joint meeting with Milly.

Mediator: In thinking about 'The Inconsistency' it sounds like consistency is important in your life and in your work. Is that something that was present before in your relationship with Milly?

Lori: Yes it was, and I would really like it back again.

Mediator: So if it was back again what would be happening, what would it look like?

Lori: Well I would look forward to going to work. I would be able to ask questions without fear and to give input that would be valued. I'd like it to be a professional relationship and that together we would explore problems and strategies. It would also be good to have the team meetings back again and for them to be productive.

At this point the mediator was curious about what Lori might call this working relationship. She named this as 'Working Together' and mediator and participant engaged in an externalising conversation around the preferred story of relationship.

This conversation is an example of how the problem is unpacked and objectified in narrative mediation. The externalising conversation provides the space for the person to take up an alternative position in relation to the problem, one that offers the possibility for collaboration. The mediator returned to other things heard during the session including the importance and meaning of 'team' to Lori. The mediator speculated that for Lori the significance and meaning came from some other experience or knowledge and this was something that was now absent; that is, taking up Michael White's ideas around the absent but the implicit.

Milly

Milly began her individual meeting with revealing how shocked she was to have been accused of bullying. She said she had never had a complaint against her about anything and was shocked that it had happened and particularly that the accusation had come from Lori.

Mediator: How come it was a shock that Lori put in the complaint?
Milly: Well for a couple of reasons, and I've thought a lot about this and frankly I've thought of little else. You see I had been struggling for several months about what to do about Lori and I was about to go to the DON to get some advice when I got hit with this complaint.
Mediator: Did you want to say what it is you were struggling with that got you considering taking it to the DON for advice?
Milly: Yes, well, this might sound silly but Lori had been acting differently.
Mediator: In what way had she been acting differently?
Milly: She'd been getting quieter and quieter. Not talking at team meetings and treating me like she doesn't approve of what I do or say. I knew her mum was sick and at first I put it down to that.
Mediator: You said at first you put it down to her mum being unwell. What got you thinking differently to that?
Milly: Well I was convinced it was to do with her mum until a couple of staff told me that Lori had been going around

saying that she didn't understand how I got the acting CNM job when Martha went on maternity leave. Then she apparently starting saying that I was bullying her. She was clearly undermining me.

Mediator: Once you heard both these things what did you do in response?

Milly: I was really pissed off. I became very cautious around her. I decided not to speak to her unless I really had to.

Mediator: I hear what you said about undermining, but if it's okay I'd like to ask you what you meant when you said that 'apparently' Lori had said you were bullying her?

Milly: Really and honestly speaking I don't know if it's really true, because when I think of the Lori I knew I can't believe she would say that. I mean when I think about what they said Lori said I wondered about their intentions, you know what I mean, was it just gossip.

Mediator: I'd like to come back to the Lori you knew, but first you mentioned the gossip and earlier you talked about the undermining. If you were to name the problem that's brought the trouble between you and Lori would you call it 'The Undermining' or 'The Gossip' or something else?

Milly: Oh I need to think about that [*a fairly long silence ensued*]. It would be 'The Gossip'. Yes that's it.

Mediator: So when you think about 'The Gossip', what impact has 'The Gossip' had on you and your relationship with Lori?

Milly: Look I always thought I was really strong but since 'The Gossip' has been around I've been really worried, I haven't been sleeping well, it's like it's taken over my life. And my relationship with Lori has just deteriorated, as I said before I avoided talking to her. Why just a couple of weeks ago I lost it with Lori in a team meeting. I mean I shouted at her because she was late with a project, I couldn't believe I'd done that. I even tried to apologise.

Milly talked more about the apology and what that said about how she saw the action of shouting. She was very clear in her thinking that it was totally inappropriate and when asked how Lori might have seen it she came to the realisation that Lori may well have named it as bullying.

Mediator: Why do you think she might have seen it as bullying?

Milly: Well I'm her manager and I shouted at her in front of others.

Mediator: Is this something you might speak about when we get together with Lori.

Milly: Oh yes. It might be hard but I'll give it a try.

The mediator further explored the act of avoiding Lori and again how Lori might have named the avoidance. These questions made it possible for Milly to come to an understanding of how Lori would have named her experience of Milly as bullying and to further invite her to take responsibility for her practices and their impacts. The mediator then turned to Milly's hopes for the mediation and her relationship with Lori.

Mediator: I want to ask you about something I heard early in our conversation. You said when you were talking about the allegation of bullying by Lori that the shock came for a couple of reasons. You said that one was because you were struggling with what to do about Lori because she had changed and you were thinking about going to the DON for advice. What was the other reason?

Milly: Just that the complaint had come from Lori.

Mediator: So why was the complaint coming from Lori a shock?

Milly: Well we had gotten on so well before. She was always well organised, always so calm and if we had a problem then we would talk about it.

Mediator: So when you think about how you worked together before does that give you some clues about what you might want for the future?

Milly: Yes it does.

Mediator: Is this something you'd like to get back and if yes how would you describe it?

Milly: Some of the things I'd like back are to be comfortable together, to share ideas, to try things and be flexible.

Mediator: How might you name this preferred story of relationship?

Milly: Mmm, these questions really get me thinking. I'd name it 'Working Well Together'.

Mediator: So what plans do you think 'Working Well Together' might have for you and your relationship with Lori?

Milly: Oh they would be good plans. Coming to work would be great again.

| Mediator: | When I ask you in the joint meeting what your hopes are for the mediation and the future is this something you would be okay talking about or is there something else. |
| Milly: | Yes these are the sort of things I would mention. |

During this conversation, Milly began to see the problem differently and accepted responsibility for what had happened. Finishing each session with the hopes they held facilitated the opportunity to start the joint meeting with 'The Hopes'; in effect starting where the individual meetings left off and avoiding the risk that the first exchange between the two participants would be weighed down with the problem saturated story.

Joint meeting

The joint meeting commenced with outlining the process, the behaviour, stressing confidentiality and a reminder that the process could be stopped at any time. Although these things had been covered in the individual meetings, it was important to set the scene again when they were together. They were then each asked about their hopes for the mediation and their working relationship. Lori offered to start, saying that as this had come about because of her complaint then she should go first.

| Mediator: | Milly before I ask Lori what hopes she holds, can I ask that if you hear anything you want to know more about that you make a note of it and we can come back to that? [*Milly nodded in agreement.*] So tell me Lori what are the hopes you hold for the mediation and the working relationship? |
| Lori: | I have a few. I want to be able to go to work and to feel comfortable and to be able to ask questions. I'd like to be treated the same as the other CNEs and it would be good if you [*talking to Milly*] were open to accepting feedback without taking offence. I'd also like it if we could explore issues together as I'd like to be more involved. And finally can the team meetings be reinstated? When I think about it I want to have a professional working relationship where we communicate well. Really I want us to be able to work like we did before, before you took the acting CNM role. Really and truly I would like to leave here understanding what changed between us. |

The mediator thanked Lori and repeated what she said using her words and advised her that there would be a further opportunity to discuss these. Milly was then asked about the hopes she held. Milly said that she wanted to get on with Lori, to not be afraid, to be able to be herself, to give opinions, to have a flexible working relationship with Lori, to be treated with respect and to find out how all of this started, to find out what happened that got them to this point.

The mediator repeated Milly's words, and let her know that the discussion would return to these hopes before asking each participant if they had heard anything that they wanted to know more about. The mediator then asked each to name the story of their hopes.

Lori:	Well I had thought about 'Working Together'. What about you Milly?
Milly:	I had a similar idea but as I heard you speak the word harmony came to mind. What about 'Working Together in Harmony'?
Lori:	Yes I like that.
Mediator:	I'd like to come back to that naming, but first I was thinking about exploring what has gotten in the way of 'Working Together in Harmony'. Milly do you have any ideas about this from your experience?
Milly:	Well I don't really know. Well I mean it's difficult.
Mediator:	Would it help to think about when things, from where you sit, started to go wrong?
Milly:	Yes, well, for me it was when Lori stopped participating in meetings. At first I thought it was to do with your mum being sick Lori. At that time you just got quieter and quieter, it was like you were withdrawing.
Mediator:	Lori, is that something you recall, getting quieter, withdrawing?
Lori:	Yes I do.
Mediator:	Lori did you want to say what it was that got you withdrawing?
Lori:	Hmm, well this is difficult, but here goes. It's like you changed when you became CNM Milly. Things were different, you stopped listening, you never seemed to have time for anything I said, and you made decisions about my work without even considering what it would mean for me. I started to feel left behind. So it was easier just not to participate. I started to believe you didn't want me in the

	team, and then when you shouted at me in the team meeting I was convinced you were trying to get rid of me. That's why I put in the complaint about you bullying me.
Mediator:	Milly, what was it like hearing that, what did it get you thinking?
Milly:	I had no idea I was like that. I remember how hard I was finding the job, about not having enough time do anything properly. And yes I did shout at you and I am so sorry about that. I had no idea how isolating it felt to be CNM. I had no one to talk to.
Mediator:	You said you had no one to talk to. Before you were CNM would you have talked to anyone?
Milly:	Yes I would have. In fact I would have gone to Lori.
Mediator:	So what do you think stopped you going to Lori after you became CNM?
Milly:	A couple of things I think. In the beginning I believed it would be unprofessional of me to go to someone who was reporting to me.
Mediator:	What got you thinking it would be unprofessional?
Milly:	Well I was CNM, the boss so to speak, and as a nurse that was just a no no!
Mediator:	So are you saying that was a 'no no' in nursing culture.
Milly:	Absolutely. Nursing is very hierarchical.

The mediator followed this line of questioning to expose the discourse operating in nursing culture and to invite the participants to consider to what extent it was this discourse that informed the change in the way Milly behaved.

Mediator:	Milly, you said there were a couple of things that stopped you going to Lori. Did you want to say what the other thing was?
Milly:	Mmmm, this is more difficult. You see, Lori, I heard that you were saying I shouldn't have got the acting CNM job and then that I was bullying you. I was devastated. So I decided that I would have as little to do with you as possible.
Lori:	I never said any of these things. I did say you had changed and that I felt excluded from things.
Mediator:	Is it possible that in hearing what you said that those hearing it found their own name for it?

Lori:	Well I guess that's possible. Actually I remember now. A couple of days before I had that conversation we had all attended a Workplace Bullying Awareness session.
Mediator:	Milly, what's your thinking on this?
Milly:	Look, I always wondered if it was true and what Lori said explains why she withdrew. But I still felt I had to protect myself which I did by avoiding Lori.

The mediator explored with Lori the apology from Milly and what it was like hearing how she was dealing with the CNM role before moving to how each might now name the problem story. As each had described the problem story from their own experience, the mediator now moved to renaming the problem which had caused the discord.

Mediator:	In hearing what the other said about what had happened, what does that get each of you now thinking about how you saw the problem originally? Lori, what are your thoughts on this?
Lori:	It seems now that I came up with a reason why Milly had changed, about why she treated me differently when I didn't know the real reason.
Milly:	I can relate to that. I had no idea until today why you were withdrawing.
Mediator:	It sounds like you're both saying that you came to a conclusion about why the other acted the way they did without really knowing why. If that's the case how might each of you now name what happened?
Lori:	It sounds like I jumped to conclusions. As I said before, I even thought Milly shouting at me in the meeting was her trying to get me out of the team.
Milly:	I think I jumped to conclusions as well. And Lori I can't tell you how sorry I was about shouting at you.
Mediator:	Are you both saying that 'Jumping to Conclusions' more aptly names the problem?

Both agreed with this naming and the mediator then moved to an externalising conversation with them about the plans and intentions that 'Jumping to Conclusions' had for each of them and their relationship with one another. This brought forth descriptions of the effects with each expressing the difficulty they had sleeping, how each hated coming to work and how the problem, 'Jumping to Conclusions', had taken over their lives. In each hearing these effects presented the possibility for them, together, to take a stand against 'Jumping to Conclusions'.

The mediator then returned to the hopes each held for the mediation and their future working relationship. She checked that naming of their preferred story of relationship 'Working Together in Harmony' still fitted for each of them before engaging in an externalising conversation around this naming. The intention here was to thicken this alternative story, to give it a richer description, to dissipate the influence of the problem story of 'Jumping to Conclusions' in ways that made it possible for each to work together in their preferred way and to keep the problem out of their relationship.

From these conversations an 'agreement' was developed. This was called a 'Memorandum of Shared Understanding between Lori and Milly'. This memorandum included their shared hopes from the mediation. The shared understanding was introduced as 'The following reflects our shared understanding and was developed taking into account our hopes and the intention to keep "Jumping to Conclusions" out of our relationship.' The memorandum then described how this would be achieved and concluded with the commitment to get together in a mediation context in three months, or sooner if required, to review and to reflect on where things were at.

Alternative understandings of workplace bullying and the role of mediation

This story of Lori and Milly is not unique, and is in fact typical of many narrative mediations where bullying was in the first instance named as the problem by the complainant.

From this mediation and others, a number of themes have emerged. These themes offer an alternative understanding to the taken for granted truths of workplace bullying that have become the dominant view and to the suitability of mediation. These alternative understandings are summarised as follows:

- The person making the allegation of bullying was not singled out, was not targeted.
- The practices named as bullying were not intentional, were not systematic and were not intended to do harm.
- The effects of these practices, which are not disputed, were experienced by both the person making the claim and the person the claim of bullying is against.

- The history of relationship identified a time when the relationship was not problematic and through a process of exploration an event or events can be named that got in the way of the relationship.
- The ways of expressing personal agency and responsible action were limited because each person was subject to the traditional or dominant understandings of power relations. That is, their decision on how to respond was informed by such things as entitlement and hierarchy and the prevailing workplace culture and what behaviours it permits.
- (Narrative) mediation is a suitable intervention where there have been allegations of bullying regardless of the 'stage' of the conflict.
- (Narrative) mediation creates a space for participants to take responsibility for their actions and the effects.

Summary

The history of workplace bullying has largely been informed by a single voice. This single voice is that of those who claim to have been bullied. The voice of those who it is claimed have bullied has not been heard, and in fact this voice has not been sought. Narrative mediation offers the opportunity for both voices to be heard. This has made it possible for a different understanding, for some different proposals of workplace bullying and its practices to be considered.

In thinking about this, what might we be saying now about this thing called workplace bullying if we had recruited the voice of not only those making the claim of bullying but also the voice of those it was alleged had bullied?

Note

1 Post-structuralism proposes that our identities are constantly created in relationship with others, with institutions and within the broader relations of power and further, that our ideas, problems and qualities are all products of culture and history. It further proposes that language plays a vital role in shaping life as what is said and the meaning we give to what is said is the shaping of our lives and our identities (Russell & Carey, 2004).

References

Carey, M. (2003) *1st Dulwich Centre Summer School, Practice Seminar: An Introduction to Narrative Therapy.* Adelaide, South Australia.

Clarke, J. (2005) *Working with Monsters: How to Identify and Protect Yourself from the Workplace Psychopath.* Sydney: Random House.

de Guzman, E. B. (2010) *In Search of a Solution: A Meta-analysis of Workplace Bullying vis-à-vis Mediation*. 7th International Conference on Workplace Bullying & Harassment, Cardiff, Wales.

Hargreaves, D. A., & Tiggemann, M. (2004) Idealized media images and adolescent body image: 'comparing' boys and girls. *Body Image*, 1(4): 351–361.

Namie, G., & Namie, R. (2009) *The Bully at Work: What You Can Do to Stop the Hurt and Reclaim Your Dignity on the Job*. Naperville, IL: Sourcebooks.

Russell, S., & Carey, M. (2004) *Narrative Therapy: Responding to your Questions*. Adelaide: Dulwich Centre Publications.

White, M. (2005) *Narrative Practice and Exotic Lives: Resurrecting Diversity in Everyday Life*. Adelaide: Dulwich Centre Publications.

White, M. (2007) *Maps of Narrative Practice*. New York: Norton.

White, M., & Epston, D. (1990) *Narrative Means to Therapeutic Ends*. New York: Norton.

Winslade, J. (2003) *1st Dulwich Centre Summer School, Keynote: Narrative Mediation*. Adelaide, South Australia.

Winslade, J., & Monk, G. D. (2000) *Narrative Mediation – A New Approach to Conflict Resolution*. San Francisco: Jossey-Bass.

Winslade, J., & Monk, G. D. (2008) *Practicing Narrative Mediation: Loosening the Grip of Conflict*. San Francisco: Jossey-Bass.

Chapter 9

Coaching abrasive leaders

Contradictory tales of the Big Bad Wolf

Laura Crawshaw

Early encounters

I am thankful that I knew nothing about so-called *bully bosses* when I first encountered them over 30 years ago in Alaska. I worked as a psychotherapist in Alaska's first employee assistance programme (EAP), providing counselling to troubled employees of over 500 employers who contracted for this confidential service. It was here that I first encountered what I refer to as 'abrasive leaders'. Abrasion is generally defined as the process of wearing down by means of friction, injury, or irritation (Simpson & Weiner, 1989); an apt description for the emotional erosion experienced by those who work with an abrasive leader. When I started coaching such leaders in 1980, I was unaware of the small but growing body of literature claiming that these individuals were evil predators who intentionally set out to exterminate their co-workers, reminiscent of the evil wolves in fairy tales who delighted in devouring innocent grandmothers, children, and assorted little pigs. If I had read and accepted the big bad bully tale as fact, I never would have entertained the possibility that they could be helped to improve their management styles. Beyond that, I would have feared for my own safety, as taming savage beasts is a perilous profession – would not the same hold for taming savage leaders?

I do not use the term 'bully' when referring to interpersonally destructive individuals, for it implies an intent to harm. In the course of life's interactions, we may cause suffering in others intentionally or unintentionally, and may or may not be aware of the impact of our words or actions. To label a leader whose conduct creates suffering a bully suggests that they intend to cause harm, and thus must be fully aware of the impact of their hurtful behaviour. Instead, I refer to these individuals, who are charged with authority over others, as *abrasive leaders*, a term describing only the effects of their behaviour, without alluding to cause. We know that abrasive leaders rub their co-workers (whether subordinates, peers, or superiors) the wrong way. We do not necessarily know the facts of why.

Trained as a psychotherapist to help people address their own or other's destructive behaviours, I worked from a foundation of clinical objectivity, developing a deep respect for the individuality of my patients, paired with intense curiosity regarding the emotions that motivated their behaviours. Later, as an executive coach, I applied this same stance as I encountered abrasive leaders. Unburdened by any preconceptions, I asked them to join with me in a process of mutual inquiry that could help us understand the meaning and impact of their destructive interpersonal conduct, hopefully resulting in management approaches that no longer left a trail of working wounded in their wake. I did not believe they were hopeless, nor did I believe I was helpless to help them.

Abrasive behaviours

The behaviours displayed by the abrasive leaders I encountered shared two common denominators: others perceived their words and actions as disrespectful, and, in turn, their words and actions disrupted organisational functioning. I have interviewed more than 1000 co-workers over the past 20 years and identified a wide variety of behaviours, including, but not limited to shouting, swearing, making threats, publicly demeaning others, overcontrol (micromanagement), intimidation, and condescension, all characterised by the common denominator of disrespectful conduct. I also learned how the suffering of these co-workers, manifested in decreased morale and motivation, disrupted organisational functioning through lowered productivity, increased attrition, litigation, and, in the most extreme cases, retaliatory responses such as sabotage and workplace violence. While working in Alaska, more than one distressed employee sought help at the EAP to contain their homicidal impulses toward an abrasive leader. Only later did I learn that the abrasive leaders who caused such distress were referred to more commonly as *workplace bullies*, or *bully bosses*. But in these early encounters, I simply perceived them as individuals displaying dysfunctional behaviour.

Mutual exploration

I was filled with curiosity. Did they see themselves as abrasive? Were they aware of the negative impact of their behaviour on others, and the specific nature of the negative perceptions this behaviour generated? Did they see the costs to their employers resulting from decreased employee motivation? Did they see the costs to themselves imposed by threatened disciplinary action for unacceptable conduct? What motivated them to behave in ways that co-workers perceived so negatively? Where did they learn these behaviours, and why did they elect to use them? Did they believe that they could control the behaviours? What, if anything, would motivate them to seek to develop a less destructive interpersonal management style? And, if they chose to change, what would help them achieve and permanently maintain interpersonal competence?

In the course of the coaching conversations that now span 30 years, I explored these questions with my clients, gathering data that became the foundation for my efforts to learn why abrasive leaders behave aggressively with co-workers, and what can be done to help them change. Only later did I come to understand that this mutual exploration of these issues constituted *action research*, defined as a process in which the validity and value of research results are tested through collaborative participant-professional (in this case, client-coach) knowledge generation and application processes to increase fairness, wellness, and self-determination (Greenwood & Levin, 2000). I did not see how my clients could possibly determine what behaviours they needed to change until they had specific data on the behaviours that their co-workers found objectionable. Standard 360-degree assessments were patently unhelpful, in that they provided only very general feedback, asking co-workers to rate the leader's 'ability to create an effective team' or 'ability to build trust with co-workers'. Abrasive leaders who received low scores were at a loss to decipher which of their words or actions had led to these poor evaluations.

Responses to feedback

Provided with only general feedback, clients denied that they were abrasive, or minimised their impact on others. 'I'm not abrasive – they're the ones that can't handle direct communication!' or, 'I can be tough at times, but people accept that.' Many were mystified by their employer's insistence that they improve their interpersonal conduct: 'I don't see what the big issue is here – I'm the only one around here that gets results, and now I'm getting punished for it?!' This initial denial or minimisation is a characteristic response of abrasive leaders when they receive general feedback. Instead of debating whether or not they are abrasive, I instead offered the coaching client an appealing proposition:

You have told me that you don't understand why your employer is demanding that you change your management style – that you don't have clear information on the complaints people have made about you. I can help you with this. I would like you to engage me as your co-researcher, to interview your co-workers and discover what the negative perceptions are and what causes them. That data will give us an opportunity to develop strategies to eliminate these negative perceptions – to manage them out of existence, so that they never again disrupt your professional effectiveness.

Assured that the findings of our research would remain confidential, clients were eager to have me discover the exact nature of the negative perceptions through interviews with co-workers. In the majority of cases, these leaders had received only minimal feedback prior to the referral to coaching, and what they had heard was usually phrased in generalities: 'People have been complaining that you're hard to work with – that they don't feel you treat them with respect.' When asked for specifics regarding the complaints, employers understandably tended to withhold detailed information from the individual for fear that he or she would retaliate against the complaining co-worker(s). To solve this problem, I conducted individual interviews with co-workers (selected separately by both the leader and the employer) and asked for detail regarding the words and actions that they perceived as abrasive. 'What exactly did he/she do or say?' 'When you say that he/she can be rough on people, can you describe that in more detail?' This data was then purged of identifying information, aggregated into behavioural themes, and provided only to the abrasive leader. This commitment to confidentiality for all parties served to protect co-workers and allowed the leader to examine the negative perceptions without fear of immediate repercussions from the employer.

Abrasive leaders' reactions to the lengthy, highly detailed lists of negative perceptions reinforced my initial impression of their blindness to the emotions of others. As these blinders came off, the leaders voiced shock and bewilderment at the nature and degree of the perceived destructive impact on co-workers: 'I can't believe that people think I'm out to get them. I'm just trying to get the job done – it's nothing personal.' Second, they appeared to have little or no insight into why their behaviours alienated others. 'Calling someone's idea stupid doesn't mean that I actually think they're stupid – why would they take offence at that?' In summary, they were astonished by the volume and negativity of the perceptions, and especially confounded by accusations that they caused distress out of malicious intent. 'The hardest thing to deal with in all of this feedback is the perception that I don't care about people – that I want to hurt them.'

The power of perceptions

In the course of their feedback sessions, clients quickly came to understand the power of perceptions. The initial debate over whether or not the client was abrasive was silenced by this incontrovertible evidence that the client was *perceived* to be abrasive. This they could not deny. Once they recovered from their shock, clients expressed immediate motivation to eliminate the negative perceptions and replace them with positive ones. 'I want to do what it takes to turn this around. I do not want people seeing me this way. It's no good for them, and no good for me.' Many spontaneously abandoned those behaviours that cause the most obvious damage. 'I stopped swearing – I haven't done it since.' 'I'm careful to issue criticism privately, now that I realise how much damage I did dressing people down in meetings.' Those who were unable to devise appropriate replacement behaviours asked for help developing more effective strategies that are more effective: 'So how do I get people to do what I want done without yelling at them?' Previously unaware, they were now motivated to gain insight into the negative perceptions that mystified them: 'People say that they can't trust me. I've always seen myself as honest and straightforward. I just don't get it – I'm going to need help to understand what this is all about.'

Defence against threats to competence

As we worked together to understand the origins of these negative perceptions and the interpersonal dynamics that generated them, clients related their own frustrations in trying to achieve their work objectives. Over time, I observed that these abrasive individuals reflexively experienced any perceived co-worker incompetence as a direct threat to their own competence: 'I struggle with people who can't move ahead – I have the patience of a wounded rhino. I can't deal with people who stand in the way of my vision.' They defended against this perceived threat to their professional competence with aggression: 'I have trouble when people put blocks in front of me. I am ruthless; I hang them out to dry.' Additionally, abrasive leaders viewed their use of aggression as both necessary and even noble to achieve organisational goals: 'Sometimes, you've got to kick people to get them moving – I want this company to succeed.' As coaching progressed, clients came to understand the critical importance of monitoring and managing their own and other's emotions in the workplace. *Emotional intelligence* is another term for this capacity to read and manage one's own and others' feelings 'so that they are expressed appropriately and effectively, enabling people to work together *smoothly* [emphasis added] toward their common goals' (Goleman, 1998: 7). Finally, I was continually struck by the rapidity with which these abrasive leaders realised that riding roughshod over co-workers' emotions constituted interpersonal, and ultimately, managerial incompetence.

These discoveries controverted the aforementioned popularly held belief that abrasive leaders are predatory creatures who are intent on doing harm, are fully aware of the impact of their actions, and inflict interpersonal wounds as a result of impaired moral or mental functioning. On the contrary, I found that the great majority of these individuals were interpersonally *blind*. Insecure regarding their own competence, they also displayed a profound lack of psychological insight into the dynamics and impact of their defensive aggression toward co-workers. These discoveries also explained the characteristic denial that organisations encountered when they attempted to intervene with abrasive leaders. 'We've tried to talk to her, but she denies that she's the problem – she blames co-workers and doesn't see her role in it.' These coaching clients did not view their interpersonally aggressive behaviour as unacceptable or abnormal. Instead, many would relate that they either grew up with such behaviour or encountered it in their earlier work experiences and considered their aggression to be the optimal (and often only) strategy. The origins of this abrasive style, as well as specific organisational strategies to deal with this denial, are discussed further in *Taming the Abrasive Manager: How to End Unnecessary Roughness in the Workplace* (Crawshaw, 2007).

Having coached over 400 abrasive leaders, on only two occasions have I encountered individuals who manifested symptoms of sociopathy. They stood out almost immediately as they contemplated their feedback, one dismissing the negative perceptions expressed by co-workers as worthless, the other elaborating on the pleasure she took in tormenting her male co-workers (suggestive of sadistic tendencies). Both found ways to avoid the coaching process, one by leaving the company, the other by seeking protection from a superior whose own professional survival was entirely dependent on her technical competence. Compare these two 'big bad bullies' to the preponderance of abrasive leaders who reacted very differently when they learned of the negative perceptions held by their co-workers. They expressed shock: 'I can't believe people see me this way.' They expressed remorse: 'I never meant to hurt anyone – I was just trying to get the job done.' They were mystified: 'Why would they take my words so personally – they weren't meant to be taken personally!' And they were embarrassed: 'It's horrible to think that people see me as so out of control, as a figure of ridicule.'

These findings are phrased as generalisations, and I am the first to acknowledge that these coaching encounters with abrasive clients do not constitute formal research that could yield conclusive empirical data on this population or conclusive evidence of the Boss Whispering method's (Crawshaw, 2010) efficacy. In view of this, one could look upon these reports as yet another tale, not of big, bad wolves, but of highly anxious humans, blindly defending against those whom they perceive as threats to their workplace competence and professional survival.

The psychodynamic of defence

Defensive behaviour follows a fairly predictable course in all members of the animal kingdom, humans and wolves included. When an organism perceives a physical *threat*, the perception generates fear (*anxiety*), which mobilises the target to *defend* against this threat through *fight or flight*. For the benefit of my clients, I describe this dynamic of *threat* → *anxiety* → *defence* as the *T-A-D* dynamic. Sigmund Freud (1923, 1926) and later Anna Freud (1936) proposed that this same dynamic applies to the psychological realm (e.g. when a human perceives a psychological threat, this perception generates anxiety, which in turn mobilises the individual to defend against the threat through the mechanisms of *fight* or *flight*). 'He was always barking at employees, implying they were stupid or worthless. Some would fight back and try to defend themselves, with no success. Others would just clam up – they'd withdraw.'

In the course of my work with abrasive leaders, I discovered that they vigorously defend against any perceived threats to their professional competence (and thus, survival) with the *fight* mechanism: with interpersonal aggression. Driven to demonstrate their superior competence (a defence against unconscious self-perceptions of inadequacy), they experience immediate and intense anxiety when co-workers do not meet their expectations, and defend against these threats to their competence with aggression.

As individuals develop a somewhat stable self, that self becomes the 'filter mechanism' through which he perceives himself and his world, and by which he evaluates his and others' effectiveness in it. The individual will tend to accept those experiences consonant with his self, and he will tend to distort, deny, and reject that behavior that is different from, and not immediately integratable with, his self. The latter is usually described as defensive behavior. Behavior is 'defensive' when it is a response to a perceived threat to the self.

(Argyris, 1962: 18)

I eventually concluded that the majority of these abrasive leaders were neither evil nor insane; instead, they were *afraid*, fearful of perceived threats to their competence, which, in their view, could jeopardise their workplace survival. Insight into the critical role of the threat-anxiety-defence dynamic underlying abrasive conduct proved instrumental in the formulation of the Boss Whispering coaching method (Crawshaw, 2010). This psychodynamic, drawn from sociobiological and psychoanalytic theories, was shared with abrasive leaders as a conceptual framework to help them better understand their aggressive responses to co-workers. Looking through this interpretive lens of psychological defensiveness also gave abrasive leaders insight into why co-workers resisted (defended against) their initiatives. They came to see that co-workers manifested resistance was not because they were stupid, slothful or insolent (the leaders' earlier primitive theories); they resisted because they perceived the abrasive leader as a threat, and defended against this threat through fight or flight. The next stage of the coaching process encouraged clients to test this new hypothesis by constructing non-aggressive management strategies (including mentoring and other forms of support) to reduce co-worker fight/flight reactions as well as ensuing negative perceptions. 'Now people listen to what I say, instead of complaining about how I say it.'

Instilling of insight

To my continued astonishment, clients demonstrated the value of this insight through increased empathy and decreased aggression. Before, they considered themselves crusaders for competence and viewed their aggression as necessary, ethical, and admirable. They took pride in communicating without tact (which they previously viewed as duplicitous 'sugar-coating') or consideration for others' emotions ('useless touchy-feely stuff'). In summary, abrasive leaders felt that threats to their competence could only be overcome through force, through aggressively wielding the sword of power to decapitate co-worker resistance (Crawshaw, 2005). Once they grasped the T-A-D dynamic, they shifted from the 'crusader for competence' stance to a more empathic perspective, exemplified in comments such as 'Now I understand why they didn't speak up when I asked them to – they were afraid I'd criticise their input', or 'As soon as he pushed back, I could feel myself wanting to attack, but I didn't – it wouldn't solve the problem'.

Coaching continued through repeated iterations of mutual analysis of co-worker and client behaviours through the T-A-D lens. By the third or fourth session, clients consistently displayed insight into the impact of their behaviours: 'I thought that by criticising one person's performance in front of the team, everyone would learn from those mistakes. Now I realise that it only alienated them – they all felt threatened.' Once clients displayed the ability to apply this newfound insight in the construction of non-abrasive management strategies (usually by the sixth session), I then re-interviewed co-workers to gather data on their current perceptions of the leader's style. They reported improved conduct: 'The shouting has stopped'; examples of improved emotional control: 'She doesn't lose her temper anymore'; as well as surprise and gratitude for the leader's willingness to work to change: 'I never would have believed this could happen – it means so much to me that he's really trying.'

Reduction of suffering

Am I spinning yet another tale, one of magical transformation and happily-ever-after endings? In reality, I observed a fairly consistent pattern: as these leaders integrated and applied their new insight, co-worker suffering was dramatically reduced, if not wholly eliminated. The leader's conduct achieved an acceptable level: 'Paul will always have his rough edges, but now he treats people decently.' Co-workers were grateful that the employer intervened, dispelling any prior perceptions that management condoned bullying behaviours. Beyond this, formerly abrasive clients expressed gratitude and increased loyalty as a result of their employers' willingness to intervene and offer help through coaching (vs. demotion or termination). Employers were thankful to have found a way to retain the leader's expertise without risking further damage to the organisation through impaired productivity, increased attrition, and harassment litigation. Follow-up with employers confirmed that their formerly abrasive leaders were able to sustain acceptable levels of conduct. As a practitioner who is interested in reducing suffering in the workplace, I was thankful when employers referred more abrasive clients as soon as they detected a problem: 'We've got another one for you – we hired him six months ago, and we're already getting complaints about his interactions.'

As I noted earlier, I knew nothing about workplace bullies or workplace bullying when I began coaching abrasive leaders. I only knew that I was working with these individuals in a manner that appeared to be helpful, and determined to explore this phenomenon further in my doctoral studies. I was eager to review the literature and learn of other intervention methods developed for this population. I found a few theoretical analyses of abrasive leaders, but had no success locating coaching or training methods specifically designed to help them improve their management styles. Kaplan (1991) described *expansive* executives as those whose insatiable appetite for mastery reflects underlying insecurity. 'Fundamentally, they do not have a secure feeling of their own worth. For this reason they are inordinately concerned with performing well' (Kaplan, 1991: 58). In a *Harvard Business Review* article entitled 'The Abrasive Personality' Levinson (1978) described these leaders as 'people who puzzle, dismay, frustrate, and enrage others in organisations' (p. 86), and as 'men and women of high, sometimes brilliant, achievement who stubbornly insist on having their own way and are contemptuous of others' (p. 87). From his perspective as psychoanalyst and management consultant, Levinson theorised that such leaders were driven by the desire for perfection, reflective of an unconscious self-perception of inadequacy, and a resulting need to see oneself as extraordinary. These conceptualisations resonated with my findings. Encouraged by this discovery, I contacted the Levinson Institute to get more information on their method, only to be told that their consultants did not utilise a specific method, instead coaching each individual leader 'according to their individual needs'. Undaunted by my inability to locate other defined methods for helping abrasive leaders, I then contacted the top 20 executive education programmes (from *Business Week* magazine's annual ranking) to ask if they offered training interventions specifically designed for this population. The 14 programmes responding stated that they did not offer any such programmes, with one respondent (who wished to remain anonymous) noting that their general leadership development course had jokingly been referred to as a 'charm school for assholes'.

Tales of the Big Bad Bully

This pejorative reference to abrasive leaders signalled my first encounters with the less objective, more hostile popular literature on workplace bullying and those who engage in bullying behaviours. Descriptions of abrasive leaders in the popular literature shared strikingly similar characteristics. Typically, these leaders were portrayed as the 'Big Bad Wolf' of the workplace – as morally or mentally deranged predators intent on perpetrating harm. Book titles reflected this savage characterisation: *Brutal Bosses and Their Prey* (Hornstein, 1996), *Snakes in Suits: When Psychopaths Go To Work* (Babiak & Hare, 2006), *Corporate Hyenas at Work: How to Spot and Outwit Them by Being Hyenawise* (Marais & Herman, 1997), and *A Survival Guide for Working With Bad Bosses: Dealing With Bullies, Idiots, Back-stabbers, and Other Managers from Hell* (Scott, 2005). Books and articles in this genre offered dramatically derisive categorisations of these leaders, such as *bully, paranoid, narcissist, bureaucrazy, disaster hunter* (Bing, 1992), *constant critic, two-headed snake, gatekeeper, screaming mimi* (Namie & Namie, 2003), or more simply, *assholes* (Sutton, 2007). Remarkably, even the authors of one of the earliest scholarly examinations of abrasive leaders (Lombardo & McCall, 1984) could not resist the impulse to classify these individuals as *snakes in the grass, Attilas, heel grinders, egotists, dodgers, business incompetents, detail drones, not respected*, and *slobs*.

These impassioned descriptions of 'Big Bad Bully' behaviours were inevitably accompanied by the assertion that these individuals deliberately and intentionally set out to harm co-workers because they are evil, crazy, or some combination of the two. Definitions of workplace bullying often incorporate this perspective; in his book *Adult Bullying: Perpetrators and Victims*, Randall (1997) defined bullying as 'aggressive behavior arising from the deliberate intent to cause physical or psychological distress to others' (p. 4), while Namie and Namie (2003) defined bullying at work as 'repeated, malicious, health-endangering mistreatment of one employee (the Target) by one or more employees (the bully, bullies). The mistreatment is psychological violence, a mix of verbal and strategic assaults to prevent the Target from performing work well' (p. 3).

I was fascinated by this assertion, as it differed so dramatically from my findings on the motivation underlying abrasive conduct. The abrasive leaders I encountered in the course of my coaching and research (aside from the two possible sociopaths) bore no resemblance to these bloodthirsty workplace wolves malevolently calculating strategies to prey upon their co-workers. On the contrary, the individuals I coached seemed blinder than bats – most were entirely unaware of their destructive impact on others, and those who had some slight awareness minimised the degree of impact: 'I know I can be hard on people, but they don't take it personally – They know it's just business.' There is no question that abrasive leaders can cause terrible suffering – I learned of the deep wounds as I interviewed co-workers contemplating suicide and homicide in response to the pain they experienced. But how was I to understand the dramatically differing perspectives on the motivation of abrasive leaders? Was their aggression the result of anxiety or malevolence? Were we dealing with big bad wolves, or anxious humans who knew no better ways to manage their work-related anxiety? What could explain these contradictory perceptions?

Contradictory interpretations of behaviour

The Boss Whispering coaching method is based upon the premise that the exercise of empathy can generate insight. In this approach, abrasive leaders are asked to put themselves in the psychological shoes of co-workers to gain insight into how the leader's words and actions could be perceived as threatening. This method evolved from my determination to walk in the psychological shoes of my clients, the abrasive leaders. In doing so, I gained insight into their experience of their work habitats, perceived to be fraught with threats to their competence that they warded off with defensive aggression. Why not attempt to put myself in the psychological shoes of victims (also known as *targets*) of workplace bullying in the hope of gaining insight into the 'Big Bad Bully' perspective they held? Pursuing this line of thought in the context of wolves, it dawned upon me that victims of wolf attacks could understandably draw very different conclusions about wolf behaviour than conclusions drawn by wolf researchers. Victims could report that they had been singled out by the wolf, targeted as the victim, and conclude that the wolf intended to attack. These perceptions seem very reasonable. Victims could also conclude that wolves commit terribly destructive acts. This, too, is true. It is possible that fairy tales involving big wolves were based upon the realistic danger posed by these predators. The wolves in these fables are depicted as calculating and malevolent – as forces of evil. They do bad things, and therefore must be bad.

Yet, researchers of wolf behaviour might hold a very different perspective. Wolves attack not because they are bad, but because they are defending against threats to their survival, namely, starvation. I envisioned interviewing these wolves (as I had interviewed abrasive leaders), and suspected that, if they could talk, they would sound much like my clients: 'Yes, I can bark and bite – I'm known to chew on others, but they understand it's strictly business – nothing personal.' Research of wolf behaviour reveals that their aggression toward victims is borne not out of evil, but as a defence against threats to physical survival. I suspect that further research on abrasive leaders may support a similar conclusion: that their aggression serves as a defence against perceived threats to professional survival, and is, in the majority of cases, not enacted with the intent to harm but to survive. Research of human behaviour indicates that the majority of people who inflict distress do not intend to hurt others. In Leary *et al.*'s (1998) study, over 80 per cent indicated that they had no intention to hurt others' feelings, and that the hurt had been accidental or the result of inconsiderateness and insensitivity. Miller (2001) noted that people engage in abrasive behaviours out of sheer ignorance, lacking awareness of the appropriate relational rules (Metts, 1994), or because of some type of social skill deficit on the part of the perpetrator (Miller, 2001). I present my findings not as definitive empirical evidence, but to encourage others to consider alternative theories – other 'tales' or theories on why leaders resort to bullying behaviours. The Boss Whispering Institute, dedicated to research and training in the field of coaching abrasive leaders, is now gathering such data to submit to external scientific scrutiny.

How, then do we account for the scenario in which one person is singled out for extreme aggression? I propose we term this phenomenon *focused bullying* as opposed to the aforementioned generalised bullying displayed toward multiple individuals. Listen to this tale, related by an employee of an abrasive executive. The executive engaged in a variety of abrasive behaviours directed toward his entire team, including shouting, public humiliation, and over-control; constituting generalised bullying. In an effort to enlighten her boss, this employee gently explained to him that his motto 'Believe or Leave' did not, as he believed, motivate his team, but only served to reduce morale. 'Looking back, I know that was the turning point – the moment when he decided I wasn't "on board" and needed to go. From that point on, he did everything he could to drive me out of there. After I left, I learned that his plan was to replace me with a past colleague of his who "never gave me [the boss] any trouble".'

Here we see generalised bullying intensify into focused bullying, focused on those employees who are perceived to pose a greater threat to the abrasive leader. They may have directly challenged the leader, failed to fulfil the leader's expectations, or in the case of this unfortunate employee, pointed out the leader's incompetence in an effort to help. For highly insecure abrasive leaders, perceived extreme threats to one's professional survival must be annihilated, or, as we say in the business world, terminated. They must be driven out of the pack to ensure the leader's continued dominant status.

Obstacles to research

Stepping into the victim's perspective helped me understand the intensely hostile stance of those who have been subjected to abrasive leadership behaviour. It also explained why I felt like such a lone voice in the wilderness of workplace bullying, as I proposed that abrasive leaders do bad things not out of malevolence, but as a defence against threat. Although there are legions of victims of abrasive leadership conduct, there are woefully few researchers of perpetrators of workplace bullying. Unlike wolves, abrasive leaders are almost impossible to access as research subjects. Since they do not perceive themselves to be abrasive, they would not tend to volunteer to be research subjects. Employers, too, would be understandably reluctant to respond to a researcher's request for access to that company's abrasive leaders; what company wants to publicise its inability to solve the problem of workplace bullying? Rayner and Cooper (2003) described this dilemma:

> Gathering data about black holes is difficult because we cannot see them. . . . We know that black holes exist only because of celestial bodies around them. . . . For those who study negative behaviour at work, the *bully* is the parallel of black holes – almost invisible to us. We gain all our data regarding bullies from other people and events that happen around them. . . . Finding and studying the bully is like trying to study black holes – we are often chasing scattered debris of complex data and shadows of the past.
>
> (Rayner & Cooper, 2003: 47)

As we contemplate these contradictory tales of big bad bullies (related by victims) and anxious, defensive leaders (related by this researcher-practitioner), it is important to acknowledge that we are still in the dark as we seek to find solutions to workplace bullying. The bully-busting genre of books mentioned earlier is strong on describing symptoms, but simplistic as far as offering solutions. Employers are instructed first to establish anti-bullying policies, and then admonished to avoid hiring abrasive leaders. Finally, if one should somehow infiltrate the organisation, he or she is to be terminated immediately upon detection. I am unaware of any screening tool that reliably predicts abrasive behaviour in humans; if such an instrument existed, one would think it would be universally applied prior to finalising today's employment or marital contracts.

Little empathy is displayed for employers who fail to take these measures. They are portrayed as depraved masterminds of abuse, caring only about profit and nothing about their employees. In this scenario, prosecuting and penalising these organisational offenders will compel them to exterminate their big, bad work wolves on sight. Unlike wolves, terminating abrasive leaders will not lead to their extinction, as they will only go on to cause distress in future employment situations. Nor will litigation provide a complete solution to the problem of workplace bullying, as redress occurs only after the trauma has occurred, and the inevitable financial and psychological costs of this process risk further traumatisation of victims.

Solutions: a tripartite approach

Most civilised societies have chosen to address other forms of abuse through a tripartite approach of prevention, intervention, and prosecution. In the realm of child abuse, prevention consists of education and policy development for those who interact unacceptably with children. Intervention takes many forms, including removal of the child, and specialised training and/or counselling for abusive parents. Laws enacted against child abuse are considered effective only in conjunction with prevention and intervention approaches. Perpetrators of child abuse are researched with clinical objectivity, producing effective intervention strategies. We see no books titled 'Toxic Tot Tormentors' or 'Baby Bashers and their Prey', for in this field there appears to be an understanding that we cannot help perpetrators if we demonise them.

As we contemplate tales of big, bad wolves and abrasive leaders, I would like to ask readers to consider another tale, one that offers one solution to workplace bullying. Imagine workplaces in the here and now, where employers have declared that all employees shall be provided with a physically and psychologically safe environment in which to work. These employers do their best to hire technically and interpersonally competent individuals who are productive and treat one another respectfully. Because they lack magical powers to predict who might display abrasive behaviour in the course of work, they are alert for any reports of disrespectful conduct voiced by employees, and do not hesitate to take these negative perceptions seriously. Identified abrasive leaders are informed of the proliferation of complaints, and charged with improving their management styles, to end further distress and disruption to the smooth functioning of the organisation. At the same time, these employers offer help in the form of specialised coaching, and monitor the leaders' interpersonal conduct. If an acceptable level of interpersonal conduct is achieved, suffering ends and all parties live happily ever after. Employers maintain productivity and avert the risk of employee litigation, while employees appreciate their employers' early intervention, and are heartened by the leaders' willingness to change. These now interpersonally competent leaders also experience appreciation for their employers' willingness to offer help instead of immediately moving to termination, and look upon the coaching process as an enjoyable and empowering experience. However, not all tales (fairy or otherwise) have happy endings. What about those occasions when leaders fail to benefit from coaching and must be terminated? In these rare cases, employee suffering ends, and employers will rest assured that they did (and, in the case of litigation, can demonstrate they did) everything in their not-so-magical powers to help these abrasive leaders resolve the situation successfully.

This particular tale is a true tale. It takes place not once upon a time, nor in a land far, far away; it is a living reality experienced by organisations that seek out coaches specifically trained to work with abrasive leaders. Thanks to my ignorance of tales about big, bad, bully bosses and the supposedly evil organisations that employ them, I was able to develop one method to help abrasive leaders relinquish their destructive management strategies and increase their interpersonal competence. I look forward to the evolution of this and other approaches designed to address the problem of abrasive leadership. We are humans, not wolves, and we can all be abrasive at different times and under different circumstances. Only by maintaining an objective and empathic stance toward all parties involved in the phenomenon of workplace bullying will we find a way to address the symptoms with true solutions.

References

Argyris, C. (1962) *Interpersonal Competence and Organizational Effectiveness.* Homewood, IL: Dorsey Press.

Babiak, P., & Hare, R. (2006) *Snakes in Suits: When Psychopaths Go to Work.* New York: HarperCollins.

Bing, S. (1992) *Crazy Bosses: Spotting Them, Serving Them, Surviving Them.* New York: William Morrow.

Crawshaw, L. (2005) *Coaching abrasive executives: exploring the use of empathy in constructing less destructive interpersonal management strategies.* Unpublished PhD dissertation, Fielding Graduate University.

Crawshaw, L. (2007) *Taming the Abrasive Manager: How to End Unnecessary Roughness in the Workplace.* San Francisco: Jossey-Bass.

Crawshaw, L. (2010) Coaching abrasive leaders: using action research to reduce suffering and increase productivity in organizations. *International Journal of Coaching in Organizations*, 29, 8(1): 60–77.

Freud, A. (1936) Ego and the mechanisms of defense. In *The Writings of Anna Freud*, Vol. 2. New York: International Universities Press.

Freud, S. (1923) The ego and the id. In J. Strachey (ed.) *Standard Edition of the Complete Psychological Works of Sigmund Freud* (Vol. 19: 3–182). London: Hogarth Press.

Freud, S. (1926) Inhibitions, symptoms and anxiety. In J. Strachey (ed.) *Standard Edition of the Complete Psychological Works of Sigmund Freud* (Vol. XX: 87–172). London: Hogarth Press.

Goleman, D. (1998) *Working with Emotional Intelligence*. New York: Bantam.

Greenwood, D. J., & Levin, M. (2000) Reconstructing the relationships between universities and society through action research. In N. K. Denzin & Y. S. Lincoln (eds) *Handbook of Qualitative Research*, 2nd edn. Thousand Oaks, CA: Sage.

Hornstein, H. A. (1996) *Brutal Bosses and their Prey: How to Identify and Overcome Abuse in the Workplace*. New York: Riverhead Books.

Kaplan, R. E. (1991) *Beyond Ambition: How Driven Managers Can Lead Better and Live Better*. San Francisco: Jossey-Bass.

Leary, M. R., Springer, C., Negel, L., Ansell, E., & Evans, K. (1998) The causes, phenomenology, and consequences of hurt feelings. *Journal of Personality and Social Psychology*, 74(5): 1225–1237.

Levinson, H. (1978) The abrasive personality. *Harvard Business Review*, May–June: 86–94.

Lombardo, M. M., & McCall, M. W., Jr. (1984) *Coping with an Intolerable Boss*. Greensboro, NC: Center for Creative Leadership.

Marais, S., & Herman, M. (1997) *Corporate Hyenas at Work: How to Spot and Outwit Them by Being Hyenawise*. Pretoria: Kagiso.

Metts, S. (1994) Relational transgressions. In W. R. Cupach & B. H. Spitzberg (eds) *The Dark Side of Interpersonal Communication*. Hillsdale, NJ: Lawrence Erlbaum Associates, Inc.

Miller, R. S. (2001) Breaches of propriety. In R. M. Kowalski (ed.) *Behaving Badly: Aversive Behaviors in Interpersonal Relationships*. Washington, DC: American Psychological Association.

Namie, G., & Namie, R. (2003) *The Bully at Work*. Naperville, IL: Sourcebooks.

Randall, P. (1997) *Adult Bullying: Perpetrators and Victims*. London & New York: Routledge.

Rayner, C., & Cooper, C. L. (2003) The black hole in 'bullying at work' research. *International Journal of Management and Decision Making*, 4(1): 47–64.

Scott, G. (2005) *A Survival Guide for Working with Bad Bosses: Dealing with Bullies, Idiots, Back-Stabbers, and other Managers from Hell*. New York: AMACOM.

Simpson, J. A., & Weiner, E. S. C. (eds) (1989) *The Oxford English Dictionary*, 2nd edn. Oxford: Clarendon Press.

Sutton, R. (2007) *The No Asshole Rule*. New York: Business Plus.

Chapter 10

An integrated counselling approach

Noreen Tehrani

Introduction

Whilst most bullying policies recommend counselling for the targets of bullying and occasionally for the perceived bullying offenders, there is little information on when counselling is appropriate and what kind of counselling is most suited to supporting employees affected by bullying or other unacceptable behaviours. It is becoming well established that the consequences of bullying can have devastating effects on the health and well-being of the exposed workers (Hogh *et al.*, 2011). Employees of severe and long-term bullying can find themselves suffering from a range of psychiatric conditions including: anxiety, depression, phobias, panic attacks and traumatic stress (see Part I). Employees considering using counselling to help them deal with their responses may have little knowledge or experience of counselling and find themselves searching the internet for information, only to be faced with bewildering lists of names and qualifications leaving them uncertain and left to choose their counsellor or therapist on the basis of the sound of their name, the location of their office or attractiveness of their website. Without a clear road map to help troubled employees to go through the process of identifying their needs, understanding what is on offer, choosing an approach, ensuring that the counsellor is competent, and finding someone with whom they can work and get the right kind of help can be hit and miss. In this chapter we will look at the nature of counselling and show how it differs from other pre-, peri-, and post-bullying training, mentoring, coaching and other interventions. Different kinds of counselling will be described together with what each model or approach to counselling has to offer. Research will be presented to demonstrate the key factors in determining the success of the counselling and the benefits of blending or integrating counselling and other interventions for dealing with bullying. Guidance is provided for identifying those people who would benefit from a counselling approach.

What is counselling?

At its simplest level counselling is a helping relationship which enables the counsellor to work with one or more people to explore a difficulty that is being experienced. It is provided at the request of the people involved and is entered into voluntarily. Organisations may send employees for counselling. However, if the counselling relationship is to work it needs to be entered into freely. Whilst there are hundreds of models or types of counselling, there are some basic principles which underpin a successful counselling relationship: 'a warm concern for and acceptance of the other, openness and attunement to the other's experiential reality; a grasp of what the other needs; an ability to facilitate the realization of such needs and an authentic presence' (Heron, 2001: 11). In counselling sessions the person seeking assistance should be treated as a client and not as a patient or customer. This relationship is therefore one of equality and mutual respect. During the counselling process clients are encouraged to explore the difficult or troubling aspects of their lives, behaviours and feelings. The nature of the counselling relationship makes it easier for the client to talk freely and openly in a way that is rarely possible with family members or friends. Whilst there is little objective evidence to show any significant difference between the effectiveness of different counselling models, three important success factors have been identified:

- The qualities and capabilities of the individual therapist (Okiishi *et al.*, 2003).
- The strength of the relationship between the counsellor and client (Cooper, 2008).
- The extent to which the client has been willing to engage in the counselling process (Orlinski *et al.*, 1994).

How does counselling differ from other forms of intervention?

For any relationship to work there is a need for at least one member of the relationship to be capable of using interpersonal skills. Regardless of the nature of the relationships, the core skills are the same for employees whether they are working in mediation, conciliation, mentoring, coaching or counselling. These skills include the following abilities:

- to establish rapport – building a strong relationship
- to listen and respond – using open questions, paraphrasing and summarising
- to reframe and reflect – providing feedback which encourages growth and development
- to explore and challenge – identifying strengths and weaknesses
- to be confidential and ethical – behaving professionally
- to be non-judgemental – accepting and respecting.

These skills will support a range of very different activities. Table 10.1 provides an outline of five interventions, each of which may be appropriate in some conflict or bullying circumstances. Mediation and conciliation are most appropriate where the conflict has been clearly defined and the participants are prepared to engage in finding a solution. This can be the most productive way of dealing with conflict and bullying as at the end of a successful mediation all parties will have learnt a lot about themselves and about the other employees involved (DeDreu *et al.*, 2004; Desivilya & Eizen, 2005).

Mentoring can have an influence on reducing the incidence of workplace bullying by enhancing the skills of managers and leaders in dealing with conflict and through building organisational or team socialisation and encouraging employees to acquire the attitudes, behaviours and knowledge that help them to become an effective team (Payne & Huffman, 2005; Madlock & Kennedy-Lightsey, 2010). Where a worker believes that they have been treated unfairly, a trained mentor or supporter can help them deal with the situation and offer a safe place to discuss options (see Chapter 13, Dix *et al.*). Coaching can be an effective approach for working with abrasive managers involving their colleagues and their teams (see Chapter 9, Crawshaw). The coaching approach is appropriate when those involved are able to engage in the process, look at their behaviour and recognise the benefits of working in a way which meets their needs whilst also meeting the needs of their teams. However, some employees involved in workplace bullying as offenders or victims are unable to benefit from the issue or the skills-led approaches provided by mediation, mentoring or coaching. These difficulties are often due to the employee being too emotionally or psychologically distressed to engage in the process or where there are pre-existing emotional or psychological difficulties which block all attempts to resolve the problem. On occasions the person may be suffering from a psychiatric condition which pre-exists or has been exacerbated by the bullying relationship. For these employees a counselling or psychiatric intervention may be necessary.

Table 10.1 Comparison of types of informal support available in the UK to individuals affected by workplace bullying

Domain	Mediation/conciliation	Mentoring	Coaching	Counselling	Psychiatry
Intention	Resolve conflict and differences.	Pass on experiences and knowledge.	Increase potential to achieve identified goals.	Identify and remove blocks to achievement.	Diagnose and treat psychopathology.
Underpinning beliefs	Conflicts can be resolved through supported constructive negotiation.	Guiding less experienced people will help to build their skills and competence.	Skills to deal with issues/situations can be learnt through systematic engagement.	People are resourceful and given support will solve their problems and achieve their goals.	Some mental conditions are caused by underlying medical or psychiatric malfunctions.
Benefits	Can resolve conflicts when both parties are willing to engage.	The mentor will have experience in dealing with bullying and share those skills.	Forward looking in increasing the range of skills and abilities based on the needs of the individual.	Recognises and addresses patterns of behaviour which may get in way of achieving goals.	Can identify and treat psychiatric disorders which may contribute to unwanted behaviours.
Disadvantages	Can be abused by a party who uses the process for their own ends.	The mentor may promote their solutions to problems without understanding what else is available.	Most coaching models do not deal with the complexity of bullying. Coaches may not recognise the psychological/ psychiatric problems.	Some counselling may not pay attention to organisational issues or be aware of the skills required to deal with bullying issues.	Psychiatrists may adopt a medical model approach, ignoring the impact of the bullying and other social issues.

Training	Although some mediators and conciliators are lawyers this is not always the case. Min. requirement for a certificate in dispute resolution is four days.	No specific training required to become a mentor although one-day courses are available to refresh the skills which should be used in the mentoring process.	No standardised training or minimum entry qualification. Certificates normally five days training, Diplomas an additional ten days. Coaching psychologists need a degree in psychology and MSc in coaching.	No minimum qualification for counsellors in UK. Prof. bodies generally require a minimum of two to three years part-time theory and practice training. Counselling psychologists need a degree in psychology and MSc in counselling.	A psychiatrist is a qualified medical doctor who has obtained additional qualifications to become a specialist in the diagnosis, treatment and prevention of mental illness and emotional problems.
Professional bodies	There is no dedicated professional body, however Acas (Advisory, Conciliation and Arbitration Service) can provide training and mediators. Law Society for lawyers.	No dedicated professional body. However, the use of mentors is supported by the Chartered Institute of Personnel and Development (CIPD).	International Coach Federation; European Mentoring and Coaching Council; Assn. For Professional Executive Coaching; Assn. for Coaching Psychology; British Psychological Society (for coaching psychologists).	British Assn of Counselling and Psychotherapy; UK Council for Psychotherapy; British Assn for Behavioural and Cognitive Psychotherapies; British Psychological Society (for counselling psychologists).	Royal College of Psychiatrists; General Medical Council.

(Continued overleaf)

Table 10.1 Continued

Domain	Mediation/ conciliation	Mentoring	Coaching	Counselling	Psychiatry
Standards	Law Society has a code of ethics which lawyers have to abide by in order to retain their practice certificate.	The CIPD has a code of ethics for its members. It is possible to work in HR without belonging to the CIPD.	All the above professional bodies have codes of ethics. Coaching psychologists are regulated by the Health Professionals Association (HPA).	All the above professional bodies have codes of ethics. There is no regulation, although this is being investigated currently. Counselling psychologists are regulated through the HPA.	Psychiatrists come under the jurisdiction of the General Medical Council (GMC).
When appropriate	When the participants are willing to work together for a mutually acceptable solution.	Where a peer or supporter helps a colleague to identify the options open to them.	When there is an openness to explore and self-awareness and an ability to accept some responsibility for actions.	Where there are some unresolved issues from the past which may be getting in the way of a positive solution and personal growth.	Where the underlying problem relates to a psychiatric disorder which has caused or been caused by the bullying.

Counselling models

There are many schools and approaches to counselling. Wampold (2001) undertook a meta-analysis of counselling outcomes and estimated that only 1 per cent of the variance in counselling effectiveness could be accounted for by the counselling model or approach. Despite this evidence it appears that when working with employees affected by bullying there are some approaches which are less successful in practice (see Chapter 11, Hirigoyen). The reason for this is that in some traditional forms of counselling there is a tendency to focus on the individual divorced from their environment or organisation. Unfortunately, few counselling courses deal adequately with organisational relationships and dynamics, with the result that when the problem involves a systemic failure or flaw in the organisational culture this goes unrecognised and unexplored. Systemically and organisationally trained counsellors will deal with the issues raised by the individual employee, but their focus will go beyond the employee to include subordinates, colleagues, managers and the organisation or system which may have caused, facilitated or supported the bullying behaviours. Organisationally aware counsellors are in a good position to identify potential flaws within a team, section or the whole organisation. These flaws can be addressed through team training, mentoring, coaching or counselling employees, or working with the organisation to create a culture which is more respectful and able to deal creatively with the normal clashes and conflicts that arise in relationships. Counselling offers the client an opportunity to explore his or her responses to the bullying within a safe relationship in order to gain an understanding of why the bullying had occurred, what can be learnt from the experience and what needs to be done to regain a sense of autonomy and self-worth. During the counselling the counsellor will be alert to the presence of hidden or repressed thoughts, feelings and responses which may have gone unrecognised or unacknowledged by the client. Depending on the counsellor's orientation and method of working, appropriate training and supervision should help them to accept and reflect upon their client's problems without becoming burdened or injured by them (BACP, 2009).

An integrated counselling approach

There are many hundreds of counselling theories available to counsellors, let alone the variations that counsellors introduce to adapt a particular model to meet their own preferences or needs. For many counsellors the ability to adopt an integrated approach allows a certain freedom of practice to suit their style of work, an approach appearing to be one of the most popular approaches in contemporary counselling practice (Dryden, 1992). Whilst to the outsider the choice of technique or approach may appear random, to the experienced integrative counsellor this could not be further from the truth. Integrative counselling approaches have developed out of the lack of any strong evidence to indicate that any one approach is significantly more effective than others (Norcross & Arkowitz, 1992).

In simple terms, counselling falls into three main groups. The first group includes the psychodynamic schools which have their origins in the work of Sigmund Freud. These approaches recognise and deal with the unconscious conflicts relating to instinctual drives and repression. The second group, the behavioural school, has its origins in the work of Pavlov and Skinner and is characterised by conditioned learning. Finally, there are the humanistic/existential schools with their roots in the work of Aristotle, Maslow, Rogers and Berne, with a belief in self-actualisation. Whilst counselling training tends to teach each of the counselling models in isolation, many counsellors will pick and choose between models or approaches to address an identified need, a client preference or perhaps blend several theories together and form a hybrid approach (Lapworth et al., 2004). This integrative movement can be observed in recent developments within cognitive behavioural therapy (CBT) with its origin within the behavioural school. Over the past few years CBT has begun to incorporate aspects of attachment theory which is more closely associated with the psychodynamic school and mindfulness with its origin in spirituality and self-actualisation.

An integrated model of counselling

Whilst there is no evidence to support a particular model of counselling, some models lend themselves more easily to the organisational need for a clearly defined process, ease of access and speed of recovery. The following outline has been used by the author for many years with positive outcomes. The model involves five main elements which are utilised throughout the counselling process. As the emphasis or importance of a particular element may change during the counselling progress, the counsellor will need to be continually aware of the process, the elements, and the ultimate ending of the counselling relationship and contract. The five elements involved in this approach are: (a) assessment; (b) education; (c) symptom reduction and other interventions; (d) integration and understanding; (e) rehabilitation and return to work.

Assessment

Employees attending a counselling assessment session tend to fall into one of three groups. First, there are those employees who come to the assessment unaware that their symptoms of distress are related to an oppressive or negative relationship. For these employees it may come as a surprise to recognise that the behaviour which they are experiencing is unacceptable and that they have the right to be able to ask for it to be stopped. The second group comes because they have been referred by management following a disciplinary hearing in which the employee has been identified as the perpetrator or victim of bullying. Finally, there are employees who recognise that they are involved in a conflict with one or more employees and want to find out what they can do to resolve it. Regardless of the reason for attending the assessment, each employee is made aware of the boundaries within which the counselling will take place, including that within certain limits the counselling will be confidential,[1] that the employee needs to attend voluntarily and that the counselling is not an easy option and will require the employee to fully engage in the process.

The assessment begins with an outline of what will happen during this first session and the agreement that depending on the outcome of the assessment a decision will be made on whether there is a basis for the client and counsellor to work together. In addition to the initial contracting assessments there are three further sections. First, there is a structured interview, which involves the counsellor taking a life history of the employee, providing an opportunity for the client to describe what has caused them to seek counselling. Second, there is a review of the results of questionnaires which the client has completed previously. The questionnaires measure clinical symptoms including anxiety, depression and post-traumatic stress, in addition to a set of well-being and occupational questionnaires which assess general health and lifestyle, locus of control, behavioural style, coping skills and personality. During the assessment the counsellor provides feedback on the questionnaires. Finally, there is an opportunity for the employee and counsellor to talk about what the employee would like as an outcome and to decide on the best approach. It is important to ensure that prior to commencement of the counselling the employee is not exposed to any further bullying or other negative acts. Attempting to undertake counselling whilst the client is in real danger of further traumatic exposures undermines the counselling.

Following the assessment the counsellor provides the employee with a written report of the assessment and, where appropriate, an agreed programme or plan for future sessions. Only when the counsellor and client have agreed on the content of the report and counselling programme, does the counselling begin.

Education

Education is an important part of this integrated approach. The education process is continual and fully integrated into all the other counselling activities. In the assessment, typically there will be a description of the biological basis of stress and trauma including the use of drawings and descriptions of how the brain copes with aversive events by locking the sensory memory traces within the amygdala where they are inaccessible to conscious review or understanding (Damasio, 2006). This education is augmented by other information taken from the psychometric results with, for example, a client being shown where they may be lacking a basic coping skill and what they need to do to develop this ability. For clients, the whole counselling experience is one of action learning in which they are asked to seek answers and meaning from their experiences. Many clients will also take the opportunity to read recommended books or formulate hypotheses on their reactions and responses by drawing on information from their own areas of expertise, family feedback and reading. The action learning process encourages the client to become intrigued by their responses and reactions rather than a victim of them.

Occasionally the trauma response to the bullying situation involves strong physical reactions including panic attacks, palpitations, diarrhoea and trembling. Where this occurs the education will include information on the nature of human responses to strain and how these are important to survival. A simplified version of Damasio's tree (Damasio, 2003) which shows the intimate relationship between the immune responses, pain and pleasure behaviours, drives and motivations and their connection to the expression of emotions and feelings is often used to illustrate the way that early life traumas may be restimulated without conscious awareness.

Symptom reduction

The main body of counselling work involves symptom reduction. Each activity will be discussed with the client and introduced flexibly in response to the client's needs. The initial work tends to be a response to the needs identified in the psychometric testing and personal history, particularly where the client has been found to have an issue which may be making them vulnerable to distressing symptoms. When the assessment has shown, for example, that the client has a poor lifestyle, this will be addressed by talking about the benefits of reducing the caffeine intake, taking regular exercise, cutting out excessive alcohol and eating regular meals. The inadequate use of a particular coping skill will be addressed by organising training or coaching in the required skill. Whilst these practical steps may not be regarded as a normal part of the counsellor's role, particularly by those counsellors who take a non-directive stance to their work, in this pragmatic approach to counselling there are clear benefits for the client engaging in some practical activities which provide them with relief from their symptoms and increases their self-confidence.

Typically, one of the first tools to be offered to a client is an ability to relax and create a 'safe place'. This is achieved by the use of a relaxation script in which the client is encouraged to find an imaginary place where they feel at home and at peace. Only when this has been achieved is it safe to go to the next stage where some of the re-experience symptoms are addressed. Re-experience comes in a number of forms including flashbacks, nightmares, hallucinations and emotional or physical reactivation. A re-experience is different to recall or remembering a distressing event; within the re-experience the client responds as if the incident is actually occurring. The main task involved in reducing the power of the re-experienced responses is to encourage the client to summon up the trigger of this reaction, which may be an upsetting image, sound, smell, body response or taste. For each of the five senses the process is similar, involving the client going through the relaxation exercise, then gradually, and at their own pace, purposefully bringing the feared stimuli to mind, and then finding ways to manipulate it by changing its size, shape, colour, smell or intensity. Through this process the conscious mind comes to recognise that the feared perception is a construction rather than a real event. At the end of each exercise the client is asked to switch off the stimuli and to check that it remains off until they decide to visit the stimuli once more. Through this process of desensitisation the client becomes aware that the feared flashbacks, hallucinations and sensory reactivations can be brought under their conscious control.

Integration and understanding

Throughout the counselling, clients need to learn how to reflect upon and become interested in their responses to events. The mindfulness approach to reactions requires them to adopt a concentrated awareness of their present thoughts, actions and motivations without becoming emotionally attached or distressed by them (Brown & Ryan, 2003). Writing and keeping journals encourages clients to reflect on their changing perceptions through the identification of repeating patterns of behaviours, events or emotions. This process is helpful in creating deeper meanings and reducing distress (Pennebaker & Chung, 2007). For many clients it is difficult to accept that they may have played any role in the bullying drama apart from being the innocent victim. It may be difficult to contemplate that one of the more negatively perceived roles is anything but bad. However, despite the view, it is clear that the seemingly negative roles involve qualities that are not in themselves negative, but can possess positive elements (Karpiak, 2003). The bullying drama model predicts that where clients are able to accept their shadow side through the expression of their vulnerability, power, responsiveness and need for justice, all virtues inherent within the victim, oppressor, rescuer and avenger roles, this acceptance will enable them to gain self-awareness and wisdom.

Returning to the workplace

The counsellor also has an important role in preparing their client for returning to work. Although many employees involved in bullying do not return to the same role or even the same organisation, the workplace is the place where the traumatic bullying experiences took place. Therefore it can hold the triggers to memories which have not been fully processed. The use of visualisation prior to the actual return to work can be extremely helpful to flush out some of these triggers and deal with them. Walking along a corridor, going into a meeting room or coming face to face with a person associated with the bullying can reactivate high levels of distress. It is helpful to practise the return to work through the medium of the visualisation prior to the actual return. This virtual return to work can identify areas of counselling or practical steps that need to be undertaken if the return is to be successful. Even if the initial return to work is successful, it is important to arrange for the counselling to continue during the first few weeks following the return in order to deal with the unexpected responses to the working environment.

Emotional competence and bullying

Whilst many employees, particularly those who regard themselves as victims of bullying, hold the view that there is a clearly defined group of antisocial workers and these workers engage in bullying wholly innocent and unsuspecting colleagues, the reality is less clear. Certainly there are some personality disordered psychopaths within organisations who, through their use of charm, manipulation, ruthlessness and lack of any feelings or conscience, selfishly take what they want and do as they please without a thought for their victims (Hare, 1993). However, this is not the situation found by the author when working in a wide range of organisations dealing with formal and informal investigations of bullying as well as counselling distressed employees. The experience of dealing with organisations and employees caught up in the warp and weft of bullying indicates that it is rare to find a totally innocent victim or a wholly guilty oppressor (Page, 1999). Frequently, players describe themselves as the victim of the other party whilst attributing their own behaviour to the circumstances in which the behaviour occurred, both sides providing evidence to support their version of events. How is it possible for employees to have such disparate views of what are, on the surface, the same events? It appears that this phenomenon is due to the way people view the world and the actions of others (Kelley, 1972) with a bias to viewing one's own negative actions as due to situational factors ('I was very cross that day because the baby was teething and I did not get any sleep'), whilst viewing the negative actions of others as indicative of a persistent trait or intent ('That is typical of Jenny, she always gets angry when she does not get her own way').

Fortunately, the principles underpinning most of the counselling models provide counsellors with some insight into how individuals become engaged in and maintain negative behaviours. It has been suggested that the reason for this displacement of personal responsibility on to others lies within society, particularly in those cultures where there is little or no emphasis on enabling children to learn how to recognise, accept and deal with their negative emotional responses (Heron, 2001). Child-raising patterns frequently place on the child the requirement to control their emotional responses in order to be socially acceptable. This emotional control is achieved without the child or its parent recognising or understanding the important purpose of the emotional expression as a mechanism for responding to and meeting basic human needs. As a result of this suppression of emotional process, children are left with the distress of their unmet needs. Instead of the child achieving a healthy understanding of their deeper needs, they are taught to control their emotions through a toxic mix of suppression, repression and denial. Children begin to release their emotional distress resulting from displacing their emotions into a range of behaviours including aggression, demanding, blaming, clinging and whining. This pattern of learnt behaviour continues into adult life with the earlier life traumas being added to and triggered by new traumatic events. Unless as adults people come to recognise and meet their hidden needs, this process continues throughout life and emerges in automatic, compulsive, unwarranted, unacceptable and unexpected forms of behaviour.

Most adults are unaware of the influence of these intra-psychic processes, and as a result their rational and sensitive responses to situations become mixed with compulsive, distress-driven reactions powered by a hidden inner distress. These displacement behaviours are often reinforced within the workplace where they may become valued and legitimised with the result that the rational and compulsive become intertwined. Employees become skilled at dressing up irrationally driven behaviours as being reasonable. For example, being driven to succeed in achieving career goals regardless of the cost to themselves or their families they justify their behaviour on the grounds of business need rather than recognising that this hyperactivity is a displacement of the unexpressed distress or anger they experienced as a child when they did not achieve the recognition or validation they craved. On the other hand, where an employee has been found to have reported being a victim of bullying behaviours of colleagues or managers in every team or organisation they join they will blame others for causing their distress whilst failing to recognise that their difficulty in establishing positive working relationships originates from a repressed destructive anger which has followed the unexpressed feelings of the loss of a loved parent or sibling, and manifests itself in an insatiable need for reassurance and support and feelings of being rejected.

People develop emotional competence through understanding and accepting their drives, responses and reactions to their environment and their relationships. The emotionally competent individual is able to accept their positive and negative emotions and is willing to recognise that their experience of distress is a mechanism of self-healing rather than providing evidence of their imminent psychological breakdown. Emotional competence requires people to identify when old emotional pain and distress is being re-enacted in displacement or other forms of distorted behaviour, and then to attempt to recognise, understand and deal with the original hurt. To achieve emotional competence therefore people need to:

- gain an insight into their early traumatic experience and the influence it is having on their adult behaviour
- notice when the conditioned or obsessional forms of displacement prevent more rational and flexible behaviours

- learn how to appropriately challenge others who are unconsciously acting out their denied distress in negative and other forms of disrupted behaviour (Steiner, 1999; Heron, 2001).

Presenting a distraught employee with what may seem to them to be an approach which blames them for their own distress is not helpful. The first goal of counselling would be to work on reducing the distress and recognising that for whatever reason the employee has been experiencing behaviours which have been damaging and distressing. Only when the employee has regained some sense of personal well-being and autonomy is it possible to look at ways to deal with some of the underlying vulnerabilities. The counselling relationship, if it is working well, should provide a model for the ways to deal with differences and conflict in a positive way. Many clients when they become stronger will be able to look at their own part in the negative relationships and learn ways to deal with conflict. This is not to say that employees may not be severely mistreated at work by others who abuse their power, or who accept or condone bullying behaviours.

The wounded helper

When working with bullying, a counsellor needs to be able to use a number of different models of intervention, continually monitoring the value and benefit of a particular intervention. Knowing how and when to move from one style of working to another and understanding how to maintain the creative balance in the use of their own personal power and vulnerability, while simultaneously capturing and responding to the power and vulnerability of their client, is essential. However, counsellors and other helpers are not immune to experiencing the anxiety and distress of their own unresolved traumas. Indeed, some practitioners unconsciously choose to work with victims of bullying or their oppressors as a means of dealing with their own unresolved and hidden distress. Fundamental to counselling training and ongoing personal development is the professional requirement for all counsellors to present their client work in supervision. The supervisor will not only deal with the nature and appropriateness of the counselling process and techniques used, but also spend time looking at the impact of the content of the counselling on the counsellor, including any of the counsellor's hidden drives or motivations which may be influencing their behaviour within the therapeutic relationship (McNab, 2011). The professional requirement for all counsellors to attend regular supervision sessions is essential in protecting clients from the abuse of power that could so easily occur within the counselling room, and should be adopted by others involved in dealing with workplace bullying.

Conclusions

Counselling has an important role to play in dealing with workplace bullying. However, it should be regarded as only one of a number of interventions that can be used. Counselling is most appropriate for employees who are resistant or unable to resolve their difficulties through conflict resolution, mediation, mentoring or coaching. If there is to be a co-ordinated approach to supporting victims of bullying, it would be beneficial for each of the groups of supporters to recognise and value the unique contribution of other interventions and not to work outside their remit or area of competency. Where the employee is experiencing extreme distress, clinical anxiety, depression, panic attacks, phobias or symptoms of traumatic stress, it is unlikely that they will be able to engage in processes which require them to be cool and unemotional. Counselling provides a means for employees to gain self-awareness and understanding of what has happened to them and what resources they are able to tap to build their resilience in the future.

Note

1 Confidentiality is only broken if there is a serious risk to the life or health of client or another person or a crime has been committed.

References

BACP (2009) *Ethical Framework for Good Practice*. Lutterworth: British Association of Counselling and Psychotherapy.

Brown, K., & Ryan, R. (2003) The benefits of being present: mindfulness and its role in psychological well being. *Journal of Personality and Social Psychology*, 84: 822–848.

Cooper, M. (2008) The facts are friendly. *Therapy Today*, 19(7): 8–13.

Damasio, A. (2003) *Looking for Spinoza – Joy, Sorrow and the Feeling Brain*. London: Heinemann.

Damasio, A. (2006) *Descartes Error*. London: Vintage.

DeDreu, C. K. W., van Dierendonck, D., & Dijkstra, M. T. M. (2004) Conflict at work and individual well-being. *International Journal of Conflict Management*, 15(1): 6–26.

Desivilya, H. S., & Eizen, D. (2005) Conflict management in work teams: the role of social self-efficacy and group identification. *International Journal of Conflict Management*, 16(2): 183–208.

Dryden, W. (1992) *Integrative and Eclectic Therapy – A Handbook*. Buckingham: Open University Press.

Hare, R. D. (1993) *Without Conscience: The Disturbing World of the Psychopaths Among Us*. New York: Guilford Press.

Heron, J. (2001) *Helping the Client – A Creative Practical Guide*. London: Sage.

Hogh, A., Gemzoe-Mikkelsen, E., & Hansen A. M. (2011) Individual consequences of workplace bullying/mobbing. In S. Einarsen, H. Hoel, D. Zapf, & C. L. Cooper (eds) *Bullying and Harassment in the Workplace: Developments in Theory, Research and Practice*. London: CRC Press.

Karpiak, I. E. (2003) The shadow: mining its dark treasury for teaching and adult development. *Canadian Journal of University Continuing Education*, 29(2): 13–27.

Kelley, H. H. (1972) Attribution in social interaction. In E. E. Jones, D. E. Kanouse, H. H. Kelley, R. E. Nisbitt, S. Valins, & B. Weiner (eds) *Attribution: Perceiving the Causes of Behavior*. Hillside, NJ: Lawrence Elbaum Associates, Inc.

Lapworth, P., Sills, C., & Fish, S. (2004) *Integration in Counselling and Psychotherapy – Developing A Personal Approach*. London: Sage.

McNab, S. (2011) One disaster after another: building resilience in the trauma therapist and the role of supervision. In N. Tehrani (ed.) *Managing Trauma in the Workplace: Supporting Workers and Organisations*. London: Routledge.

Madlock, P. E., & Kennedy-Lightsey, C. (2010) The effects of supervisors' verbal aggressiveness and mentoring on their subordinates. *Journal of Business Communication*, 47(1): 42–62.

Norcross, J. C., & Arkowitz, H. (1992) The evolution and current status of psychotherapy integration. In W. Dryden (ed.) *Integrative and Eclectic Therapy*. Oxford: Oxford University Press.

Okiishi, J., Lambert, M. J., Neilsen, S. L., & Ogles, B. M. (2003) Waiting for the supershrink: an empirical analysis of therapist effects. *Clinical Psychology and Psychotherapy*, 10: 361–373.

Orlinski, D. K., Grawe, K., & Parkes, B. (1994) *Process and Outcome in Psychotherapy and Behavior Change*. New York: Wiley.

Page, S. (1999) *The Shadow and the Counsellor – Working with Darker Aspects of the Person, Role and Profession*. London: Routledge.

Payne, S. C., & Huffman, A. H. (2005) A longitudinal examination of the influence of mentoring on organisational commitment and turnover. *Academy of Management Journal*, 48(1): 158–168.

Pennebaker, J. W., & Chung, C. K. (2007) Expressive writing, emotional upheavals, and health. In H. Friedman and R. Silver (eds) *Handbook of Health Psychology*. New York: Oxford University Press.

Steiner, C. (1999) *Achieving Emotional Literacy*. London: Bloomsbury.

Wampold, B. E. (2001) *The Great Psychotherapy Debate: Models, Methods and Findings*. Mahwah, NJ: Lawrence Erlbaum Associates, Inc.

Chapter 11

Healing the wounded soul

Marie-France Hirigoyen

> A lion can kill a man with a single bite of its teeth, but if you throw this man in a pit full of fleas, he will end up dying from a thousand bites.
>
> (Saint Augustine, sermon)

Introduction

Anti-bullying legislation in the labour and the penal codes was introduced in France on 17 January 2002. Under French law, workplace bullying involves 'repeated actions that have, as their aim or effect a deterioration of working environment likely to infringe upon the employee's rights and dignity, to alter their physical or mental health, or compromise their professional future' (Stievenard, 2010). The legal statutes refer to '*harcèlement moral*' (moral harassment), a term originally coined by Marie-France Hirigoyen (1998), which reflects the unjust and unfair nature of the behaviour affecting the target's moral status and integrity. These civil and criminal provisions were the first steps taken in France to protect employees' mental health and well-being. Bullying is characterised by repetitive hostile behaviour taking place over a long period of time. Such behaviour includes verbal aggression, mockery, intimidation, humiliation, refusal to communicate and professional undermining. When examined individually, these behaviours may appear harmless. However, their cumulative effect creates the aggression. Bullying can involve an individual's behaviours undertaken with the intention of harming or destroying a fellow worker or the actions taken by an organisation in terms of procedures or policies which have the effect of undermining or distressing one or more employees.

An insidious progression

Despite the legislation against moral harassment that is found in many countries, bullying remains difficult to identify and to prevent. The common denominator being the definition: how can a look charged with hatred be defined, a feeling of being ostracised and rejected measured, or the implied threat of violence recognised? The destructive process is created by an accumulation and repetition of these and other aggressive acts. Bullying rarely involves open conflict where people clash, but rather an insidious, one-sided violence made more dangerous because it is virtually invisible. At first, those targeted are unwilling to take offence, and will give little importance to the initial cutting remarks or humiliations. They may question their perception of events, being unsure whether they are exaggerating what happened. However, over time the attacks will escalate and the target becomes subjected to the increasing belittling, hostile and degrading manoeuvres of their aggressor. Whatever the origin of the conflict and whoever the perpetrators may be, the process tends to follow a similar pattern: the problem is never clearly identified, but underhand actions are initiated to expel the target rather than seeking a solution. The process is amplified as colleagues and others witness and become involved in the process.

Bullying creates a vicious circle, whether organisational or individual in nature. Hostile behaviours cause the target to become increasingly anxious, isolated and defensive, which in turn attracts further aggression from the perpetrator. Initially, perpetrators, targets and witnesses will deny what is happening, ignoring the emergence of an all too visible conflict. Perpetrators do not question their behaviours, and witnesses become too nervous to get involved. The targets withdraw from the situation becoming submissive, fearing that they will be unable to deal with any escalation of the conflict. After a period of time, a reciprocal phobic phenomenon emerges in which the perpetrator becomes increasingly irritated at the sight of the target, while at the same time contact with the perpetrator triggers extreme states of fear in the target, with the result that targets will be viewed as behaving in a confused and chaotic manner. However, creating this behavioural change in the target is the main objectives of the perpetrator as it causes the target to appear ineffective and inefficient, enabling the perpetrator to justify their requests for the target to be dismissed. By this stage the reason for the conflict may have been forgotten, with onlookers seeing the target as difficult or bad-tempered and the perpetrator as taking reasonable steps to deal with the target's defensive attitudes and behaviours. This process makes it easy for the target to be seen as responsible for what is happening to them, their responses to the bullying being regarded as personality flaws with a total disregard for the reason these behaviours had become established.

Submission

Whilst important, the fear of unemployment may not be the primary reason for a target's submissive behaviour. Bullying managers and other petty tyrants constantly seek power, consciously or unconsciously using perverse tactics to cause the victims to feel psychologically bound, controlled and unable to respond. The target is disrespected, abused, put under pressure, scolded, watched or timed, causing them to feel a need to maintain a constant state of vigilance. Typically, employees will not be given the appropriate information or support to enable them to change this situation, leaving them cornered and deprived of the ability to think rationally about their situation and causing them to accept the unacceptable, incapable of confronting the unreasonable behaviour. Targets frequently describe the difficulties they experience in trying to concentrate when in close proximity to their tormentor. These problems in thinking and the inability to focus lead to impairment in their work performance. Interestingly, targets frequently report that their anxiety is not triggered by openly aggressive behaviour but rather by those situations where the aggression is more hidden and they feel they may have had some responsibility. They may feel relieved when an attack is out in the open and obvious to everyone. The urge to display a submissive attitude towards a perpetrator causes enormous inner tensions for the target as they attempt to adapt their behaviour to reduce the likelihood of angering the perpetrator, defusing hostility by remaining passive even when provoked. The tension caused by the increased level of stress resulting from the target's ability to react to provocation brings about a state of emotional and cognitive numbing. Curiously, anger or fight responses are seldom reported, despite their ability to bring about a reduction in tension. Whilst targets can perceive the injustice of their situation, they are usually unable or unwilling to fight. However, occasionally bullying may trigger fierce emotional reactions in response to aggressive provocations and frustrations at not being heard. Targets may be seen to engage in angry impulsive gestures such as breaking office equipment, destroying databases or confronting their tormentor with insults. However, such behaviours will later serve to justify the aggressive behaviours.

Denial of the reality of bullying

As bullying is difficult to quantify, people attempt to construct rational explanations to explain its occurrence. Perpetrators will refuse to accept that their behaviour is bullying, asserting that the target is incompetent, fragile or oversensitive, and that in these circumstances their 'firm' behaviour is reasonable and appropriate. Faced with this kind of denial, targets will try to understand what they have been doing wrong. They will attempt to find reasons for the negative behaviours, but as nothing makes sense they begin to lose self-confidence. Targets will continue to seek logical explanations, even when the bullying is clearly a phenomenon independent of them. They feel isolated and ashamed of what has happened to them while their tormentor will be seen as innocent of any inappropriate behaviour. This feeling of responsibility is reinforced by observers and bystanders who may become confused by the situation and unable to provide non-judgemental support, frequently commenting or advising inappropriate actions. Once this one-sided, destructive process is underway, only a radical change of approach from one of the protagonists can bring it to a close. However, in a crisis, behaviours tend to become intensified and fixed with rigid organisation becoming more rigid, aggressive individuals more aggressive and depressed employees more depressed.

Whilst this situation may bring out the best in some targets, motivating them to seek an escape, more commonly this hidden violence causes the targets to sink into deeper apathy, experiencing a permanent state of arousal, perceiving a hostile stare, gesture or tone of voice as a hidden or unspoken aggression. Targets begin to anticipate the perpetrator's negative reactions, rebukes and coldness should they fail to meet an unreasonable request, anticipating the aggressor to become sarcastic, contemptuous or deriding. To escape this cycle of distress, targets become slavish and diligent in their work, trying to adapt or comply with what they believe is expected of them, resulting in a permanent state of hyper-adaptation which the perpetrator can use to justify their aggressive behaviour. Whatever action the target takes, it will always be viewed as wrong by the perpetrator, whose aim is to disconcert, confuse and drive the target to make mistakes. This inability to make sense of the world is destructive and unbearable, in bullying the target is unable to find any reason for the suffering they are experiencing. In moral harassment there is no reason or rationality.

For many observers the saying that there is no guilt without fault is applied. How can colleagues begin to understand what is happening when they cannot recognise the reality of the aggression? Colleagues find themselves too embarrassed or fearful to become involved in providing support for the target or to engage in looking for ways to resolve the situation. Targets may be told that they are responsible for what happens to them, it is they that have a problem. Targets can become paralysed by contradictory instructions; they are criticised for being ineffective whilst not having the means to perform their work or facing blocks put in the way of them being able to achieve their goals. Targets may be given impossible tasks, conflicting orders and unreasonable deadlines. When confronted by this situation, they can find themselves paralysed, unable to react, with family, friends and therapists coming to believe that they are complicit in their own suffering.

The presence of humiliation and undermining of dignity distinguishes bullying-related distress from other workplace difficulties including work-related violence. Bullied targets feel ashamed of being bullied and of their inability to respond appropriately. The loss of self-esteem and self-confidence causes them to doubt their own feelings and to begin to believe they may be responsible for the situation. The hostility makes it impossible for them to distinguish what is normal and what is not, what comes from their frailty and what has been caused by the tormentor's destructive behaviour. Targets dream of being rehabilitated, hoping for an acknowledgement or recognition of the bullying behaviour. Rather than for any wish for revenge, they want the apology that will never come.

Consequences on health

During the early stages of bullying when it may be possible to find a solution, targets exhibit symptoms of stress. However, as the hostility escalates these symptoms are joined by feelings of helplessness, humiliation and injustice. If the bullying continues for several months or years, the body's resistance begins to wear out, giving way to a permanent state of anxiety which is constantly reactivated by the repeated bullying attacks. This constant state of intense stress can cause a generalised anxiety disorder, characterised by permanent apprehension and anticipation, anxious ruminations, permanent tension and hypervigilance. Often this will be accompanied by severe depressive states which the target may attempt to hide from family, friends and their doctor. Targets feel empty, exhausted, lacking in energy and motivation. They may find it difficult to think or focus, even on the most banal of issues. Targets are depressed not because of any prior vulnerability or fragility, but rather because the bullying has affected their self-esteem, causing them to feel worthless and hopeless. These depressive states need to be recognised early as there is a high risk of suicide in targets of bullying. Interestingly, bullied women usually consult a health practitioner sooner than men and are also more likely to take sick leave and use medication. However, bullying-related suicides are more common in men than in women.

Where a target commits suicide or attempts to take their life, the perpetrator is likely to feel comforted by the belief that the target was weak or insane, thus reinforcing their perception of not being responsible for what has happened. During the past two years in France there has been a very high rate of work-related suicides: 58 suicides in France Telecom between 2007 and 2009 (Guardian, 2009). However, the main investigations have been to look at the personal circumstances of the workers rather than any meaningful examination of the working environment as an explanation for these tragic events.

Because bullying is long-lasting and severe, the risk of post-traumatic stress is high (see Chapter 3, Tehrani). The traumatic event is constantly relived in memories and repeated intrusive dreams, provoking distress and physiological reactions. Targets of bullying respond in a similar way to the military involved in war, having been placed in a virtual state of siege creating in them a constant state of alarm. These symptoms trigger avoidance behaviours, which reduce the likelihood of the trauma needing to be relived. Targets may find their responses triggered by anything which reminds them of the aggression, causing phobic responses which may prevent them from returning to their workplace or meeting colleagues, and may result in them leaving the organisation. They may also experience a loss of interest in activities that used to bring joy, causing social isolation and limited emotion and affect, which can have major repercussions on family life.

A less well known consequence of the bullying trauma is the development of dissociation symptoms which prevent the target from coming to terms with the traumatic event (Classen et al., 1993). Dissociation is a defensive response to the fear, pain or helplessness of the traumatic event as when an experience is of such a magnitude there is a tendency to distort it or to remove it from the consciousness. Dissociative behaviours accentuate the magnitude of the response, creating additional difficulty for the therapist. Psychosomatic manifestations are also common, as what cannot be said will be expressed through the body. The body records the attack before the brain has an opportunity to refuse to see what it cannot comprehend. The stream of psychosomatic ailments becomes significant and of increasing severity. These disorders are not a direct result of the aggression itself but a consequence of the individual's inability to respond to the aggression. Targets become weaker, experience weight loss, expressing through their body a psychological damage of which they are unaware, but which is destroying their identity.

Life-changing impact

When targets cannot break free from the perpetrator's control, the trauma changes their lives. Vitality is numbed, joie de vivre disappears and personal initiative is impossible. Consequently, they become embittered, irritable, touchy and socially withdrawn. The constant reliving of events puts strain on their relationships. Unfortunately, most targets only consult a specialist when it is much too late, by which stage the target is suffering from a generalised state of anxiety, psychosomatic ailments or depression. Yet it is common to see them refuse a prescribed sick leave, for fear of the consequences on their future, or for fear of retaliation. When the exposure has been intense or has continued for a long time, targets may become incapable of fleeing or fighting the bullying behaviour. They consult a psychotherapist or psychoanalyst but refuse to examine the fundamental questions about the reason for their condition. They just want to cope with their submissive situation without too much suffering and continue to keep up appearances. They will prefer medication to entering a therapeutic process. Yet when a target suffers one depression after the other or when he uses medication to excess, only therapy can help in breaking the state.

The scarring and permanent damage of bullying may only be recognised when, after a long period of sick leave, an employee seems well enough to return to work. On their return symptoms reappear and the health problems return. This is the beginning of a vicious circle: there will be a relapse, renewed sick leave, then back to work, followed by another relapse. The long-term harassment process will in most cases end with a premature exit from the workplace, as the target makes their final attempt at survival. Initially, targets will self-medicate but when this does not work therapists will prescribe treatment. If a target has multiple symptoms, the therapist may not identify their real origin, especially if questions have not been asked about working conditions, or due to the difficulty the target has in describing what has been happening to them. However, the nature of the symptoms should be sufficient for experienced therapist to identify the presence of moral harassment from the impact it has had on health.

Implications for healing

Moral harassment is an insidious process with its recognition coming late, providing little time for targets to defend themselves. However, defending oneself alone is difficult and access to practical and legal assistance is important. Psychotherapeutic assistance is essential when the bullying has lasted a long time or has been particularly destructive. The target's problem lies in the fact that they were unable to recognise when their personal boundaries were transgressed, and they did not find themselves respected. An important task is to identify what is acceptable to them, necessitating the need to redefine themselves.

Choosing a therapist is a first step in allowing the target to be in a position where they are able to act. Targets whose ego has been wounded should not be faced with the benevolent neutrality or coldness in the approach of some therapists. Ferenczi, a one-time disciple and friend of Freud, broke away from him on the subjects of trauma and analytical method. In 1932 he wrote: 'The analytical situation – i.e. the restrained coolness, professional hypocrisy and – hidden behind it but never revealed – a dislike of the target which, nevertheless, he felt in all his being – such a situation is not essentially different from that which in his childhood had led to the illness.' The psychotherapist's silence echoes the perpetrator's refusal to communicate and brings a source of secondary victimisation.

Working with individuals who have experienced bullying should lead therapists to question their therapeutic methods and knowledge, to empathise with their client rather than place themselves in a position of power. Psychoanalysts must learn to think differently, beyond the boundaries of their usual frames of reference and question Freudian dogma. They must consider not only the client's psyche but also the factual context of events. Therapists should adopt a more interactive, stimulating and understanding process for therapy. For as long as the target remains under the control of the bully, conventional psychoanalysis, with all the frustration that implies, will not help. The target will merely surrender to another form of control. Psychotherapy centred exclusively on the intra-psychic aspects will cause the target to revisit and dwell on the events, reinforcing his depressive state and feelings of guilt, making him feel more responsible for a process that involved two people.

To seek an echo of the target's trauma exclusively in his past is dangerous because it gives a linear explanation to his present suffering, and would mean he was responsible for his misfortune. In a context of bullying, psychotherapy aims to understand how to escape the situation before understanding why the situation actually occurred. It is essential as a precondition that therapists recognise that the trauma results from an external aggression, and to identify it as abnormal. Some targets report trying to explain their ordeal to therapists who are primarily interested in the intra-psychic aspects rather than in the actual aggressive behaviour and torture they have experienced. Targets often find it difficult to express the violence of their experience, either because they are suppressing the painful memories or because what they need to say is beyond their mental capacity and they need time to reflect. The therapist's scepticism merely adds to the trauma and his silence, by extension, likens him to the aggressor's accomplice. Naming the bullying does not condemn the target to constantly revisiting the traumatic situation; on the contrary it allows an escape from denial and guilt and legitimates the suffering. Enabling the target to understand and evaluate the aggressor's strategies will help in the avoidance of being placed in a similar situation in the future, lifting the weight of ambiguity of words and allusions is to access freedom.

Psychotherapy, at least in the beginning, must be reassuring and help the target in abandoning feelings of fear and guilt, and regaining self-esteem. Targets should understand that the therapist is available to understand and is not indifferent to their suffering. By accessing and using the undamaged areas of the psyche, the targets will have the self-confidence to set personal boundaries and refuse what is not good for them. Building awareness and raising self-esteem takes time, and aims to improve assertiveness and ultimately give strength to confront the bully. The therapy should never reinforce the target's feelings of guilt by burdening him or her with the responsibility for what happened. Whilst still under the control or influence of the bully, the target may be overwhelmed by doubt and guilt which can prevent any movement, this is particularly true if the bully has questioned or raised doubts about the target's mental health.

The American psychotherapist Spiegel (1988) summarises the changes that need to be made to traditional psychotherapies to adapt them to working with victims: 'In traditional psychotherapy the target is exhorted to take greater responsibility for life problems, when the victim should learn to take lesser responsibility for the trauma.' Only when the healing process has been completed and the targets have recovered their sense of identity is it possible to revisit the bullying situation and try to understand why this destructive process occurred and why it was not possible to defend oneself. The therapist must help the targets to regain confidence in their resources and inner knowledge. Whatever the theoretical framework used, the psychotherapist must feel sufficiently free in the tools and protocols used to communicate this freedom to the targets, releasing them from the control exerted by the bully. The therapist must give the target the possibility of expressing the anger and other emotions that could not be expressed during the bullying process: if the target cannot find words to do so, then the therapist must help to describe the repressed emotions.

In post-traumatic stress, the target relives the trauma of the bullying through recurrent and intrusive recollections of the events. To relieve the anxiety generated by these memories, targets will try to control their emotions. However, in order to return to normal life the target must come to terms with this anxiety and understand that it will not disappear overnight. There must be an acceptance of this feeling of helplessness to enable the start of the grieving process. Only then can the targets accept the suffering and experience of violence within their lives, respecting and recognising the damage and the wounds. Acceptance provides an opportunity to transcend this depressive and morbid state. As in all forms of trauma, targets of workplace bullying will tend to focus on one detail of their ordeal that prevents them from alleviating their anguish; the memory of the conflict monopolises their thoughts. Targets need to be heard and believed, without judgement. Reliving the events should not be considered a source of pleasure, as is often the case in therapy, as this will only add to the trauma. The wounds must first be healed and only later can they be interpreted when the target can revisit events from a new perspective.

In treatment, an atmosphere of trust can create a relationship in which the target can revisit the violence, explore their reactions to events, and begin to understand the role they played in it and the weapons they may have given their aggressor. Therapists can help the targets identify which aspects of the violence are related to vulnerability, and which to the external aggression, helping in the reappraisal of past events in the light of this new learning. Targets often have an inaccurate understanding of the bullying context as, despite being dissociated, they have registered a mass of information which whilst incomprehensible at the time has now become meaningful and clear, making sense of the communication and the context. Targets may be aware of things they may have said or done which they felt, according to their personal codes of conduct, were inappropriate at the time. In therapy, the target need not suppress these memories, but be encouraged to accept and re-examine them in a new light.

Although the therapist is aware that the targets may have surrendered to the bully, often re-enacting an event from childhood, it would be dangerous to sensitise them too quickly to the dynamics of their psyche. Aggressions and violence at the workplace often echo incidents from the target's personal history. This may be the tyranny of their father or mother or other aggressions and humiliations experienced in childhood. The bully, with a good deal of intuition, connects to the target's childhood wounds. Therapists can help targets understand and identify the link between the bullying incidents and childhood wounds. This can only be done once the healing process has begun and the targets are sufficiently strong enough to acknowledge their roles in the bullying situation without falling into a state of pathological guilt. The psychotherapeutic process must help targets realise that they have not been relegated to the state of victim. This type of trauma implies the restructuration of the identity and a different relationship to the world as a whole. The scar will always remain, but the trauma is often the starting point of a journey to resume one's life. The targets can, for example, decide that from now on they will be respected. Ferenczi (1986) noted that extreme distress could awaken latent predispositions: 'the intellect does not find its origins in ordinary suffering, but in traumatic suffering. It is like a secondary phenomenon or an attempt to compensate for a complete psychic paralysis.' Bullying takes on a role of an initiation ritual in which healing requires integrating the traumatic events as a structural part of the life process, and which has enabled the target to reconnect to suppressed emotional knowledge. By using the strong part of their identity, their masochism, which may have kept them in the state of subordination, will let go. According to Paul Ricoeur (1995), some individuals suffer from an overactive memory, as if they were haunted by the memory of the humiliations, while others suffer from forgetting as if they were escaping from their own past. The healing process requires remembering in order to forget. When a psychoanalyst implies that a target gains pleasure from intense suffering, this is focusing on the individual and isolated psyche rather than exploring the relational problem.

It may be difficult for therapists, whose only insight into the target's professional environment is what the target has told them, to distinguish bullying from other forms of workplace suffering, or from an abusive request for sick leave or medical certificate to serve another purpose. The role of the therapist is to listen to the target's suffering and to the description of their working environment. The term workplace bullying or harassment should not be used in therapy, as in countries with anti-bullying legislation this has become a legal term and restricted in its use. It is not for the therapist to judge whether or not workplace bullying has taken place. There is always the danger that some employees may strategically use the concept to attack line managers who are not satisfied with their work. It may be the same employees who, by positioning themselves as victims, will try to obtain financial compensation. There are also hypersensitive employees who may feel persecuted even when this has not occurred. Psychiatrists refer to this as neuroticism interpreting any criticism of their work as a personal attack. As the workplace has become tougher, many employees feel insecure, living in constant fear of redundancy or being left on the side if they underperform. However much they are invested in their work, they do not feel recognised for their true value. Therapists are increasingly confronted with disenchanted employees who are exhausted from working in a context which favours individualistic objectives rather than collective values. Employees are increasingly frustrated at the lack of resources to carry out a good job and find this more difficult than the lack of personal recognition. It is therefore important to consider workplace bullying as a resonance factor of a more widespread process which can be observed in society as a whole, and the few cases of false allegations of workplace bullying should not mask the phenomenon and its real victims.

Conclusions

As the work environment becomes tougher and harder, workplace suffering has become a real mental health problem which therapists cannot ignore. Unfortunately, there are too few therapists working in the field. It requires flexible and well-trained practitioners, capable of providing treatment and support beyond the boundaries of their schools of thought. It is not so much the theoretical framework in which the therapist will provide assistance and support which is of importance, but rather the therapeutic alliance formed between the therapist and the target. There are no miracle solutions in therapy, but the therapeutic process requires that the target commits to the process and is prepared to initiate change in their life.

Acknowledgements

Translated from French by Sarah Vaughan.

References

Classen, C., Koopman, C., & Siegel, D. (1993) Trauma and dissociation. *Bulletin of the Menninger Clinic*, 57(2): 178–194.

Ferenczi, S. (1932) Confusion de langnes entre les adultes et l'enfant. Le langage de la tendresse et de la passion. In *Oeuvres complètes*, Vol. IV. Paris: Payot, 1982, pp. 125–135.

Ferenczi, S. (1949) The confusion of tongues between adults and children: the language of tenderness and of passion. *International Journal of Psycho-Analysis*, 30(4) (the first English translation of the paper).

Ferenczi, S. (1986) *Development of Psychoanalysis*. New York: International Universities Press.

Guardian (2009) Wave of staff suicides at France Telecom. Available at: http://www.guardian.co.uk/world/2009/sep/09/france-telecom-staff-suicides-phone (accessed February 5 2011).

Hirigoyen, M.-F. (1998) *Le harcèlement moral. La violence perverse au quotidien*. Paris: Syros.

Hirigoyen, M.-F. (2004) *Stalking the Soul: Emotional Abuse and the Erosion of Identity*. New York: Helen Marx Books.

Ricoeur, P. (1995) Le pardon peut-il guérir? *Esprit*, 3–4: 77–82.

Spiegel, D. (1988) Dissociation and hypnosis in post-traumatic stress disorders. *Journal of Traumatic Stress*, 1: 17–33.

Stievenard, C. (2010) Workforce management online. Available at: http://www.workforce.com/cgi-bin/login.pl?reason=3&dest=/archive/feature/news/frances-approach-workplace-bullying/index.php (accessed February 5 2011).

Part III

Organisational interventions

Chapter 12

Support, informing and aftercare by co-workers in the Netherlands

The role of the confidential supporter

Adrienne Hubert

Introduction

In many countries it is common practice to appoint co-workers to support and inform bullied targets. These co-workers are known by a number of different names including confidential supporter, harassment officer, confidential counsellor, dignity at work advisor, peer listener, designated contact person, contact officer and confidential advisor. In many countries this additional function has become a standard part of organisational life. In the Netherlands in 2004, 90 per cent of organisations employing more than 200 employees had a designated confidential supporter (*vertrouwenspersoon*) with more than half of all organisations having one or more designated confidential supporters (Van Dam & Van Engelen, 2004). Today most middle-sized organisations and almost all large Dutch organisations will have at least one confidential supporter, some of whom will belong to a professional association. In the Netherlands there are many training organisations offering courses designed for confidential supporters normally of two to five days duration.

This chapter will outline: (a) the importance of confidential supporters within an anti-bullying programme describing the policy, procedures and implementation of the anti-bullying process together with the tasks and duties of the confidential supporter; (b) the approach and knowledge required of confidential supporters. Both areas are important for policy-makers and to consultancies engaging in the introduction of anti-bullying policies, and also for those choosing to work as confidential supporters helping their colleagues to deal with workplace bullying.

I am writing this chapter as a managing director of a consultancy in the Netherlands, specialising in policy research and implementation related to workplace bullying, sexual harassment, discrimination, aggression and violence. During the past nine years I have trained over 1000 confidential supporters and continue to provide them with group supervision and free advice.

Law, regulations and anti-bullying policies

The Dutch Working Conditions Act (2007)[1] has been important in the introduction of anti-bullying policies and the introduction of confidential supporters. This Act states:

> The employer shall operate a policy aimed at preventing employment-related psychosocial workload, or limiting it if prevention is not possible, as part of the general working conditions policy.
>
> (article 3, sub 2)

Bullying is described as one of the risk factors involved in employment-related psychosocial workload:

> Employment-related psychosocial workload: the factors direct or indirect discrimination, including sexual intimidation, aggression and violence, bullying, and work pressure, in the employment situation that cause stress.
>
> (article 1, sub 3e)

The policy can be split into two parts:

- the prevention or limiting of work pressure
- the prevention or limiting of unwanted behaviours (discrimination, sexual intimidation, aggression and violence, and bullying).

The confidential supporter will not be involved in dealing with work pressure, as this responsibility falls to the medical officer or works council. However, the confidential supporter's role is to deal with unwanted behaviours which in the Netherlands involve bullying, discrimination, sexual intimidation, aggression and violence. In this chapter the emphasis will be on the role of the confidential supporter in dealing with bullying in the workplace. In the Netherlands bullying is defined as follows:

> All forms of intimidating behaviour of a structural nature, coming from one or more employees (colleagues, managers) aimed at an

employee or group of employees who is/are not able to defend himself/themselves against this behaviour. An important aspect regarding bullying is the repetition of that behaviour in time.

(Explanatory Memorandum, Working Conditions Act, 2007)

Organisations in the Netherlands are recommended to use this definition in their policy statements and grievance procedures. Organisations in other countries are recommended to identify the definitions of bullying used by their own legislation. It is important to have a clearly defined statement of what constitutes bullying when an employee complains about behaviour that does not meet the bullying criteria. For example, where there is a conflict about promotion without intimidating behaviour, it is clear that this will not be handled by a confidential supporter. The law and the definition of bullying are therefore important in defining the role of the confidential supporter.

Whilst the law does not prescribe exactly how the policy should be formulated, an appropriate policy is a prerequisite for the effective functioning of the confidential supporter. The Working Conditions Decree further demands the following:

1. If employees are or can be exposed to a psychosocial workload, the risks with regard to the psychosocial workload must be assessed in connection with the risk assessment and evaluation ... and, with due observance of the latest technological and scientific insights, measures be determined and implemented in the plan of action.

2. Information and instructions should be given to employees ... about the risks of psychosocial workload as well as about the measures aimed at preventing or restricting this load.

(article 2.15, Working Conditions Decree, 2007)

The 'latest scientific insights' on bullying can be found in guides on good practices which include examples of: policy statements, codes of conduct, reporting and complaints procedures, mediation procedures, the provision of support and aftercare by the confidential supporter, description of tasks and responsibilities of all involved stakeholders together with the mechanisms for implementing and evaluating the policy and procedures (Hubert, 2003a; Kolner *et al.*, 2006). In other countries similar good practices are being described (see, for example, Tehrani, 2005).

The need for confidential supporters within an anti-bullying policy

What is the need for a confidential supporter within an anti-bullying policy? There are many functions working within organisations that deal with the well-being of employees, including human resources, supervisors, occupational welfare workers, mediators and grievance committees. What is the added value of a confidential supporter?

Regulation of emotions

Employees who believe that they have been bullied feel they have been targeted and treated unfairly. If the bullying continues for a long time the targeted employees can begin to suffer from anxiety, depression and symptoms of post-traumatic stress disorder (PTSD; Einarsen & Mikkelsen, 2003). One of the major symptoms is that the target engages in repetitive behaviours such as continually talking about their experiences as targets of bullying. It is essential for the target to have someone who listens to them, accepts their account of events and provides them with acknowledgement and support. Unlike most of the other functions within the organisation that are expected to solve problems by remaining independent and taking a balanced position between the target and the alleged perpetrator, the confidential supporter stands at the side of the target. If a confidential supporter is contacted by both sides accusing each other of being the bully, the second complainant should be referred to another confidential supporter.

One of the difficulties faced by targets is identifying objective evidence of bullying behaviours. The feeling of not being believed is frustrating and can lead them to seeking support from numerous different people and functions. This shopping around behaviour, which can include pressurising and cajoling colleagues, unions, health professionals and HR to provide unrealistic levels of support, can run the risk of escalating the problem and alienating those who otherwise may have been supportive. The increasing frustration of the bullied targets may lead them to exhibit inappropriate behaviours such as openly criticising the way the problem is being handled or shouting at their HR manager.

Confidential supporters are not required to solve the bullying problem; their role is to be on the side of the person that approaches them as the target of bullying. It is expected that they regard the bullying target's story as truthful and then offer the target an opportunity to express their feelings about the bullying. The confidential supporter helps the target by acknowledging their difficulties, and if desired informing them about several interventions and preparing them for meeting the perpetrator or for presenting the grievances to other involved functions (management, HR, grievance committee). Throughout this process the confidential supporter will encourage the development of a realistic view of the options that are available within the anti-bullying policy. The confidential supporter is also able to accompany the target during these conversations which helps them to feel calmer and in control of the process.

Low profile support at an early stage

When a target of bullying reports bullying to HR, a supervisor, occupational social worker, or a grievance committee, this frequently leads to an escalation of the process with the target losing control over what actions are taken, with the result that some action may be taken which worsens the situation for the target. For example, if a bullying behaviour is still not extreme the actions taken may be too heavy handed and formal. Talking to a confidential supporter in the bullying process will not lead to action without the consent of the bullied target. In many cases the confidential supporter may be used only as a listening ear.

Victim blaming from other functions

People want to believe that the world is a secure, just and controllable place. This belief can be challenged when someone undesirably experiences a negative event, like an accident, a robbery or an incurable disease. To maintain the 'just world belief' people need to blame the victims for causing their misfortunes (Lerner, 1970). In the case of bullying, which is an undesired negative event, this unconscious process may lead to much well-meant advice for bullying targets on how they should change, such as 'You need to become more assertive', 'It's your nervousness', 'You should wear different clothes', or 'What did you do to make them treat you that way?' For traumatised or depressed targets this kind of advice is undermining and counterproductive, and for bullying colleagues it is a permit to continue their negative behaviours as they do not regard themselves as responsible for the distress of the target. Providing advice with the effect of blaming the target is a major problem with all functions involved with bullying. Even occupational social workers, coaches and psychologists are not always aware that in trying to change the target's behaviour or personality traits they may inadvertently blame the target for the bad behaviours of others.

Well-trained confidential supporters are aware of the constant risk of blaming the target. They will not try to change the target's behaviour or personality, but take the view that bullying behaviour is not to be tolerated regardless of the target's characteristics. They will talk with the target about the possibilities within the anti-bullying policy that may limit the bullying behaviours.

Conflicting interests and role conflicts

It is not helpful for the support, information and aftercare to be provided by the existing functions from the organisation as this will frequently lead to conflict of interests and roles. The next section deals with the conflicting issues that involve HR and supervisors, occupational social workers, company medical officers and grievance committees.

HR and supervisors

Whilst a supervisor could become a confidential supporter for people outside their own teams, this would not be possible for people in their own team as the supervisor needs to be independent and to be able to listen to the story of the employee at face value. In addition, supervisors may be involved in dealing with mediation or disciplinary actions which could conflict with their confidential supporting role. It may also be difficult for a supervisor to guarantee confidentiality as their primary responsibility is to the business and dealing with a case involving inappropriate behaviour may cause a conflict of interests. So if a target talks about severe bullying which includes threats to organisational property or safety, then the supervisor has no alternative but to report this, even when this is not requested by the target.

The confidential supporter has a duty of secrecy, which is often included in the anti-bullying policy but which is also based on the Criminal Code (art. 272). There are only a limited number of very serious crimes[2] for which a statutory duty of reporting exists. Naturally a confidential supporter aware of a threat may experience moral dilemmas. The confidential supporter is then not obliged to breach the duty of secrecy.

HR professionals have similar role conflicts as supervisors since they cannot fail to take action when an allegation of bullying has been made. Whilst they are able to mediate between parties, they cannot guarantee confidentiality. Moreover, HR professionals will keep records in the personnel file of the bullying target when approached about a bullying situation. In large organisations an HR professional may become a confidential supporter for a group of employees that fall under the responsibility of another HR professional.

Occupational social workers

Occupational social workers are focused on guiding employees, supervisors and management in organisations in bottlenecks in employment and private situations that have their effect on the work situation (Notenbomer *et al.*, 2009). There is, however, a mismatch between the role of the occupational social worker and that of confidential supporter. Social workers are often required to undertake mediation which can be between employee and employer or between colleagues. First, in mediation it is not possible to support the target; the role requires the mediator to maintain neutrality. Second, the occupational social worker has a general view that people seeking assistance can best be helped by giving them insight into how their own behaviour evokes bullying behaviour. This approach fails to recognise that bullying is an abuse of power, which generally requires a different kind of solution. Third, there is a tendency for occupational social workers to push the target into taking actions without being aware of possible negative outcomes of these actions on the target. However, the latter two problems can be overcome by training.

Company medical officers

One of the tasks of a company medical officer is to assess whether sick leave is due to illness or other causes, for example, a conflict in the organisation. In the latter case in the Netherlands there exist special regulations on how to act. The company medical officer has the duty to mention to the employer that sick leave is due to an employment conflict. This means that the company medical officer cannot guarantee that he will never undertake any action without the permission of the victim.

Grievance committees

In the Netherlands a formal complaint about bullying is usually investigated by a grievance committee, which normally consists of three people (Vilters, 2009). In some organisations the grievance committee consists of internal members only; in others it consists of external experts, completely or in part. Neutrality is crucial for members of a grievance committee. They must be impartial to guarantee a fair investigation of the bullying complaint. A target may choose to be accompanied by a confidential supporter to a hearing of the grievance committee. A hearing is emotionally stressful and even the grievance committee is relieved if a confidential supporter will support the complainants in emotional moments and help them to bring forward everything they want to say.

Selection, appointment and training of confidential supporters

The selection and training of confidential supporters should be discussed and agreed with the works council or union. In the Netherlands, the works council plays an important role in agreeing and implementing the anti-bullying policy.

The number of confidential supporters required in an organisation depends on its size, the number and distribution of locations and the magnitude of the bullying problems. If confidential supporters are spending more than half a day a week on this work, consideration should be given to appointing more confidential supporters. Whatever the size of the organisation, it is important to have at least two confidential supporters, as on occasion a conflict may arise where both parties see themselves as the target of bullying. A confidential supporter does not assess who is the 'real' target or even whether there is one. The role is to believe the story of the first person in the conflict situation that asks for help. However, as may happen, if a second person also wants to talk to a confidential supporter, it is essential that there is at least one other person to whom they can be referred. It is also possible that an employee may wish to complain about the behaviour of the confidential supporter. A further benefit of having several confidential supporters is that it gives the opportunity for employees to choose their own confidential supporter. There are benefits for the confidential supporters themselves in that they can bring issues to supervision where their clients agree,[3] which is invaluable in difficult cases.

Where the organisation is large and has a number of confidential supporters, it helps to have a 'confidential supporter co-ordinator' who ensures that there are adequate confidential supporting resources and advises the organisation on policy issues. Where there are a number of confidential supporters the selection should try to reflect the demographics of the organisation as, for example, it may not be easy for an older employee to talk to a young confidential supporter about a problem. Status should also be considered with all organisational levels being represented as it can be a barrier for a worker on a production floor talking to someone from management. However, a confidential supporter needs to have the intellectual capacity to be able to identify the potential legal and other consequences of their interventions and to be able to undertake the work without any possibility of personal or role conflicts.

The confidential supporter may be employed inside or outside the organisation. In the Netherlands there are occupational health services and other consultancies from which confidential supporters can be hired. The external confidential supporter has the advantage of being less likely to be influenced by people within the organisation than the internal confidential supporter. As an outsider the external person is not part of the organisational culture and more able to identify the underlying reasons for the bullying behaviour than an internal co-worker. On the other hand the internal confidential supporter is familiar with the organisation and people which may help in creating realistic informal resolutions for bullying problems. An internal confidential supporter is usually easier to meet in terms of time and location. In some organisations there is a combination of internal and external confidential supporters.

It is important for a person seeking assistance to have easy access to the confidential supporter. To achieve this, the employees' confidential supporters must have the opportunity to introduce themselves and their role using a range of channels of communication within the organisation. For example, they may introduce themselves personally during staff and management meetings, through articles in staff magazines, posters, email and intranet. The introductions should explain the function of the confidential supporter and include photographs and contact details. Confidential supporters should be contactable by phone to make an appointment, ideally with some opportunities for contact outside normal working hours. Employees need to know that they can arrange a meeting with a confidential supporter without the awareness of anyone else in the organisation; this will require a private room being made available before or after work or the opportunity to meet in a neutral place outside the organisation.

The appointment of an internal confidential supporter should be made by the CEO or equivalent in the organisation as it is this person who is responsible for ensuring the respectful behaviours of all employees. It is also the person to whom the confidential supporter should render account. The confidential supporter should be given an appointment letter that sets out the following:

- starting date and duration of appointment
- list of unwanted behaviour recognised by the organisation
- job description
- tasks and responsibilities
- safeguarding of juridical status[4]
- statement of confidentiality
- hours and compensations.

What a confidential supporter needs to know

Tasks and obligations

Confidential supporters should be confident in undertaking their roles and responsibilities which include:

- promoting their role
- providing initial support to employees who believe they have been bullied
- informing and supporting targets of bullying considering informal and formal procedures
- supporting the target during the procedures
- providing aftercare
- referring targets for professional help as necessary
- recording reports and complaints about bullying
- preparing anonomised statistical reports to management and works council on workplace bullying
- advising management and works council on resourcing issues relating to the anti-bullying procedures.

However, the most important task of a confidential supporter is to support the target by listening attentively to the story of the target and enabling the expression of emotions. The confidential supporter will not give advice on what to do in a particular situation, but rather will examine different actions that can be taken and discuss the potential advantages and disadvantages of each intervention with the target. It is therefore the target who decides whether he or she wants to do something about their situation. It is this aspect of the confidential supporter's role which adds value to existing functions and therefore it is important that the confidential supporter sticks to this task.

Relevant regulations

A confidential supporter must be very familiar with the policy and complaints procedure of the organisation and be able to explain the whole procedure to the target. It is also important to have some knowledge of the opportunities for taking legal actions outside the organisation and the process by which this is achieved.

Relevant background on bullying

Prior to fulfilling the job, a confidential supporter should be trained on the nature and impact of workplace bullying. The chapters in this book provide a lot of the essential information which should be known to the confidential supporter. The main areas essential to training include the following:

1 *Consequences of bullying.* Due to the symptoms of PTSD, bullied targets may exhibit strange behaviour. If a confidential supporter does not know about these consequences he or she is likely to get overwhelmed by this behaviour, or might think that the behaviour has been caused by the bullying (blaming the victim). The confidential supporter needs to know how to react to this behaviour and when it is time to refer the target for professional help.
2 *Required attitude towards targeted co-workers.* (See Tables 12.1 and 12.2 for checklists for dealing with targeted co-workers.)
3 *Origins of bullying and suitable interventions.* Some background on the distinction between predatory and conflict-related bullying (see Chapter 1) may be helpful in practice when confidential supporters need to discuss interventions with the target. In the case of predatory bullying, for example, interventions like giving feedback, norm setting and penalties are suitable. In the case of conflict-related bullying, interventions like mediation or separation of the conflict parties are more obvious (Hubert, 2003b).

Chances and risks of different interventions

Confidential supporters must be able to think along with the victim about the chances and risks of different formal and informal interventions. Especially the risks of interventions are easily overlooked when a victim is emotional. Often the confidential supporter believes that 'something simply must happen' without examining whether the step to be

Table 12.1 Checklist for dealing with targeted co-workers: things to do

Active listening	Confidential supporters need training in communication skills, e.g. listening, paraphrasing, summarising, digging deeper, following the story of the target and not being afraid of silences.
Acknowledging	Confidential supporters provide acknowledgement by saying things like: 'That is awkward. I can see that this is difficult for you.'
Accepting the story as true	Confidential supporters do not have to investigate whether the bullying actually occurred or to what extent the story is true. Any lack of acceptance would damage the mutual trust.
Emotional space	It is important that the target of bullying feels able to express any emotions (e.g. feelings of anger, distress, guilt, shame).
Education	Targets exhibiting symptoms of post-traumatic stress or depression are often shocked by them, themselves. A confidential supporter can reassure them that these are normal reactions to a shocking experience and that generally these symptoms diminish over time.
Affirming	Confidential supporters are recommended to make positive remarks, where appropriate, like: 'It is good that you have had the courage to come and talk to me about this.'
Ongoing support	At the end of a first meeting the confidential supporter should offer prospect: 'Thank you for coming, you are not facing this alone anymore. If you wish we can meet again when we can discuss if there are ways to improve the situation.'
Respect	Confidential supporters should treat the target with respect and also respect the limits set by the target. There should be no pressure put on the target to reveal more than feels comfortable.

taken can offer comfort at all and which negative consequences it involves.

The chances and risks of an intervention are different in every situation. Much depends on the culture of the organisation and the hierarchical positions and character of the persons that are involved in the bullying

Table 12.2 Checklist for dealing with targeted co-workers: things not to do

Trivialise	Even if a bullying seems to be very innocent, the confidential supporter must not make well-intentioned remarks like 'It might have been worse' or 'No offence was meant.'
Be judgemental	Confidential supporters should not question the story or give their own opinion, interpretation or judgement about the situation.
Blame	Confidential supporters should not blame the target for being bullied, by giving advice on how to change behaviour, personality or other characteristics.
Take over	Confidential supporters should not try to 'rescue' the target and take over direction (see, for example, Proctor & Tehrani, 2001). It is important that targets make their own choices. Also the conversation should be mainly directed by the target.
Intellectualise	Confidential supporters are not psychologists. They must not try to explain current experiences by events in the past ('So you have been bullied at school as well, maybe you have become an easy target').
Push solutions	It is a common pitfall for confidential supporters to propose interventions too quickly. If the target is still emotional it may be difficult to think of interventions. Confidential supporters need to gather information prior to proposing interventions. Ideally, interventions should not be discussed in a first conversation with the target.
Escalate process	The more people involved in a bullying case, the more likely it will escalate. Confidential supporters have to be very cautious in involving other people in the bullying situation.

situation. The bullying target often knows best how his environment will react to certain steps. His assessment of how an intervention will affect his situation is therefore of crucial importance. The discussion of interventions in which the confidential supporter describes the possibilities and general chances and risks and the victim assesses how the different possibilities in his own specific situation will turn out is a skill in itself.

Conclusion

The confidential supporter has an added value on the existing functions in organisations. The support given by a confidential supporter to the bullying target helps in dealing with the shocking bullying experience and ensures that the bullying target is well prepared to undertake steps within the anti-bullying policy. For the quiet progress of formal and informal procedures within the organisation, it is essential that this supporting task is carried out by a separate function, the confidential supporter.

In practice we see, however, that untrained confidential supporters forget their real task and take on the tasks of other disciplines. They try to mediate, take corrective action against the accused, get involved in taking over the complaint or starting to fight the organisation. As a result, the confidential supporter now loses their added value within the anti-bullying policy and the existing functions are unable to undertake their tasks. In extreme cases the attitude of the confidential supporter can even contribute to a further escalation of the bullying situation. For the success of an anti-bullying policy it is essential that all functionaries understand their role and task together with the role and tasks of others. To deal with bullying effectively everyone should stick to their own task.

Notes

1 Since 1994 the Working Conditions Act has obliged employers to protect employees from sexual harassment and violence and aggression. Bullying was seen as an element of aggression until it was included as a separate subject in the law in 2007.
2 Like: manslaughter, murder, rape, abduction, inciting to (or help in) suicide, crimes in which the general safety of persons is endangered (such as arson and deliberate exposure to radioactive contamination), crimes against the safety of the state and specific crimes against royal dignity and abuse of power by a civil servant.
3 Agreement from the target is important because the other confidential supporter is a co-worker as well and it may feel uncomfortable for the targets if another person with whom they are working knows about the situation and their feelings about it.
4 In the capacity of their role, confidential supporters may not experience any disadvantage of their juridical status.

References

Einarsen, S., & Mikkelsen, E. G. (2003) Individual effects of exposure to bullying at work. In S. Einarsen, H. Hoel, D. Zapf, & C. L. Cooper (eds)

Bullying and Emotional Abuse in the Workplace: International Perspectives in Research and Practice. London: CRC Press.

Hubert, A. B. (2003a). To prevent and overcome undesirable interaction. A systematic approach model. In S. Einarsen, H. Hoel, D. Zapf, & C. L. Cooper (eds) *Bullying and Emotional Abuse in the Workplace: International Perspectives in Research and Practice*. London: CRC Press.

Hubert, A. B. (2003b) *OR en ongewenste omgangsvormen op het werk* [Works Council and unwanted behaviour in the workplace]. Alphen aan den Rijn: Kluwer.

Kolner, C., Nauta, O., Van Soomeren, P., & Steinmetz, C. H. D. (2006) *Goede Praktijken tegen Geweld. Preventie en bestrijding van ongewenste omgangsvormen op de werkplek* [Good practices against violence. Prevention and control of unwanted behaviours at the workplace]. The Hague: Ministry of Social Affairs and Employment.

Lerner, M. J. (1970), The desire for justice and reactions to victims. In J. Macaulay & L. Berkowitz (eds) *Altruism and Helping Behaviour*. New York: Academic Press.

Notenbomer, K., Alphen, W. van, Groot, G. de, & Weel, A. (2009) *Dossier Arbodienstverlening* [Dossier Occupational Health Services]. Available at: http://www.arbokennisnet.nl/kennisdossier_arbodienstverlening.html (accessed March 6 2011).

Proctor, B., & Tehrani, N. (2001) Issues for counsellors and supporters. In N. Tehrani (ed.) *Building a Culture of Respect: Managing Bullying at Work*. London: CRC Press.

Tehrani, N. (2005) *Bullying at Work – Beyond Policies to Culture of Respect*. London: Chartered Institute of Personnel and Development.

Van Dam, Y., & Van Engelen, M. (2004) *Evaluatie van de arbowet inzake ongewenste omgangsvormen* [Evaluation of the effectiveness of the Working Conditions Act with respect to undesired behavior]. The Hague: Ministry of Social Affairs and Employment.

Vilters, H. J. (2009) *Omgaan met seksuele intimidatie. Juridische praktijkgids ongewenst gedrag* [To deal with sexual harassment. Legal practical guide unwanted behaviour]. The Hague: Boom uitgevers.

Chapter 13

Bullying and harassment at work

Acas solutions

Gill Dix, Barbara Davey and Paul Latreille

Preventing conflict, resolving disputes, and seeking strategies for work-place improvement: this spectrum of activity reflects the work of the British Advisory, Conciliation and Arbitration Service (Acas). It also represents the range of activities provided by Acas in response to bullying and harassment in the workplace. This chapter describes Acas 'solutions' to a problem of perceived growing significance in the modern workplace:

- how behaviours that manifest in the form of bullying or harassment can be addressed
- what mechanisms have most positive impact
- how approaches may be adapted for the future to ensure more robust outcomes for parties directly and indirectly involved.

Established in 1976, Acas is state-funded but independent of govern-ment. Its impartial status is ensured by a governance arrangement that involves a tripartite council comprising representatives of employers and employees, as well as independents. This independence and impartiality allows Acas to address workplace matters in a manner that can support both sides of the workplace. This is as important in dealing with conflict over workplace behaviours as it is in dealing with outright disputes. Acas is perhaps best known for the latter: resolving collective disputes between managers and employees, including actual or threatened strike action. But Acas also plays a significant role in responding to conflict of a more individual nature through its telephone helpline, mediation and concilia-tion. Acas also seeks to prevent conflict and promote best practice through a range of services including: publications; a website offering guidance and toolkits; via statutory Codes of Practice; a comprehensive training programme for managers; and in-depth consultancy with organ-isations and employee representatives.

Since the creation of Acas over 30 years ago, bullying and harassment have assumed increased significance. The next section discusses evidence on the incidence of bullying and harassment generally, and then on the work of Acas. The following sections consider strategies practised by Acas to address bullying and harassment at work, reviewing evidence on Acas training provision and mediation. The final section draws together some conclusions and reflections on how workplace conflict solutions might be calibrated in the future.

Incidence of bullying and harassment and Acas

Finding a comprehensive measure of the incidence of bullying and harassment is problematic. The largest survey of workplaces in Britain – the Workplace Employment Relations Survey (WERS) – reported that 3 per cent of workplaces (with ten or more employees) had experienced at least one grievance relating to bullying and harassment in the year prior to the 1998 survey; by 2004 this had risen to 7 per cent (Kersley *et al.*, 2006). However the WERS data give no sense of the prevalence of grievances within a workplace, nor the detail of cases, nor the incidence of bullying and harassment. Moreover, the source of the grievance data cited here is the manager, whilst it is arguably more appropriate to look at employee accounts.[1] However, there is limited reliable data on individuals. One reason for this shortfall is that surveys covering these issues tend not to be based on random samples, the more prevalent being within workplaces or by sector. One large-scale random survey that does give a recent measure of incidence is the government-funded *Fair Treatment at Work Survey* which in 2009 reported that 7 per cent of employees had experienced bullying and harassment over the previous two years (Fevre *et al.*, 2009).

Another challenge to finding an accurate measure, and one which has been the subject of considerable debate, is the issue of definition – how to define bullying and harassment in a way that receives a consistent response. The Fair Treatment Survey (Fevre *et al.*, 2009) refers to bullying and harassment 'that create a hostile working environment'. Overall, the features of bullying most prevalent in the literature are frequency, intensity, duration and power disparity (Lutgen-Snadvik *et al.*, 2007). These aspects are also encapsulated in Acas definitions where bullying is: 'offensive, intimidating, malicious or insulting behaviour, an abuse or misuse or power, through means intended to undermine, humiliate, denigrate or injure the recipient'. The Acas definition of harassment is:

'unwanted conduct affecting the dignity of men and women in the work-place . . . related to age, sex, race, disability, religion, sexual orientation, nationality or any personal characteristic . . . and may be persistent or an isolated incident'. Harassment, then, relates to an individual's dignity and 'unwanted' behaviour. Though not explicitly mentioned in the context of bullying, in reality both bullying and harassment are 'unwanted acts'.[2]

Whilst no substitute for statistics, in its day-to-day dealings with work-places Acas provides a useful barometer of the significance of the wide range of workplace issues including bullying and harassment. One of the most sensitive to the swings in everyday concerns is the Acas national tele-phone helpline. The helpline handles around one million calls annually from employers, employees and representatives, helpline advisers deal with a diverse range of subjects. Analysis of call patterns reveals that around one call every two and a half minutes relates in some way to bullying and harassment. In 2009–10, this amounted to 80,000 (8 per cent of calls) and around four in five of these calls are from employees or employee repre-sentatives.[3] The take-up of Acas publications relating to bullying and harassment is also significant: in the financial year April 2009–10, 20,000 free advice leaflets were ordered on the subject of bullying and harass-ment,[4] again with employees as the predominant customer.

Aside from help and guidance, Acas has a statutory duty to offer conciliation in claims made to the Employment Tribunal.[5] While not covered directly in legal provision protecting employees, bullying may be a feature of claims brought under specific jurisdictions such as constructive dismissal. Alternatively an employee may bring a claim relating to the effects of damaging behaviours, under health and safety legislation. Legal precision is greater around harassment, at least where it applies to behaviours covered by the Equality Act 2010 (age, sex, gender, race, disability, sexual orientation and religion or belief). A key development was the UK's adoption in 2002 of the Equal Treatment Amendment Directive which altered the 1975 Sex Discrimination Act to allow 'free standing harassment claims'. However, knowledge of the incidence of bullying and harassment in the legal context is poorly served by public records because there is no requirement for parties to record the factors underlying a tribunal claim and research surveys of tribunal claimants are rarely sufficiently detailed to uncover the complexity of issues that lie behind a claim. The only evidence on tribunal claims then relates to the jurisdictions of claims (Ministry of Justice, 2010): in 2009–10, for instance, 18,200 claims (6 per cent of the total) related to sex discrimination, 5700 related to race discrimination and 7500 concerned disability (2 per cent and 3 per cent respectively).[6]

These statistics provide limited insight. For this reason, in 2007 Acas undertook detailed research on claimant experiences under the 2003 Employment Equality Sexual Orientation and Religion or Belief Regulations (SORB). Around 1000 claims had been brought by the time of the research. In-depth exploration of 470 tribunal application forms in sexual orientation cases found bullying and harassment to be the most common source of the claim (Savage, 2007). The alleged behaviour took different forms, including verbal abuse, exclusion from informal social networks, physical attacks, sexual harassment and unfair treatment such as making claimants undertake 'menial tasks' or exclusion from informal perks or benefits enjoyed by other employees. Savage (2007) also undertook analysis of claims relating to religion or belief discrimination. Here allegations that barriers had prevented religious observation were among the most common claims, but bullying and harassment again featured strongly, in the form of name-calling, abusive language, shaming people into not practising faith, or not facilitating their observance. Further research with SORB claimants revealed that they tended to have experienced harassment in a number of different ways, and often over long periods of time (Denvir *et al.*, 2007).

The volume of work associated with bullying and harassment coupled with the complexity of the problems place this area high on the agenda for Acas. The following sections consider some of the solutions practised by the organisation, reviewing first training services, then mediation.

Training – from a managerial to a collective response

Organisations need to ensure that clear and effective policies are in place for responding to employee grievances, and for enforcing disciplinary sanctions as the first step in preparing managers for handling conflict of a serious nature. Following the Gibbons Review of Dispute Resolution in Britain (Gibbons, 2007) and the subsequent Employment Act 2008, Acas issued a new statutory *Code of Practice on Discipline and Grievance* in April 2009. In place of statutorily required procedures, the new Code sets out basic principles for handling disciplinary and grievance situations. To accompany the new principles-based *Code*, non-statutory *Guidance* provides detailed information on handling discipline and grievance in the workplace. In the 18 months following its introduction, Acas trained around 6700 delegates in the new Acas *Code* and *Guidance*.[7]

In 2009–10, 2245 delegates attended Acas training on developing anti-bullying and harassment policies. But Acas recognises the limitations of simply putting in place a formal policy. Embedding change is complex and requires an holistic approach focusing on the responsibilities and roles of all parties – senior and line managers, employees and representatives, 'victims' and 'perpetrators'. The Acas approach to training reflects the need to triangulate these different perspectives whilst encouraging a sense of social and corporate responsibility, alongside an understanding of the legal infrastructure. This approach underpins the Acas emphasis on improving employment relations in the widest sense. So whilst one of the outcomes of an intervention may be a new policy on bullying and harassment, it is the joint working to achieve a shared policy and the shared learning that forms the heart of the approach. Joint working, involving managers, employees and employee representatives is in some sense the hallmark of the Acas approach to problem solving in the workplace, and to ensuring positive lasting arrangements (for further discussion, see Kessler & Purcell, 1994, 1996; Purcell, 2000; Broughton et al., 2010).

One methodology that encapsulates this 'collective approach' is 'facilitated discussions'. Particularly apt in addressing team behaviours or wider cultural issues, the approach involves a joint working session (typically a day) with a group or team and an Acas adviser. The day might start with an introductory session on the organisation's obligations and liabilities under discrimination legislation; the employment rights of the individual; and the laws covering prosecution of perpetrators and protection against victimisation. But the core of the session emphasises self-realisation and mutuality. A session designed to create an understanding of what constitutes inappropriate and appropriate workplace behaviours may be used for participants to reach their own definition of bullying and harassment as fits their workplace. This might involve gaining an understanding of why bullying or harassment has occurred, including a review of organisational and external issues that may be contributory factors. This is an important dimension to unlocking individual and organisational cultures and in the experience of Acas might identify issues such as problematic work organisation, poor line management, competitiveness, job insecurity, and 'in and out groups'.

Full acknowledgement of the serious nature of negative behaviours and the implications for disciplinary sanctions is taken as given. But the emphasis is on tackling problems informally, promoting 'an open ear and open eye' approach, and for line managers the benefits of 'nipping situations in the bud'. The session also focuses on the future, the importance of setting review dates to monitor progress and updating the policy and its implementation; of keeping confidential records of complaints; and following up individuals (perpetrators and victims). The Acas facilitated discussion approach has resonance with Altman's work which applied Novak's theory of learning to workplace bullying and training (Altman, 2010). According to Altman, trainees can engage in 'meaningful learning' where new concepts of bullying may be constructed through learners hearing the views of others. Similarly, Acas training serves as a 'meaning construction process' which favours learners formulating their own understandings of the issues and ideas for future action.

Case study evaluations of Acas training specifically on bullying and harassment have provided further insights (see www.acas.org.uk/ casestudies). Common themes include the potentially damaging effects of office banter; the importance of 'buy-in' to policy changes; and the need for improving communication arrangements. Box 13.1 provides a case study illustrating some of these outcomes.

13.1 Acas facilitated discussion on bullying and harassment at Volorg

Volorg (the company name has been anonymised) is a medium sized, voluntary sector organisation. It has a Dignity at Work policy which covers bullying and harassment. Overall there had been few incidences of bullying and harassment at the organisation. However, an investigation following allegations against a line manager revealed the use of inappropriate 'banter' on the part of the manager, and more widely across the team. The investigation also highlighted aspects of favouritism and some 'inconsistent operational activity', whereby some staff felt forced to work additional hours for fear of losing their jobs. Following the investigation, the manager involved left the organisation, but a rift had developed in the team, and concerns remained about negative behaviours. Managers invited Acas as an impartial, external organisation, to assist in tackling the bullying culture, and building relations. An Acas workshop focused on five questions:

1   What would you classify as acceptable/unacceptable behaviours in the workplace?
2   What kinds of behaviour do you feel are acceptable in terms of pro-social role modelling?
3   What does the term 'professional boundaries' mean to you? Can you provide examples of good and bad practice?

4   What is banter? When is it acceptable and unacceptable?
5   How can behaviours impact on effective team working and relation-
     ships?

The Acas adviser set some ground rules for the day: participants were asked not to interrupt each other and to respect each other's opinions, and whilst being free to disagree, not to be judgemental. Participants worked in groups to address the five questions. Practical examples were cited by employees of types of behaviour and banter that caused offence to some. An employee participant commented that this brought about a realisation for some individuals that their own language had been unacceptable and resulted in plans to change in the future:

> Yes, but it was done in a pretty [. . .] supportive open way and I think most of the people involved in [banter] kind of went: 'That's me you're talking about' and they were able to say 'Right, fair do's, I take your point and I can work on that'.
>
> (Employee)

The process had helped the team see some of the problems more clearly and accept that they would have to work together to resolve them:

> What did come out is the realisation that whatever they felt about what happened, their focus of activity needed to be more professional about work [. . .] and you could see almost like people thinking in their heads 'Right I might not like her but I need to work with her because that's what I need to be here to do [. . .]'.
>
> (HR representative)

After the workshop Acas produced a report for senior managers highlighting what was considered acceptable or not in terms of banter and behaviour. This formed the basis of a second Acas workshop with a wider group of employees to develop a set of standards of behaviour that could be used to improve the existing code of conduct.

Overall there was felt to be a deepening awareness of the seriousness of the issues, and appreciation of the impact of banter, and a better understanding of what constitutes professional behaviour:

> I think the biggest thing I took away from it was just under-
> standing the impact of some of the kind of joking and banter
> can have on other people. [. . .] See I think it raised every-
> body's awareness which really helped.
>
> (Employee)

The HR representative felt that the initiative had helped achieve a 'real settlement' within the team. Thanks to the new code all employees should be more aware of appropriate behaviour within the workplace and their responsibility to identify and report any problems.

Mediation – an individual focused response

Acas has a long-standing tradition of mediating[8] in cases brought to the employment tribunal system. It also provides mediation in cases which have not been submitted for legal recourse. Mediation is defined as a voluntary process involving a third party, the mediator, whose role is to help two or more people in a dispute reach an agreement. Any agreement comes from the parties, not the mediator; the mediator does not judge or say who is right. The volume of non-tribunal mediations carried out by Acas is relatively low with just over 200 mediations completed in indi-vidualised disputes in 2009–10. In the same year just under 87,500 Employment Tribunal claims were passed to Acas, and 33,500 Acas settlements were achieved (Acas, 2010).[9] Acas also trains people in workplace mediation, and in 2009–10, 339 people attended certificated mediation courses run by Acas (Acas, 2010).

Mediation has become a subject of growing policy interest. The Gibbons Review (Gibbons, 2007) highlighted the value of mediation, and it has also been promoted in the foreword to the aforementioned *Code* (Acas, 2009) emphasising the benefits of an early response to disputes and more use of alternative dispute resolution (see also, Acas, 2005). In spite of this policy focus, the evidence base and academic literature in the UK remain slight, particularly in comparison with the USA. Partly to address this, in 2007 Acas joined with the Chartered Institute of Personnel Development (CIPD) to undertake a number of research projects on mediation, including surveys of managers and case studies. The results were synthesised to produce a new employer's guide on the subject (Acas/CIPD, 2008). Some of the findings from the joint Acas/CIPD work are reported below discussing the prevalence and value of mediation, and its application to bullying and harassment.

In short, findings to date suggest that while mediation is not widespread, it is perceived to be valuable in dealing with workplace conflict, and especially in tackling relationship breakdown. A 2007 Acas poll of managers from small and medium sized enterprises (SMEs) found that 7 per cent had used mediation to address a workplace problem, rising to a third of medium sized organisations (Johnston, 2008; Latreille *et al.*, 2010). Just over a third had used mediation to address difficulties associated with 'relationship breakdown' and 31 per cent had used mediation to deal with 'bullying and harassment'. A contemporaneous CIPD survey used a purposive sampling strategy targeted at its members and others likely to have experience of mediation. Whilst not representative, this provides 'an informed response' from larger employers (CIPD, 2007; Acas/CIPD, 2008; Latreille, 2010) on aspects of mediation. Of 766 respondents, 327 indicated their organisation had experience of using mediation to resolve workplace conflicts. Like the SME poll, 86 per cent said that mediation was most suited to relationship breakdown, and 74 per cent said it was suited to bullying and harassment cases.

In the CIPD survey, nine out of ten said it had been successful in resolving the issues it sought to address; and in the SME survey, referring to the last mediation that had taken place, 82 per cent of respondents said that mediation had either 'completely' or 'partly' resolved the case. As Roehl and Cook (in Kressel & Pruitt, 1989) argue, the real benefits of mediation should be judged less on the wider impacts, including organisational outcomes, and more on the parties' views: how satisfactory did they find mediation, and were the outcomes durable? More evidence is needed on this dimension (Fox, 2005; Seargeant, 2005). Latreille (2011) summarises the challenges of measuring 'success' in mediation. First, there is the difficulty of 'self selection bias': the voluntary nature of mediation means those who opt for mediation are likely to be predisposed to settling their case using this approach (Roehl & Cook, 1989; Fox, 2005; Poitras, 2007), rendering non-mediated cases inappropriate comparators for judging success. Even if success is defined by the rate of settlement, there is still no single index of outcomes, with success varying by measures of time and cost savings, perceived fairness and satisfaction, and rates of compliance to name a few. Surveys are notoriously poor at capturing these complexities. It is through case study research that more illuminating material emerges. The benefits and challenges described in the literature are wide-ranging: summarised below are those most relevant in the context of this chapter.

One of the most frequently articulated benefits of mediation is its potential to keep or reopen communication channels, especially in circumstances where managers may not be well placed to deal with a problem. Across the Acas/CIPD case studies mediation was considered versatile: it provides a mechanism for addressing relationship problems between colleagues in similar roles, employees and line managers, and senior managers and those highest within an organisation. In dealing with bullying and harassment, mediation was praised as providing an open environment encouraging participation, compared with the more adversarial nature of grievance and disciplinary hearings. It gave people time to reflect and to re-evaluate their own feelings and to see how their actions impacted on others (Fox, 2005; Seargeant, 2005). Mediation, it was argued, had the benefit of seeking jointly agreed resolutions, rather than the conventional approach to disputes, which focus on apportioning blame (Pope, 1996; Reynolds, 2000). In summary, mediation gave a genuine chance to consider the attitudes, motivations and feelings of the individual and the opposing party (Acas/CIPD, 2008; Latreille, 2011).

The evidence base, though, is not universally positive. One important issue stressed in case study interviews was that mediation should not be seen as an alternative to encouraging people to speak to one another and seeking personal resolution of difficulties. The role of line managers remains important, and mediation should not be the default mechanism for responding to conflict. Mediation may not suit people who, for one reason or another, find language and communication a barrier, since they may misunderstand the parameters of mediation, at least without the support of a representative. Mediation may not suit if one party is especially intransigent or is using mediation to raise unrealistic expectations. There was also a view that the relative 'informality' of mediation might be used against the parties (although in reality the mediation practised by Acas and other providers is a formalised process). Such 'allegations' of informality may refer to a number of factors, including the private nature of mediated outcomes and hence that they cannot establish precedent (Green, 2006). In relation to areas such as bullying, harassment and discrimination, the danger is that mediation may be a screen hiding (possibly repeated) misconduct and, more importantly, a deviation from the pursuit of a workplace's disciplinary or grievance procedures.

> In sexual harassment, the less formal tone of mediation might make sensitive issues easier to deal with and confront, than more formal procedures; yet equally as an approach there are concerns about it privatising or creating a barrier to justices, for instance, in sexual harassment cases where it may perpetuate a significant power imbalance.
>
> (Private sector company)

Thus one of the strengths of mediation – to iron out misunderstandings – may also be its weakness in relation to bullying and harassment.

Such reservations have been mirrored in the wider debate on workplace mediation, with particular concern centring on power imbalances (Hunter & Leonard, 1997; Dolder, 2004). In contrast, Gazeley (1997) discusses how mediation may be especially beneficial in the sexual harassment context by virtue of providing a safe and empowering environment for parties to deal with emotional and sensitive matters. Mediation's capacity to allow parties to articulate their feelings is also important and may lead to greater mutual understanding, especially where (as in several of the case studies), perceptions of bullying or harassment arise from personality clashes or interpersonal conflict. Importantly, it 'allows for catharsis and creative solutions that may be more meaningful for the plaintiff and at least somewhat less costly for the employer and the harasser ... [allowing the transgressor to] seek forgiveness for unconsciously hurtful acts' (Gazeley, 1997: 632–633).

In certain circumstances mediation has therefore proven a powerful tool. It may be that it is most effective in addressing underlying behaviours and attitudes, rather than dealing directly with the act of bullying or harassment per se. Most clear among the case study respondents was the view that matters of overt misconduct should not be the subject of mediation. That aside, mediation is especially relevant in laying a foundation for ensuring an ongoing relationship, avoiding the emotional and economic costs associated with staff turnover.

Conclusions and the future

The serious nature of bullying and harassment at work and the implications for individual and organisational well-being are profound. It is paramount that managers are therefore trained in the early identification of behaviours which are offensive and unwanted, and equipped in both policy and practice terms to respond to allegations using established discipline and grievance procedures. But this chapter has also explored other Acas methods designed to respond to bullying and harassment at a fundamental level in order to both preserve work relationships where they have broken down, and to improve employment relations. By offering training to affected parties, the opportunity is presented for a collective response to behaviours; and via mediation individuals are assisted in resolving their own conflicts.

As far as evidence allows, the chapter has sought to evaluate particular approaches. However, further evidence is needed to evaluate approaches on a case-by-case basis. For example, Hoel *et al.* (2006) argue that evaluation should include pre- and post-training measures of bullying prevalence and wider organisational measures, for example, absenteeism, turnover and grievances and complaints as well as longer term impacts.

In respect of improving support to workplaces, finding a way of involving the perpetrators, though potentially contentious, may be especially important if relationships are to be maintained. The experience to date suggests that mediation might involve encouraging self-reflection and allowing individuals to reform their behaviour without reprimand. Provided that actions do not involve disciplinary offences, the latter would seem especially significant in creating positive workplaces and in reducing staff turnover. The tendency to focus on managers' rather than individuals' accounts has perhaps been misguided in that managements' agenda, whilst overlapping with the interest of employees, may be weighted to wider organisational-level outcomes and benefits. Indeed, Saam (2010) argues that the private nature of mediation may mean that the outcomes cannot reverberate to reach the group or organisational level.

Encouraging conflict management – a cultural response

Whilst the issues might be outflanked by matters of dismissal and redundancy handling, bullying and harassment are concerns that are frequently placed at the door of Acas. Most importantly, they represent aspects of negative behaviours that may not be easily labelled and thus may not be transparently reported. It is only when bullying or such negative behaviours reach disciplinary or grievance procedures, or are found to underpin allegations of specific legislated areas of discrimination, that the potential for 'counting' can begin. This is not to say that the ramifications of detrimental behaviours and outright bullying are not significant if they do not manifest via formal mechanisms. On the contrary, they can have a pervasive effect on the well-being of individuals, the culture and potentially the productivity of a workplace. It is for this reason that Acas has an interest in developing an understanding of how workplaces can approach conflict and discontent in a more strategic way, embracing both manifest and underlying disputes.

This approach resonates with 'conflict management systems' theory from the USA, in which dissent is welcomed, and the approach to conflict is proactive and comprehensive, involving a wider range of organisational players than is the case with dispute resolution strategies (Lipsky *et al.*, 2003; Dix & Oxenbridge, 2004). Wholesale imposing of conflict management strategies in the UK is likely to be problematic, not least because of the historic differences in employment relations regimes between the two countries, but equally seeking individual strategies for alternative dispute resolution (ADR) in isolation may have a lesser overall impact that can be achieved from a more 'integrated' approach.

How can Acas support a culture of workplace conflict management, and how can this be applied to the management of bullying and harassment at work? Again, turning to evidence, in 2008, Acas commissioned a study to identify strategies for better management of sexual orientation and religion and belief, in response to the findings from the research mentioned earlier. A deliberative approach was used to identify problems and seek solutions (Dickens *et al.*, 2009). The findings provide important signposts to practical steps that could be promoted by Acas and others, in seeking a more proactive approach to handling conflict and preventing negative behaviours.

Debate centred around two key areas: improving knowledge and understanding; and tackling organisational culture. Managers identified best practice in respect of both. On the former, the emphasis was on creating a positive environment in which issues such as bullying and harassment could be addressed, but not perceived purely as 'a problem'. In workplaces, this would involve having open discussions on the subject, with clear and transparent policies on terms and conditions, whilst acknowledging change in social and legislative context. The objective would be to create a culture of respect and fair treatment by identifying the nature and impact of bullying and harassment (and other negative behaviours), and, as described earlier in the chapter concerning the Acas training function, seeking to establish a new code of behaviours bespoke to the individual workplace. The use of compulsory training, reflective learning, networks and impact assessment are all vehicles for advancing learning and understanding.

But how might this translate into culture change? Three levels of change were identified. First, change via leaders and senior managers, who should be transparent in their acceptance of the case for equality and diversity, and visible in their commitment to the ethical, legal and business case for fair treatment. If processes are to be embedded, their design and implementation should involve other workplace constituencies, such as trade union (Saundry et al., 2011; Latreille, 2011) and key figures (Dickens et al., 2009). Second, overt signalling of support for positive behaviours and equality might include, in relation to sexual orientation, holding celebration events and encouraging networking. Less public, but also important was the process of embedding support through job descriptions, induction processes, appraisals and performance indicators. The third step was seeking to mainstream and cascade the importance of positive behaviours beyond human resource teams to the wider workforce, achieved, for instance, by giving managers and staff direct ownership of issues.

The agenda set by the research was ambitious in respect of better handling of sexual orientation and religion or belief. But the proposition represents a paradigmatic shift to finding an all-embracing set of integrated solutions to improved behaviours in the workplace and ensuring more effective conflict management. Acas has played a key role in developing practical responses to conflict at work, including bullying and harassment, over the last 30 years in a rapidly evolving employment relations landscape. It will be key to developing and delivering future change.

Disclaimer

This chapter reflects the views and interpretations of the authors which may not coincide with those of Acas Council.

Acknowledgements

We are grateful to Acas Research and Evaluation Section, especially Nick Wainwright and Jon Cooper, for the evaluation and monitoring data and case study. Thanks also to Acas Adviser Suzanne Sheils for information on Acas training, and to Steve Williams, Head of Acas Equality Services, for sharing his thoughts on this subject.

Notes

1 WERS includes a survey of managers and worker representatives. The 1998, 2004 and 2011 surveys include a survey of employees, though this covers neither grievances nor bullying and harassment.
2 *A Guide for Managers and Employers: Bullying and Harassment at Work* (Acas, 2010b); *Guidance for Employees: Bullying and Harassment at Work* (Acas, 2010c).
3 Estimates are based on call volumes for 12 months from Acas management information, and the pattern of call and caller types from the report of the *2009 Acas Helpline Evaluation* (Thornton & Fitzgerald, 2010).
4 See Note 3.
5 The UK employment relations framework involves a system of legal rights underpinning individual employment relationships. Acas has a statutory role to encourage parties involved in disputes over alleged breaches of individual employment rights to reach a settlement and so avoid the need for an employment tribunal (labour rights court) hearing.
6 Figures relate to the number of jurisdictions, not number of individual claims, since applications can be submitted identifying more than one jurisdiction.
7 Figures taken from Acas management information system.
8 Though this service is traditionally known as 'conciliation', the process and objectives are the same as the Acas mediation service, the latter being a charged service.
9 In 2009 Acas introduced a service offering conciliation to parties who were considering submitting an employment tribunal claim – so-called 'pre-claim conciliation'.

References

Acas (2005) *Making More of Alternative Dispute Resolution*. Acas Policy Discussion Papers 1. London: Acas.

Acas/CIPD (2008) *Mediation. An Employer's Guide*. London: Chartered Institute of Personnel and Development.

Acas (2009) *Acas Code of Practice: Disciplinary and Grievance Procedures*. London: Acas.

Acas (2010a) *Acas Annual Report and Accounts, 2009–2010*. Available at www. acas.org.uk.

Acas (2010b) *A Guide for Managers and Employers: Bullying and Harassment at Work*. London: Acas.

Acas (2010c) *Guidance for Employees: Bullying and Harassment at Work*. London: Acas.

Altman, B. A. (2010) Workplace bullying: application of Novak's (1998) learning theory and implications for training. *Employee Responsibilities and Rights Journal*, 22: 21–32.

Broughton, A., Pearmain, D., & Cox, A. (2010) *An Integrated Evaluation of Acas Workplace Projects*. Acas Research Paper Series 01/10. London: Acas.

CIPD (2007) *Managing Conflict at Work*. London: Chartered Institute of Personnel and Development.

Denvir, A., Broughton, A., Gifford, J., & Hill, D. (2007) *The Experience of Sexual Orientation and Religion or Belief Employment Tribunal Claimants*. Acas Research Paper Series, 02/07. London: Acas.

Dickens, S., Mitchell, M., & Creegan, C. (2009) *Management Handling of Sexual Orientation, Religion and Belief in the Workplace*. Acas Research Paper Series, 01/09. London: Acas.

Dix, G., & Oxenbridge, S. (2004) Coming to the table with Acas: from conflict to co-operation. *Employee Relations*, 26(5): 510–530.

Dolder, C. (2004) The contribution of mediation to workplace justice. *Industrial Law Journal*, 33: 320–342.

Fevre, R., Nichols, T., Prior, G., & Rutherford, I. (2009) *Fair Treatment at Work Report: Findings from the 2008 Survey*. Employment Relations Research Series 103. London: Department for Business, Innovation & Skills (BIS).

Fox, M. (2005) *Evaluation of the Acas Pilot of Mediation, Appeals and Employment Law Visit Services to Small Firms*. Acas Research Paper Series, 05/05. London: Acas.

Gazeley, B. J. (1997) Venus, Mars and the law: on the mediation of sexual harassment cases. *Willamette Law Review*, 33: 605–648.

Gibbons, M. (2007) *Better Dispute Resolution: A Review of Dispute Resolution in Britain*. London: Department of Trade and Industry.

Green, M. Z. (2006) Tackling employment discrimination with ADR: does mediation offer a shield for the haves or real opportunity for the have-nots? *Berkeley Journal of Employment and Labor Law*, 26: 319–356.

Hoel, H., Giga, S. I., & Faragher, B. (2006) *Destructive Interpersonal Conflict in the Workplace: The Effectiveness Of Management Interventions*. Manchester: British Occupational Health Research Foundation and Manchester Business School, The University of Manchester.

Hunter, R., & Leonard, A. (1997) *Sex Discrimination and Alternative Dispute Resolution: British Proposals in the Light of International Experience*. London: Sweet and Maxwell.

Johnston, T. (2008) *Knowledge and Use of Mediation in SMEs*. Acas Research Paper Series 02/08. London: Acas.

Kersley, B., Alpin, C., Forth, J., Bryson, A., Bewley, H., Dix, G., & Oxenbridge, S. (2006) *Inside the Workplace: Findings from the 2004 Workplace Employment Relations Survey*. London: Routledge.

Kessler, I., & Purcell, J. (1994) Joint problem solving and the role of third parties. An evaluation of ACAS advisory work. *Human Resource Management Journal*, 2: 34–55.

Kessler, I., & Purcell, J. (1996), The value of joint working parties. *Work, Employment and Society*, 10: 663–682.

Kressel, K., & Pruitt, D. (1989) *Mediation Research: The Process and Effective Third Party Interventions*. San Francisco: Jossey-Bass.

Latreille, P. (2010) *Mediating at Work: Of Success, Failure and Fragility*. Acas Research Paper Series, 06/10. London: Acas.

Latreille, P. (2011) *Workplace Mediation: A Thematic Review of the Acas/CIPD Evidence*. Acas Research Paper Series, 13/11. London: Acas.

Latreille, P. L., Buscha, F., & Conte, A. (2010) *SME Attitudes Towards Workplace Mediation: The Role of Experience*. Acas Research Paper Series 05/10. London: Acas.

Lipsky, D., Seeber, R., & Fincher, D. (2003) *Emerging Systems for Managing Workplace Conflict*. San Francisco: Jossey-Bass.

Lutgen-Snadvik, P., Tracy, S. J., & Alberts, J. K. (2007) Burned by bullying in the American workplace: prevalence, perception, degree and impact. *Journal of Management Studies*, 44: 837–862.

Ministry of Justice (MOJ, 2010) *Employment Tribunal and EAT Statistics 2009–10 (GB) 1 April 2009 to 31 March 2010*. Available at: http://www.justice.gov.uk/employment-eat-annual-stats.htm.

Poitras, J. (2007) The paradox of accepting one's share of responsibility in mediation. *Negotiation Journal*, 23 (3): 267–282.

Pope, S. (1996) Inviting fortuitous events in mediation: the role of empowerment and recognition. *Mediation Quarterly*, 13: 287–295.

Purcell, J. (2000) After collective bargaining. In B. Towers & W. Brown (eds) *Employment Relations in Britain: 25 years of the Advisory, Conciliation and Arbitration Service*. Oxford: Blackwell.

Reynolds, C. (2000) Workplace mediation. In M. Liebmann (ed.) *Mediation in Context*. London: Jessica Kingsley Publishers.

Roehl, J. A., & Cook, R. F. (1989) Mediation in interpersonal disputes: effectiveness and limitations. In K. Kressel & D. Pruitt (eds) *Mediation Research: The Process and Effective Third Party Interventions*. San Francisco: Jossey-Bass.

Saam, N. J. (2010) Interventions in workplace bullying: a multi-level approach. *European Journal of Work and Organizational Psychology*, 19: 51–75.

Saundry, R., McArdle, L., & Thomas, P. (2011) *Transforming Conflict Management in the Public Sector? Mediation, Trade Unions and Partnership in a Primary Care Trust*. Acas Research Paper Series, 1/11. London: Acas.

Savage, B. (2007) *Sexual Orientation and Religion or Belief Discrimination in the Workplace*. Acas Research Paper Series, 01/07. London: Acas.

Seargeant, J. (2005) *The Acas Small Firms Mediation Pilot: Research to Explore Parties' Experiences and Views on the Value of Mediation*, Acas Research Paper Series, 04/05. London: Acas.

Thornton, A., & Fitzgerald, N. (2010) *Acas Helpline Evaluation 2009*. Acas Research Report Series, 03/10. London: Acas.

Chapter 14

Addressing bullying in the workplace

Maarit Vartia and Noreen Tehrani

Introduction

Interpersonal conflicts, bullying and harassment in the workplace should be identified, investigated, and resolved where it occurs, that is, within the organisation or place of work rather than in an employment tribunal or court of law. Whilst managers and safety and health professionals have the primary responsibility for dealing with interpersonal conflicts, it is important that everyone within the workplace plays their part in the process. Unfortunately, many organisations lack the knowledge and skills to recognise and deal with bullying or fail to provide managers with the necessary recourse and support required to develop cultures capable of handling interpersonal conflicts, leaving them feeling unprepared and uncertain about what to do or how to choose an appropriate intervention. Without this support managers either fail to take action or overreact with the risk of making matters worse.

Where managers are asked why they fail to take action to reduce or tackle bullying despite clear evidence of bullying and conflict being provided from employee surveys, it turns out that they believe that they can only act when there are reported cases of bullying. This is, however, a very limited view of their responsibility for creating positive and respectful teams. Managers in co-operation with their staff are able to do a lot to prevent and reduce inappropriate behaviour including bullying without the need for named targets or identified bullies.

Organisations have two main pathways for reducing or managing bullying. First, there is awareness raising including developing and consulting on policies and procedures (Einarsen & Hoel, 2008; Vartia & Leka, 2011), raising awareness through the use of surveys, promoting positive behaviours, training for managers and leaders and education for employees (Mikkelsen *et al.*, 2008). The second pathway relates to the way in which individual cases of bullying are handled including the confidence that employees have in management to undertake fair, balanced and timely investigation and to resolve concerns over abrasive and destructive behaviours (Hoel & Einarsen, 2011). These two pathways require different approaches; however, they can be undertaken in parallel when necessary. Despite the absence of many systematically evaluated interventions for the prevention and reduction of bullying, there is a wide body of knowledge and experience gained from work undertaken in many countries on the way in which organisations deal with workplace bullying. The outcome of this work has shown that although a lot can and should be done to address bullying it is a complex task (Einarsen *et al.*, 2011a).

This chapter describes some of the ways in which organisations can put workplace bullying on to the agenda by emphasising the importance of encouraging discussions on acceptable and unacceptable behaviours with the aim of creating workplace environments where bullying becomes unacceptable and unaccepted by the workforce. The importance of educating managers and team leaders in handling individual reports of bullying will be described, together with actions required when responding to surveys which highlight problems with interpersonal conflict or bullying. A case study involving an educational organisation demonstrates some of the factors involved in achieving a successful outcome and finally some thoughts are presented on future directions for organisational interventions.

Putting bullying on the agenda

Managers and supervisors receive information on the presence of bullying from a range of sources including complaints from targets and bystanders and indirect notifications provided by health and safety managers, union representatives or occupational health professionals. Often the first time a manager becomes aware of a bullying problem is when the employees, work environment or exit survey show that members of their team report being bullied or observing bullying. However, as survey information is generally gathered anonymously it is impossible to identify individual targets or the perceived bully, or even for the manager to recognise that they are perceived as the bully. Whilst researchers have hotly debated the prevalence levels of bullying and harassment in the workplace (Zapf *et al.*, 2011) there is no safe or acceptable level of bullying and the starting point for every manager and organisation should be a zero tolerance to any form of damaging behaviour. Managers and supervisors should always take any report of bullying seriously and with the support of senior management and specialist resources (e.g. occupational health and safety, human resources and psychologists) work together with employees to recognise, respond to and address the causes of workplace bullying.

Conversations and consultation to establish policies and procedures

One of the best ways to create engagement in dealing with workplace bullying is to have policies, systems and procedures which define and deal with the problem. The policy and procedure documents can also be used as the basis for developing educational and promotional programmes to educate and inform the managers and employees. It has been shown that the process for consulting upon, drawing up and implementing the policy is as important as its contents (Einarsen & Hoel, 2008; PRIMA-EF, 2008). When designing the policy, consultations should take place between managers and employees at all levels and from all areas of the organisation to ensure that the policy is fit for purpose and not something which demonstrates no real understanding of what is required to meet the specific needs of the organisation and its workforce. The process by which the policy is drawn up and implemented provides a clear message to employees and managers on the importance that the company gives to dealing with workplace bullying and demonstrates the level of organisational commitment to tackling this problem.

The policy should emphasise a zero tolerance towards all forms of harassment and bullying and outline the behaviours which the organisation expects from all its employees. There should also be a clear outline of the process and procedures for preventing, reporting and dealing with workplace bullying. The policy should include a definition of the standards of behaviour required from all employees, the roles and responsibilities of management, health and safety, human resources and occupational health professionals (Einarsen & Hoel, 2008).

Communication is crucial: if employees are unaware of the anti-bullying and harassment policy it is unlikely that they will seek help when they find themselves having to deal with unfair or unreasonable behaviours from their manager or colleagues. In a study in a Finnish city it was found that only 12 per cent ($N = 575$) of employees were familiar with their organisation's anti-bullying policies, 33 per cent had superficial awareness and 15 per cent were totally unaware of a policy being in existence (Vartia, 2009).

It has been shown that the existence of a written anti-bullying policy has a preventive effect (Rayner & Lewis, 2011). But well-written policies can fail if senior management are not supportive or there are failures to handle complaints adequately and impartially or to investigate them within a reasonable timescale. In Finland, it has been suggested by some lawyers that line managers should take action within 14 days of being informed of a potential bullying case (Kess & Kähönen, 2010).

Clarifying roles and responsibilities

The employer carries overall responsibility for assessing and managing work environment risks and taking action to reduce or eliminate existing risks including bullying. However, the roles of line managers, safety and health officers, occupational health professionals, personnel managers, union representatives, external consultants and counsellors may differ between countries and organisations, resulting in employees becoming confused about whom to approach when they feel that they have been treated unfairly (see Chapter 12, Hubert). It is therefore important for organisations to clarify the roles and responsibilities of all groups of players. Health and safety personnel and union representatives are often best suited for monitoring the adherence to policies and procedures and looking for ways to prevent or manage work-related bullying. Occupational health professionals, including occupational health psychologists, can work as coaches and/or become involved in investigating bullying situations and act as mediators, and may be able to carry out surveys. They also give individual support for targets and, if needed, for perpetrators whose health and well-being have been injured because of bullying (Vartia *et al.*, 2003). Human resource practitioners may become involved in investigating and resolving bullying situations. However, regardless of the involvement of specialist resources, managers must always be involved as they have the responsibility, power and opportunities to examine and improve working practices, allocate work and tasks and be a model of respectful behaviours and also to use sanctions when necessary.

Encouraging employees to identify and report bullying

It is often difficult for employees to talk about workplace bullying. Organisations tend to see the introduction of anti-bullying policies and procedures as a single event at which time they provide training for managers and employees believing that their work is then done and that having introduced the programme there is not a need for retraining or revisiting the issue within the workforce. If the topic is not revisited, many employees will begin to find bullying a difficult subject to raise or discuss with their managers or colleagues. Team members may fail to recognise or accept that bullying is taking place within their team or workplace.

The term bullying is emotive and can cause violent reactions in targets, observers and managers. It may be necessary to use other terms such as inappropriate or negative behaviour or abrasive management styles (see Chapter 9, Crawshaw) if the issue is to be addressed openly. Many employees describe feeling shocked and ashamed at being bullied, believing that they must be responsible for doing something wrong to deserve this kind of treatment. With bullying being regarded as bad behaviour, witnesses of bullying may experience a range of complex and difficult emotions, particularly when they feel unable to intervene or to take action due to fear of retaliation (see Chapter 6, Bloch). Bullying at work is sometimes associated with school bullying and seen as a childish behaviour which may make it more difficult for adults to recognise and admit that it happens in one's own workplace. Given the nature of the impact of bullying it is not uncommon for participants in training or feedback sessions to challenge the results of work environment surveys by playing them down or ridiculing the findings. Employee's may sneer or laugh, suggesting that the discussion is stupid and a waste of time, and discounting the bullying behaviour by suggesting that the people who said that must have been mistaken or over-sensitive. Others may express difficulty in understanding the nature of the reports by suggesting that they cannot understand which behaviours have been perceived as bullying, or may suggest that although things had been bad before there was not a problem anymore. Facilitating a feedback session can be difficult and it is essential that the facilitator is fully prepared with the evidence from the data collected and is experienced in dealing with group dynamics. It is also important that the survey itself is well designed and provides evidence of the actual behaviours which are regarded as inappropriate rather than generalisations. One approach to increasing engagement is to move away from measuring negative behaviours to those that describe valued or positive behaviours (Tehrani, 2005).

Organisational culture and procedures should encourage regular discussions of behaviours and the challenge of inappropriate or destructive behaviours, with opportunities to report instances when necessary. During these discussions the potential causes of bullying should be explored including the need to develop social and communication skills (Einarsen *et al.*, 2009), the role of provocation (Matthiesen & Einarsen, 2007), the impact of organisational culture (Rayner *et al.*, 2002) and organisational change (Hoel & Cooper, 2000). Unless bullying and other destructive behaviours are put into context it is understandable that people will be hesitant to talk about their experiences, particularly when they feel that they may be blamed. For employees to be comfortable in talking about conflict and bullying they need the following:

- a clear understanding of what kinds of behaviours are not appropriate
- someone they can talk to in confidence about their experience
- managers who openly challenge inappropriate behaviours
- training on the organisation's policies and procedures
- information on the context or organisational causes of bullying
- a recognition that individual characteristics are not the main cause of becoming a target of bullying.

These measures should be supported by:

- the discussion of organisational anti-bullying policies at least annually in team meetings
- forums for individual employees to discuss the workplace atmosphere, relationships and bullying with their manager/supervisor
- surveys of organisational, work environment factors and employee's interpersonal skills which have been shown to increase the incidence of bullying.

Awareness raising and training

It has been found that awareness, knowledge and definitions of workplace bullying differ between EU countries and organisations (Leka *et al.*, 2008; Einarsen *et al.*, 2011b). Training provided for all employees should include a description of the nature of bullying, and a characterisation of the forms of bullying, including what is and what is not bullying. This requires a clear differentiation to be made on the differences between poor leadership, firm management and bullying or harassment. It should also include empirical evidence on the causes of bullying, the individual and organisational consequences of bullying, as well as information and handouts on organisational policy and procedures informing the employee on what to do if subjected to bullying, how to make a complaint and who to contact for information and support. During the induction period, new employees should be provided with the policy, procedures and support information as part of their induction training.

Training for line managers is central to dealing with bullying in the workplace. Managers require a basic knowledge on the phenomenon together with a clear understanding of their responsibilities to create a safe working environment and to adhere to health and safety, employment, discrimination and other legislation, regulations and agreements involved in the management of the risks caused by workplace conflict and bullying. Managers also need information on suitable means to tackle bullying; for example, an organisation-wide work conditions survey does not suit in a situation where an individual employee provides a notice on bullying, as well as training to help them effectively investigate and hearing bullying cases. Clarifying to managers the difference between bullying and strong management (see Chapter 1, Tehrani) is also important. Managers have the right and responsibility to organise work, delegate tasks and deal with underperformance, and organisations have the responsibility to run an economic and profitable operation which may require restructuring, the reduction of workforces and other changes. These managerial and organisational decisions, whilst being upsetting to employees, are not bullying. However, the lack of leadership, use of discrimination and favouritism in carrying out organisational decisions can be bullying, particularly when employees have not been involved or their views taken into account. Bullying is not always what is done but rather how it is carried out (see Chapter 1, Tehrani).

Importance of work organisation and leadership

A number of studies have found that deficiencies and problems in the psychosocial work environment – including role conflicts, low level of satisfaction with leadership, lack of discussion on tasks and goals for the work team, tyrannical or laissez-faire leadership styles or stressful work situation – promote bullying (Einarsen *et al.*, 1994; Vartia, 1996; Hauge *et al.*, 2007). Interventions aimed at improving the functioning of the work team by the use of agreed ways of working and leadership practices decrease some of the underlying causes of bullying. The onset of interpersonal conflicts, inappropriate behaviour and bullying are frequently situation specific, varying between organisations, types of work and employee characteristics including social skills. It is therefore necessary for the risk factors and situations to be established through open and honest discussion between employees and managers.

Organisational preparedness

Introducing a programme to reduce the incidence of bullying or other bad behaviours in a workplace requires careful planning if it is to be successful. It is important to be aware of the existing organisational culture and how it might support or undermine the introduction of policies and procedures aimed at improving employee behaviours. There can be problems and benefits to using internal and external consultants to deal with reports of bullying. External consultants will need to recognise that organisations have different cultures and that this will need to be taken into consideration when looking for ways to resolve a conflict. Internal consultants may be so used to the culture that they fail to recognise the role culture plays in bringing about interpersonal conflict and strife. Always when outside trainers and counsellors are used in an organisation it is essential to check their competency and expertise in relation to workplace bullying. Counsellors with no expertise and experience on working with bullying and who have no idea what they are doing may end up making matters worse for everyone.

Three cultural dimensions – focus, power and style (Hofstede, 1991) – have been found to be particularly useful in identifying the style of organisational intervention (Figure 14.1). Recognising the kind of interventions that might work best can be difficult. Below are examples of some common organisational types, together with the ideas on the kind of interventions that may be effective.

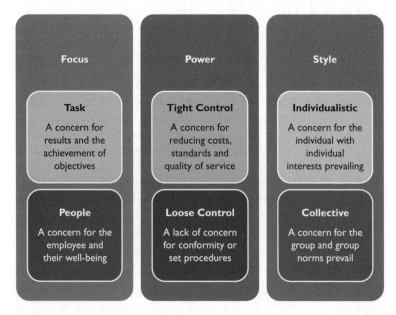

Focus	Power	Style
Task	**Tight Control**	**Individualistic**
A concern for results and the achievement of objectives	A concern for reducing costs, standards and quality of service	A concern for the individual with individual interests prevailing
People	**Loose Control**	**Collective**
A concern for the employee and their well-being	A lack of concern for conformity or set procedures	A concern for the group and group norms prevail

Figure 14.1 Cultural dimensions.

Organisation 1 (task, tight control, individualistic)

This organisation is totally focused on getting things done and will choose people who are tough minded and prepared to take a risk to get there. It is not an organisation that would want to spend much time talking about the emotional benefits of a cultural change programme. What the organisation wants to see are tangible benefits which could be measured before it would commit to a cultural change programme.

Organisation 2 (task, tight control, collective)

This organisation is likely to want to use tools such as sickness absence and numbers of grievances as the way that it monitors the effectiveness of its interventions. The needs of this organisation are to have clear policies that set out behaviours which it will enforce. Bullying will only be seen as important if it can be shown that it has an impact on profitability.

Organisation 3 (task, loose control, individualistic)

This is a difficult organisation to handle. The main focus is on getting the job done and there are few rules or procedures to inform the employees on how they are to behave. If individuals are achieving the targets then they are likely to be left to get on with the job even when this means that other employees are suffering as a result. This organisation may need time to develop a greater awareness of the real cost of their lack of control through being sued or being reported to the health and safety inspectorate.

Organisation 4 (people, loose control, collective)

This organisation may appear chaotic in its ways of getting things done and would not be interested in monitoring or other forms of data. Instead it wants to know how its employees feel about the cultural programme and whether it helps people to enjoy each other's company and work together constructively and happily. It is unlikely that you would be able to undertake any monitoring within this organisation as they are unlikely to have the infrastructure to deal with surveys or absence monitoring.

Organisation 5 (people, tight control, collective)

This organisation tends to be viewed as paternalistic in its approach. The organisation wants to put in place policies and procedures to take care of its employees. It is interested in finding out what the employees think about the provisions and therefore is likely to value regular surveys or audits of the well-being within the organisation.

Organisation 6 (people, loose control, individualistic)

This organisation, if it decides to talk to you, is likely to want to give its interested employees the tools to deal with bullying themselves with a minimum of involvement of an expert. It would be important to make sure that if you do become involved in training them the benefits of some monitoring may be important to make sure that people are having their needs met.

Handling reports of bullying

Despite the best policies and procedures there will always be complaints of bullying. When an employee reports that she or he believes that they have been bullied it is important to undertake action. Procedures and ways to proceed differ between countries and organisations. An initial discussion during which the complaint can be examined allowing for a decision to be made on whether the behaviour which is being complained of actually meets the criteria of bullying and what action may be the most appropriate in resolving the problem can be undertaken. This initial meeting can, for example, be undertaken by a peer acting as a confidential supporter (see Chapter 12, Hubert) or by safety and health delegates. The most appropriate and effective approach may not be to engage immediately in a formal investigation but rather to seek alternative ways of resolving the difficulties through the use of coaching (see Chapter 9, Crawshaw) or mediation (see Chapter 13, Dix et al.).

The investigation is carried out by line manager, or by occupational health psychologist, human resources (HR) personnel or external expert. In the procedure, the employee perceiving himself or herself as bullied is interviewed following interview of the person accused of bullying. When the necessary information on the situation is gathered, a joint meeting is arranged between the parties involved. In this meeting the necessary agreements to stop the bullying are made.

At times, particularly in workplaces where the atmosphere is poor and strained, it can be hard to distinguish between the target and the perpetrator. People may experience their working life as negative and may regard themselves as having been inappropriately treated, but feeling upset or undervalued does not necessarily mean that they have been bullied or treated unfairly. A common response to complaints of bullying is to search for the guilty and to punish them. However, interpersonal relationships are more complex than simply dividing the innocent from the guilty. In reality every employee and manager is capable of behaving badly at times and the real need is to find ways to educate and train all employees in how to work together in honesty and unity with differences being valued rather than derided.

Work environment surveys

One of the best ways of monitoring the organisational climate is to undertake an employee or climate survey and many organisations carry these out annually. Some free questionnaires include questions on bullying. The QPS Nordic Questionnaire for Psychological and Social Factors at Work (Dallner *et al.*, 2000; QPS, 2000) provides a definition of bullying and then asks three questions:

1 Have you noticed anyone being subjected to harassment or bullying at your workplace during the last six months?
2 How many people have you seen being bullied or subjected to harassment during the last six months?
3 Have you been subjected to bullying or harassment at the workplace during the last six months?

The UK Health and Safety Executive Stress Management tool also deals with employee relationships (Tyers *et al.*, 2009; http://www.hse.gov.uk/stress/standards/downloads.html) including questions such as:

- 'I am subject to personal harassment in the form of unkind words or behaviour'
- 'There is friction or anger between colleagues'
- 'I am subject to bullying at work'
- 'My relationships at work are strained'.

Whenever a working conditions survey is planned in an organisation it is important to involve all the stakeholders and to agree how the results will be handled. Where bullying or other negative behaviours are identified, managers and others responsible for the health and well-being of the employees must be prepared to report and tackle the issue. When managers are unprepared or lack training in dealing with the issue of bullying they tend to keep quiet about the bullying and think that it disappears if we don't speak about it. It is worth remembering that when line managers strictly address bullying the employees' confidence in them grows.

Avoiding negative media coverage

Whilst many organisations and managers try to avoid discussion of bullying within the workplace, when things go wrong they will lose all their power in brushing the issue under the carpet. The media like nothing better than a lurid bullying case and will often give space to stories of bullying created by unhappy and disgruntled employees. Often the organisation has little or no opportunity to defend itself. How much more effective it is for the organisation to deal with bad behaviours, through education, training, effective and efficiently operated policies and procedures rather than to leave itself open to being pilloried in the newspapers or on television. Negative media visibility is followed by a negative reputation as an organisation where bullying is accepted, which may make it more difficult for the organisation to recruit new skilful employees.

Case study: Reducing inappropriate behaviour and bullying among school staff

The starting point for this one-year project was a theme year adopted by the city-led Zero Inappropriate Behaviour intervention. The decision to undertake the intervention and set up the target group was taken by the health and safety committee of the city. The intervention took place in eight primary schools with an aim of reducing inappropriate behaviour and bullying together with increasing and strengthening the levels of positive interaction between employees. The question that the research posed was: 'Is it possible to reduce inappropriate behaviour and bullying at work with a workplace level intervention among the employees?' The project was undertaken in co-operation with health and safety representatives in education and an external consultant specialising in workplace bullying, and with the agreement of eight primary school headteachers who then told their staff about the project. Bullying was a sensitive issue for the headteachers who were afraid that their staff would be unwilling to answer questions about it. Therefore it was decided that feedback from the pre- and post-intervention surveys should be given on the overall results of all eight schools.

The project involved two joint one-and-a-half-hour to two-hour meetings in every school with training, mutual discussions and group works, plus a joint half-day event involving all eight schools. In one of the schools only one meeting was held. In addition, in one of the schools a special training day was organised during which inappropriate behaviour and bullying were discussed. Joint meetings with the entire workforce were held after a normal school day. The project lasted about a year.

The pre-intervention survey (N = 318) was conducted at the beginning of the first meeting and included a list of negative acts, definition of bullying and questions on the experience of being bullied and on observing bullying, on the general atmosphere in the workplace, and on features of work, work organisation and leadership practices. After that, training on the nature and causes of inappropriate behaviour and bullying was given by the external consultants and the health and safety delegates, and the phenomenon was discussed. In the second meeting, the feedback from the overall results of the pre-intervention survey was given and discussed. In addition, risks and possible causes of inappropriate behaviour were examined in groups. How to decrease these risk situations was also discussed.

During the theme year, many activities and events were arranged in the city. A launch event was organised for all the workers in the city and a third of employees from the intervention schools attended it. Training was also offered for supervisors in which information on the nature of bullying and their role in the prevention and management of bullying at work was provided. Further training open to all the employees within the city was arranged on a further four occasions in different parts of the city and around 9 per cent of the school employees attended this training. A personnel journal also published several articles on bullying during the year.

The post-intervention survey (N = 282) was collected by the health and safety delegate in every school after the joint half-day event. It included the same questions on negative acts and bullying, and in addition questions on the effects of the intervention, and on changes in the workplace and in one's own behaviour in relation to bullying. Respondents were also asked if they thought that everything possible had been done in the workplace to root out bullying, and if not, why not.

The results showed some positive changes with experience of being exposed to inappropriate behaviour such as criticism of one's work, the spreading of gossip and rumours, being constantly reminded of one's failings and experiences of bullying decreasing from 7 per cent to 5 per cent, with the observation of bullying falling from 44 per cent to 28 per cent. One out of five reported that as a whole inappropriate behaviour had decreased, but almost half (46 per cent) thought that no change had occurred. One positive result was the finding that as many as 47 per cent said that they took more notice of their own behaviour to their co-workers than before the intervention; only 5 per cent said that they did not do this; and 48 per cent said that there was no need for it. One in four said that if they noticed somebody being treated inappropriately they intervened in the situation more easily or more often than before. In all, 42 per cent experienced that in their workplace they could have done more to root out bullying; 29 per cent thought that they had done all that was necessary; and another 29 per cent thought that there was no need to do anything. The difficulty in discussing the subject and lack of time were most often mentioned as reasons why not enough had been done. Also the difficulty in recognising and admitting the existence of inappropriate behaviour in one's own workplace was seen as a reason by many.

Although the intervention was not able to fulfil all the success factors for a successful intervention (see discussion), and it did not prove possible to do everything that was planned at the beginning of the intervention, the work with the schools gave many learning opportunities. The intervention showed that it is possible to reduce inappropriate behaviour by raising the issue, distributing information, training and joint discussions in the workplace. The process showed again that acknowledgement of bullying in one's own workplace is not at all easy. Although bullying was experienced and observed in every school, it was quite difficult for some employees to acknowledge it. Some employees said that the pre-intervention survey results did not concern them. Many shared the opinion that there had been no inappropriate behaviour in their workplace and therefore no change had occurred; they therefore thought that there had not been any need to do anything. In every school the staff said that they would have wanted their own results from the survey and could not understand the fear of the headteachers. In all, the process showed that in an intervention like this an outside practitioner is often useful.

Discussion

Successful interventions, whether the aim is to reduce work-related stress or workplace bullying, mostly share the same success factors

(Leka *et al.*, 2008). There has to be a clear understanding on the nature of bullying and its causes, as this provides a shared language with which to describe and talk about bullying across the organisation. It is also vital to see bullying as a problem that concerns the whole workplace, to involve managers, employees, union representatives and health and safety professionals, and to emphasise preventative work. The commitment, support and active participation of management and supervisors throughout intervention are crucial. Without the involvement of all these stakeholders in establishing and agreeing the aims, intervention and implementation, probability for the intervention to fail increases. Creating a sense of ownership of the process is enhanced when stakeholders are given the possibility of participating actively in being consulted during the planning and taking part in the monitoring and reviewing of the outcomes.

Organisationally, bullying needs to be seen primarily as a work environment problem, with the main organisational emphasis being aimed at introducing interventions that focus on the working environment, culture, organisational structures and training of employees and managers. Organisational interventions should respond to the needs of the situation and be tailored to the specific problems and needs of the organisation and affected employees. Therefore interventions in a workplace should be based on a thorough risk assessment and wherever possible on evidence-based practice. Depending on the situation and size of the workplace, different measures such as questionnaires and individual and (focus) group interviews can be used to assess the situation and need for change. It is important that the aims of the interventions and the overall importance of the activities are understood and agreed by both management, employees and other interested parties such as unions and health and safety representatives. Handling major disagreements on what may cause bullying at work among the social partners can undermine discussions and get in the way of implementing interventions.

Where interventions are undertaken it is essential that they are evaluated and wherever possible efforts are made to use quantitative and qualitative research methodologies to establish which interventions are most effective (see Chapter 15, León-Pérez *et al.*). Input from external practitioners and researchers can sometimes help employers and employees to reach a common understanding on bullying and the interventions required. Where external experts are used they need to work closely with the organisation's management, supervisors, employees and specialist resources. The expertise, neutrality and impartiality of external practitioners are essential.

References

Dallner, M., Elo, A. L., Gamberale, F., Hottinen, V., Knardahl, S., Lindstrom, K., *et al.* (2000). *Validation of the General Nordic Questionnaire (QPS–Nordic) for Psychological and Social Factors at Work.* Copenhagen: Nordic Council of Ministers.

Einarsen, S., & Hoel, H. (2008) Bullying and mistreatment at work: how managers may prevent and manage such problems. In A. Kinder, R. Hughes & C. L. Cooper (eds) *Employee Well-Being Support: A Workplace Resource.* Chichester: Wiley.

Einarsen, S., Raknes, B. I., & Matthiesen, S. B. (1994) Bullying and harassment at work and their relationships to work environment quality: an exploratory study. *European Work and Organizational Psychologist,* 4: 381–401.

Einarsen, S., Hoel, H., & Notelaers, G. (2009) Measuring exposure to bullying and harassment at work: validating the factor structure and psychometric properties of the Negative Acts Questionnaire – Revised. *Work and Stress,* 23: 24–44.

Einarsen S., Hoel, H., Zapf, D., & Cooper, C. L. (2011a) *Bullying and Harassment in the Workplace: Developments in Theory Research and Practice.* London: CRC Press.

Einarsen, S., Hoel, H., Zapf, D., & Cooper, C. L. (2011b) The concept of bullying and harassment at work: the European tradition. In S. Einarsen, H. Hoel, D. Zapf & C. L. Cooper (eds) *Bullying and Harassment in the Workplace: Developments in Theory, Research and Practice.* London: CRC Press.

Hauge, L., Skogstad, A., & Einarsen, S. (2007) Relationships between stressful work environment and bullying: results of a large representative study. *Work and Stress,* 4(4): 381–401.

Hoel, H., & Cooper, C. L. (2000) *Destructive Conflict and Bullying at Work.* Manchester: Manchester School of Management, University of Manchester, Institute of Science and Technology.

Hoel, H., & Einarsen, S. (2011) Investigating complaints of bullying and harassment. In S. Einarsen, H. Hoel, D. Zapf & C. L. Cooper (eds) *Bullying and Harassment in the Workplace: Developments in Theory Research and Practice.* London: CRC Press.

Hofstede, G. (1991) *Cultures and Organizations: Software of the Mind.* New York: McGraw-Hill.

Kess, K., & Kähönen, M. (2010) *Häirintä työpaikalla – työpaikkakiusaamisen selvittäminen ja siihen puuttuminen* [Harassment at work – settling and intervening in a bullying case]. Helsinki: Edita Publishing.

Leka, S., Vartia, M., Hassard, J., Pahkin, K., Sutela, S., Cox, T., & Lindström, K. (2008) Best practice in interventions for the prevention and management of work-related stress and workplace violence and bullying. In S. Leka & T. Cox (eds) *The European Framework for Psychosocial Risk Management: PRIMA-EF.* Nottingham: Institute of Work, Health & Organizations (I-WHO), University of Nottingham.

Matthiesen, S. B., & Einarsen, S. (2007) Perpetrators and targets of bullying at work – role stress and individual differences. *Violence and Victims*, 22: 735–753.

Mikkelsen, E. G., Hogh, A., & Olesen, L. B. (2008) *Prevention of bullying and conflicts at work – an intervention study*. Paper presented at the Sixth International Conference in Workplace Bullying, June 4–6, Montreal, Canada.

PRIMA-EF (2008) *Guidance on the European Framework for Psychosocial Risk Management. A Resource for Employers and Worker Representatives*. Geneva: WHO.

QPS Nordic (2000) *General Questionnaire for Psychosocial and Social Factors at Work*. Available at: https://www.qps-nordic.org/en/index.html.

Rayner, C., & Lewis, D. (2011) Managing workplace bullying: the role of policies. In S. Einarsen, H. Hoel, D. Zapf & C. L. Cooper (eds) *Bullying and Harassment in the Workplace: Developments in Theory, Research and Practice*. London: CRC Press.

Rayner, C., Hoel, H., & Cooper, C. L. (2002) *Workplace Bullying: What Do We Know, Who Is to Blame and What Can We Do?* London: Taylor & Francis.

Tehrani, N. (2005) *Bullying at Work – Beyond Policies to a Culture of Respect*. London: CIPD.

Tyers, C., Broughton, A., Denvir, A., Wilson, S., & O'Regan, S. (2009) *Organizational Responses to the HSE Management Standards for Work-related Stress*. Research Report RR693. Brighton: Health and Safety Executive.

Vartia, M. (1996) The sources of bullying – psychological work environment and organizational climate. *European Journal of Work and Organizational Psychology*, 5: 203–214.

Vartia, M. (2009) *Reduction of inappropriate behaviour and bullying at work – a workplace intervention among school staff*. Paper presented at the 13th European Congress at Work and Organizational Psychology, 13–16 May, Santiago de Compostela, Spain.

Vartia, M., & Leka, S. (2011) Interventions for the prevention and management of bullying at work. In S. Einarsen, H. Hoel, D. Zapf, & C. L. Cooper (eds) *Bullying and Harassment in the Workplace: Developments in Theory, Research and Practice*. London: CRC Press.

Vartia, M., Korppoo, L., Fallenius, S., & Matttila, M. (2003) Workplace bullying: the role of occupational health services. In S. Einarsen, H. Hoel, D. Zapf, & C. Cooper (eds) *Bullying and Emotional Abuse in the Workplace: International Perspectives in Research and Practice*. London: CRC Press.

Zapf, D., Escartin, J., Einarsen, S., Hoel, H., & Vartia, M. (2011) Empirical findings on prevalence and risk groups of bullying in the workplace. In S. Einarsen, H. Hoel, D. Zapf, & C. L. Cooper (eds) *Bullying and Harassment in the Workplace: Developments in Theory, Research and Practice*. London: CRC Press.

Chapter 15

Effectiveness of conflict management training to prevent workplace bullying

Jose M. León-Pérez, Alicia Arenas and Thelma Butts Griggs

Introduction

Workplace bullying is a complex phenomenon that affects a large number of employees. As can be seen elsewhere in this book, there is a high prevalence of workplace bullying and potentially severe consequences justify the need to have effective interventions that deal with bullying at work. Although many researchers and practitioners advocate the use of training and other interventions as a way of reducing the incidence of bullying, few studies have examined the effectiveness of these interventions. In this chapter, the authors provide insight for the development of formal evaluation of the effectiveness of a training programme designed to prevent workplace bullying. First, they establish the theoretical rationale of the intervention. In doing so, they review the theoretical evidence linking interpersonal conflict and workplace bullying. Second, they briefly describe the different models and instruments available to evaluate training programmes. Finally, they discuss the effectiveness of intervention using the well-known Kirkpatrick model.

Theoretical roots of interventions

The main goal of a study is often obvious in applied research. This is the case in this study, where the aim is to reduce the incidence of workplace bullying. However, the theoretical rationale used to underpin and guide the implementation and evaluation of the design must also be clearly stated. Shadish *et al.* (2005) have shown that the theoretical orientation of the majority of interventions is not specified or can only be inferred (approximately 71 per cent of the studies they analysed compared to 16.6 per cent which specified their theoretical orientation). Therefore, the first step in developing an intervention should be to establish the theoretical rationale behind the design, which should be based on previous empirical and clinical findings.

In the case of workplace bullying, a complex phenomenon influenced by several factors, it is important clearly to state the theoretical position adopted since different approaches can be considered when developing an intervention (see, for example, Einarsen, 1999; Baillien *et al.*, 2009). Intervention designs will include different aspects or features depending on the approach followed. For example, considering bullying as a social stressor would lead to further training in stress coping strategies, or to the modification of working conditions for those researchers interested in testing job stress models such as the Demands-Control Model (Karasek, 1979). In contrast, considering bullying as the result of personality traits of the perpetrator and/or the victim may conclude that bullying is impossible to prevent, making it necessary to intervene by implementing early detection systems of bullying behaviours together with procedures to investigate bullying complaints.

In the intervention study presented in this chapter, the authors followed a conflict escalation perspective. In this sense, workplace bullying involves a conflict escalation process caused by an interpersonal conflict that had been poorly managed or not satisfactorily resolved (Leymann, 1996). This notion is supported by evidence from case studies. For example Matthiesen *et al.* (2003) described a non-typical bullying case, where the target was successful in a lawsuit and returned to work, concluding that the bullying was an escalated conflict process. Zapf and Gross (2001) also applied the conflict escalation model of Glasl (1982) to bullying situations. They used their findings from a qualitative study which involved the semi-structured interview of 20 targets of bullying in addition to a quantitative study which compared 149 targets and 81 non-bullied individuals (control group) to show a conflict escalation pattern in which task-related conflicts escalate to more relationship-oriented conflicts. Moreover, these authors found that bullying starts with a critical incident such as a conflict, argument or disagreement between two parties which if not addressed effectively becomes more destructive, involving increasing negative acts, and which usually ends with the target leaving the organisation after a series of failed attempts to deal with the situation.

Consequently, different interventions to counteract workplace bullying have been proposed from a conflict escalation perspective, including training employees to manage conflict effectively by putting in place mechanisms to de-escalate conflicts (Keashly & Neuman, 2004). Other interventions include developing an organisational culture based on respect, and establishing a tiered conflict resolution approach ranging from direct dialogue, to mediation, to grievance, and only if necessary to arbitration or the courts; in other words, introducing alternative dispute resolution processes as organisational procedures in order to avoid having interpersonal conflict and workplace bullying issues wind up in court.

The former interventions are focused at the level of the individual since the aim is to provide employees with conflict management strategies designed to integrate their own interests with the needs of the other party. Additionally, essential components for handling conflict successfully include developing effective communication and maintaining a positive working relationship (Ury *et al.*, 1988). According to several authors, some conflict management styles or strategies are positively related to the occurrence of workplace bullying, whereas other strategies, more co-operatively oriented, make bullying less likely (Arenas *et al.*, 2011; Baillien & De Witte, 2009). Therefore, a possible intervention to prevent workplace bullying at an individual level may involve training employees to use more co-operative strategies that seek common interest to reach an agreement (for a review of conflict management styles, see Keashly & Nowell, 2003; Baillien & De Witte, 2009). These interventions can be categorised as primary interventions since they focus on the prevention of workplace bullying before its appearance (see also Glasl's model, 1982).

A second group of interventions focuses on the organisation and refers to a broad range of processes, ranging from grievance procedures to mentoring. These interventions are designed to resolve disputes and bullying complaints through formal systems within the organisation (outside publicly available administrative agencies or courts) and include roles similar to those of an ombudsman. Organisations should use constructive management to ensure that conflicts which arise at work do not escalate to destructive levels (Zapf & Gross, 2001; Keashly & Nowell, 2003). These organisational approaches to solving conflicts should be accessible to everyone in an organisation through supervisors, union representatives and human resources staff (Fox & Stallworth, 2009).

Although many researchers and practitioners advocate the use of a range of conflict management interventions as a way of reducing the incidence of bullying, there is a lack of systematic evaluation addressing the effectiveness of these interventions. For this reason, in the next section of this chapter we will provide several theoretical models and instruments that can be used to establish a proper programme evaluation.

Effectiveness evaluation

Despite programme evaluation being critical for the ongoing improve-ment of the programme, the majority of interventions do not include this phase in their design. Sometimes the absence of planned effectiveness evaluation results from practical difficulties because when the advan-tages and disadvantages of evaluation are weighed, the process is judged to be too expensive to be implemented. However, programme evaluation is vital in explaining why intervention outcomes may not be in the expected direction. As Randall *et al.* (2009) pointed out: 'when interven-tions fail, often it is unclear whether the intervention itself was ineffec-tive, or whether problems with implementation processes were to blame' (p. 1). Empirical evidence of programme impact in the workplace is also needed because it enhances the understanding of the bullying phenom-enon at a research level. From a practitioner point of view, this evidence is crucial in building users' confidence and persuading organisations and managers to invest their scarce resources in the intervention.

From the evaluation models that are available (Phillips, 1990; Basarab & Root, 1992), the widely used Kirkpatrick's Four Levels Evaluation Model (1993) is particularly useful. According to this model four levels are considered in order to evaluate the effectiveness of intervention programmes. The evaluation at each level assesses the extent to which the training programme has achieved its goals. The levels are as follows:

- *Level I. Reaction.* At this level the crucial question is: *How did participants react to the programme?* To answer this question different measurements of how participants perceive various aspects of the training programme are needed (i.e. content, method, trainer, schedule). It is common to use surveys (similar to *customer satisfac-tion surveys*) in order to quantify reactions and compare the scores to previously established standards.
- *Level II. Learning.* The main question at this level is: *To what extent did participants improve their knowledge and skills and change attitudes as a result of the training?* In our case the training aimed to improve participants' conflict management skills. Although ideally to assess this level a measurement comparing skills both before and after the training (and using a control group, if feasible) is needed, most of the evaluations at this level are based only on post-intervention measurements.
- *Level III. Behaviour.* This level measures *the extent to which parti-cipants changed their behaviour back in their workplace as result of*

the training. This level is commonly referred to as *transfer of training.* In order to assess this level it is important to gather information from different groups (i.e. trainer, trainees and their subordinates/superiors) using a multi-method approach (i.e. surveys and interviews). In addition, it is important to measure this level long enough after the training to allow behavioural change to take place.

- *Level IV. Results.* Kirkpatrick (1993) indicates that this level measures *the organisational benefits derived from the training* or *training outcomes.* It is especially important to collect baseline data prior to programme implementation. This data may be gathered as part of the initial assessment process as it will be necessary for monitoring the intervention implementation. Additional information relevant to specific desired outcomes or development objectives should also be collected in this phase. In the study described in this chapter, the outcome standards or effectiveness criteria were to reduce the number and severity of interpersonal conflicts at work in addition to decreasing the level of exposure to bullying behaviours, or the number of potential bullying cases. The study compared measures both before (baseline or pre-test, T1) and eight months after the training (post-test, T2).

It is important to recognise that one level of evaluation is never more important than another. Each level provides a diagnostic check for problems that may become evident at the succeeding level and therefore reveal barriers for a successful implementation of the intervention. For example, if participants did not learn the skills that the intervention intended to deliver and which is measured with goal or effectiveness criteria at Level II, the participant reactions gathered at Level I might have identified the potential barriers to the learning. Examples of such barriers include insufficient managerial involvement in the intervention implementation, or the organisation or team were not ready to introduce the behavioural change. In order to fully understand what is happening, it is essential to have in mind all four levels during the programme design, implementation and evaluation so that potential areas of failure can be identified and eliminated in future trials.

Some authors propose that the implementation process also needs to be assessed in addition to the intervention outcomes. For example, Randall *et al.* (2009) propose five scales to measure employees' appraisals of organisation-level interventions to cope with stress. These scales address different aspects of implementation effectiveness found in earlier studies, including employee readiness for change, employee involvement in the design and implementation of the intervention, and line manager's attitudes and actions. These scales are easy to use. However, they are based exclusively on the perceptions of the participants involved in the training and need to be complemented with data from other sources or agents involved in the intervention process, for example, managers and trainers.

When undertaking an evaluation the researcher takes into consideration several key elements to improve the effectiveness of the bullying prevention (Keashly & Neuman, 2004). The intervention process should include the following:

- be based on previous bullying assessments using instruments that capture the subtle nature of the problem
- involve all the individuals responsible for identifying and dealing with bullying including union representatives, managers and human resources professionals in order to create a support atmosphere in which to develop interventions
- systematically evaluate and follow up the intervention to obtain feedback and readjust the planned actions where necessary.

Despite the fact that several models and instruments are available to evaluate programme impact and implementation effectiveness, few studies empirically examine the effectiveness of these bullying interventions, with a few notable exceptions such as Hoel and Giga (2006) or Keashly and Neuman (2004). As Shadish *et al.* (2005) point out during their systematic review of the intervention studies conducted in Europe, interventions conducted in the organisational context are still very scarce compared to interventions in other areas such as education or medicine (accounting only for 3.3 per cent of all interventions that these authors evaluated). Moreover, most organisational interventions use a non-randomised design in which the follow-up period is usually less than six months and there is an absence of baseline data.

In order to fill this gap in intervention studies, and specifically in bullying literature, we developed an intervention study that followed a longitudinal design and used different measures to assess its effectiveness. In particular, Kirkpatrick's Evaluation Model was applied to a two-wave prospective intervention study developed in a Spanish manufacturing corporation designed to reduce the incidence of workplace bullying. The theoretical framework for the design was to consider conflict management training (CMT) as an appropriate way to decrease conflict at work and to avoid conflict escalation into a more destructive phase which could result in more extreme forms of conflict, namely workplace bullying.

Intervention design

Before taking action a formal committee responsible for the development of the intervention was created within the organisation. This committee included individuals from unions and employee representatives, human resources department, and risk prevention staff. All of them were involved to promote employees' participation as this was considered a key factor in achieving the intervention goals.

A pre-intervention (T1) baseline was established based on employees' responses to a questionnaire that encompasses a number of different scales relating to working conditions (*COPSOQ-ISTAS21: Copenhagen Psychosocial Questionnaire*; Moncada *et al.*, 2005); interpersonal conflict at work (Medina *et al.*, 2005); and workplace bullying (*NAQ-R: Negative Acts Questionnaire-Revised*; Einarsen *et al.*, 2009). The employees' psychological well-being was also measured (*General Health Questionnaire*; Goldberg, 1992). One hundred and ninety five participants completed the questionnaire with a response rate of approximately 90 per cent.

The intervention involved conflict management training, which was delivered to intermediate managers and supervisors and others involved in influencing working procedures and relationships at work. The training looked at the different types of conflict and explored ways in which conflict could be handled, including the use of strategies to manage emotions in conflict situations and the use of effective communication. The trainer used role-playing situations and group dynamics as well as constructive discussion to encourage experiential learning. A trainer who is an expert in dispute resolution provided three sessions, each lasting four hours. A total of 42 employees were trained, divided into groups of 20 and 22 participants. A follow-up session was also carried out two weeks after the second training session to assess employees' reactions and to monitor the transfer of learning.

A second set of data was collected post-intervention (T2). This occurred eight months after the training. Employees were given the same questionnaires as at T1 (baseline or pre-test). One hundred and twenty seven people of the original 195 people completed the questionnaire at T2, with an attrition level that was less than 30 per cent.

Intervention results

The effectiveness results examined two general questions, first on how participants perceived the training and the trainer and second on whether prevalence of workplace bullying was reduced.

A Likert scale ranging from one (*very low*) to ten (*very high*) was used to measure the trainees' perception of the training and the trainer. The results showed that the training was perceived as useful ($M = 7.57$; $SD = 1.60$) with the trainer being seen as an expert in the topic. This appeared to motivate participants and encourage their participation in the activities ($M = 8.33$; $SD = 2.37$). In addition, the survey measured ten items on different aspects of the training including content, method, knowledge of the trainer, and usefulness of the training. This survey was used to assess participants' reaction (*Level I*). The results suggested that the training created high levels of satisfaction and expectations that the programme would be successfully implemented, Moreover, one of the items asking participants if they thought the training would be useful in their daily working life obtained a particularly high score.

Two open questions were introduced at the end of the questionnaire asking the participants (a) which aspects of the training were not helpful or they would change in the future, and (b) which aspects of the training they found most enjoyable or interesting. The responses to the first open question found the participants suggested that the training schedule needed to be reviewed (34.6 per cent) as well as that managers of higher ranking should also be trained (7.7 per cent). However, 23.1 per cent of participants said that nothing should be changed. On the second question 53.8 per cent of participants reported that the role-playing activities and group dynamics were most interesting, 11.5 per cent said that the skills learned would improve their working conditions, and 34.7 per cent did not answer the question or reported other issues.

A survey consisting of nine items was used to measure the knowledge, skills, and attitudes learned in the training (*Level II*). This survey was administered to participants in a follow-up session two weeks after the training. Participants believed that they had gained conflict management skills to some extent and felt that they were ready to implement the skills learned. They also believed that they would be supported by their managers when these skills were used. Ideally, a multi-method approach would have been used. However, despite the limitations to this measure results still suggest that participants improved their conflict management knowledge and skills as well as having positive attitudes towards the training and the training objectives.

The training transfer (*Level III*) was measured by comparing how group participants were managing conflicts at work ('*Thinking about your job position, do you think you manage conflicts in a successful way?*'). This item was included in the general questionnaire at both T1 and T2, and it was found that there were significant differences in the trainees' perceptions of their conflict management successes before and after the training. These perceptions of success were tested by asking subordinates if they considered that their superiors, trainees in the group, improved their conflict management following the training. Around 65 per cent of subordinates reported that their superiors improved their conflict management skills after the training as indicated in their response to the following statement: '*My superior is more aware about their subordinates' interests and deals with conflicts more effectively*'; 30 per cent indicated that their superiors managed conflict in much the same way as before the training; and the remaining 5 per cent reported that their superior dealt with conflict even worse after the training. Taking these results together, it appears that the training helped to improve participants' conflict management skills in line with the training objectives.

Finally, training outcomes (*Level IV*) were established by comparing employees' responses to the general questionnaire at two different points in time. Results show that after the training the number and intensity of interpersonal conflicts at work were significantly reduced. In addition, there was a reduction in the number of negative acts reported at work; however, this was not statistically significant. The results showed that the number of bullying cases and number of bullied victims was lower after the training (T2 or post-intervention moment). However, the data did not allow for a check to be undertaken to show whether this effect was real or due to some other variables such as: (a) the sampling error that may introduce biases with bullying victims being underestimated at Time 2 since they were more likely under-represented due to leaving their jobs or being off work sick due to workplace bullying; (b) the absence of a comparison group; (c) changes in variables at a macro level (socioeconomic and environmental aspects) which might play a buffering/promoting role of social negative acts. Further research needs to be undertaken to consider additional variables in order to control their potential effect as well as collect more objective data from the organisation such as absenteeism, turnover and sickness leave indicators.

In summary, the findings show that although workplace bullying is a complex phenomenon, conflict may play an important role and therefore conflict management training appears to be an effective way to reduce the incidence of bullying (see Table 15.1).

Table 15.1 Study design, effectiveness measures taken and main findings

Intervention phases	Effectiveness measures	Main findings
Baseline measures		
Training programme implementation and employees' reaction (*Level I*)	Reaction survey just after the training	Training created high expectations (participants perceived it as useful for their daily working basis) and was successfully implemented.
Employees' learning (*Level II*)	Learning survey two weeks after the training during a feedback session	Participants perceived that they had improved their conflict management knowledge and skills as well as they showed positive attitudes towards the training objectives.
Post-intervention measures: employees' behaviour (*Level III*) and organisational results (*Level IV*)	A survey eight months after the training in order to assess transfer of training and the second-wave data collection to observe training outcomes	Although employees perceived a behavioural change in their superiors (who manage conflict in a better way), training outcomes revealed limited success of our intervention.

Conclusion

What has been shown in this chapter is a theoretical background with which to tackle workplace bullying from a conflict management perspective. There has been a review of an evaluation model using well-respected and validated instruments to assess the interventions' effectiveness. The findings relate to a particular intervention in a single organisation and should be interpreted as such. There were some limitations to the implementation of the training and methodological difficulties due to the relatively small number of employees trained and lack of time to observe the behavioural change.

Our results show that there are opportunities for bridge-building between practitioners and researchers. In this sense, there is evidence that the use of step-by-step evaluations such as those developed by

Kirkpatrick are helpful in assessing what may go wrong as an intervention is developed, and provide information on how to modify and adapt earlier intervention designs. However, standard instruments are frequently unavailable and measurement instruments are usually developed for specific situations. Given the difficulty and costs of conducting an evaluation as one moves up the evaluation levels, it is necessary to consider which level of evaluation needs to be conducted for which programme. The whole evaluation process will be enhanced if those designing the intervention take the time to establish the evaluation tools and success criteria prior to starting an intervention.

In the assessment of the effectiveness of interventions, thoughtful consideration should be given to evaluating the implementation processes; not only the outcomes are important. The use of a range of different methodologies to gather information should be considered with, for example, the gathering of qualitative data from in-depth interviews and focus groups, quantitative data from questionnaires, objective indicators from the organisation such as productivity, absenteeism or sick leaves, and responses to the question of intention to leave (Cox *et al.*, 2007). Another crucial aspect is developing longitudinal studies with data being collected in at least two points in time. We recommend the development of baseline measures during which needs analyses are conducted, together with post-intervention measures to address intervention impact and implementation effectiveness.

There is also evidence to support the view that conflict researchers can contribute to understanding and dealing with bullying in the workplace as well as the less destructive interpersonal conflicts. Van de Vliert (2010) suggests that conflict researchers can contribute to the understanding of the mechanisms of bullying since the broader arena of interpersonal conflicts and workplace bullying shares similar elements that bring together well-established theories and practice. The common factor is that in each case the parties are interdependent and have the potential to interfere with one another since 'there are two conflict parties with at least one of them experiencing obstruction or irritation by the other party' (Van de Vliert, 2010: 87). Consequently, from a preventive perspective, using conflict resolution interventions may be appropriate to prevent conflict escalation to destructive phases such as workplace bullying, or to solve possible bullying situations in their initial phases.

Conflict can be considered a general or broader category in which workplace bullying resides. Bullying is a complex and dynamic process that can be understood from a conflict management perspective. But there are also important differences between the two constructs. Mainly, conflict focuses on the perception of *incompatibility* between the parties with the potential for both negative and positive outcomes, that is, with conflict having the possibility of constructive outcomes in some situations. In contrast, workplace bullying is always regarded as a destructive process that causes negative outcomes, including the possibility of post-traumatic stress and suicide (Leymann, 1996; Van de Vliert, 2010). While parties may have similar power in a conflict, in bullying there is always a power imbalance in which the less powerful party, the victim or target of bullying, ends up unable to defend himself or herself. Therefore, when bullying is in advanced phases other interventions rather than conflict resolution may be more appropriate.

In conclusion, the study described in this chapter has shown that the effectiveness of bullying interventions can be addressed by using scientific methods. In addition, we recommend pairing strengthening individual strategies with organisational strategies since the development of anti-bullying policies or alternative dispute resolution systems may contribute to creating a constructive conflict resolution culture in the organisation and may help to prevent conflict escalation into the destructive phases found in bullying situations.

References

Arenas, A., Munduate, L., Medina, F. J., & León-Pérez, J. M. (2011) *Crossing boundaries between conflict and workplace bullying: the role of power and conflict management styles*. Manuscript submitted for publication.

Baillien, E., & De Witte, H. (2009) The relationship between the occurrence of conflicts in the work unit, the conflict management styles in the work unit and workplace bullying. *Psychologica Belgica*, 49: 207–226.

Baillien, E., Neyens, I., De Witte, H., & De Cuyper, N. (2009) A qualitative study on the development of workplace bullying: towards a three-way model. *Journal of Community & Applied Social Psychology*, 19: 1–16.

Basarab, D. J., & Root, D. K. (1992) *The Training Evaluation Process*. Boston: Kluwer.

Cox, T., Karanika, M., Griffiths, A., & Houdmont, J. (2007) Evaluating organisational-level work stress interventions: beyond traditional methods. *Work & Stress*, 21: 348–362.

Einarsen, S. (1999) The nature and causes of bullying at work. *International Journal of Manpower*, 20: 16–27.

Einarsen, S., Hoel, H., & Notelaers, G. (2009) Measuring exposure to bullying and harassment at work: validity, factor structure and psychometric properties of the Negative Acts Questionnaire-Revised. *Work & Stress*, 23: 24–44.

Fox, S., & Stallworth, L. E. (2009) Building a framework for two internal organizational approaches to resolving and preventing workplace bullying: alternative dispute resolution and training. *Consulting Psychology Journal: Practice and Research*, 61: 220–241.

Glasl, F. (1982) The process of conflict escalation and roles of third parties. In G. B. J. Bomers & R. Peterson (eds) *Conflict Management and Industrial Relations*. Boston: Kluwer-Nijhoff.

Goldberg, D. (1992) *General Health Questionnaire (GHQ-12)*. Windsor: NFER-Nelson.

Hoel, H., & Giga, S. (2006) *Destructive Interpersonal Conflict in the Workplace: The Effectiveness of Management Interventions*. Manchester: UMIST.

Karasek, R. (1979) Job demands, job decision latitude and mental strain: implications for job redesign. *Administrative Science Quarterly*, 24: 285–306.

Keashly, L., & Neuman, J. H. (2004) Bullying in the workplace: its impact and management. *Employee Rights and Employment Policy Journal*, 8: 335–373.

Keashly, L., & Nowell, B. (2003) Workplace bullying and conflict resolution. In S. Einarsen, H. Hoel, D. Zapf, & C. Cooper (eds) *Bullying and Emotional Abuse in the Workplace: International Perspectives in Research and Practice*. London: CRC Press.

Kirkpatrick, D. L. (1993) *Evaluating Training Programs: The Four Levels*. San Francisco: Berret-Koehler.

Leymann, H. (1996) The content and development of mobbing at work. *European Journal of Work and Organizational Psychology*, 5: 165–184.

Matthiesen, S. B., Aasen, E., Holst, G., Wie, K., & Einarsen, S. (2003) The escalation of conflict: a case study of bullying at work. *International Journal of Management and Decision Making*, 4: 96–112.

Medina, F. J., Munduate, L., Dorado, M. A., Martínez, I., & Guerra, J. M. (2005) Types of intragroup conflict and affective reactions. *Journal of Managerial Psychology*, 20: 219–230.

Moncada, S., Llorens, C., Navarro, A. C., & Kristensen, T. S. (2005) ISTAS21: versión en lengua castellana del Cuestionario Psicosocial de Copenhague (COPSOQ). *Archivos de Prevención de Riesgos Laborales*, 8: 18–29.

Phillips, J. J. (1990) *Handbook of Training Evaluation and Measurement Methods*. London: Kogan Page.

Randall, R., Nielsen, K., & Tvedt, S. D. (2009) The development of five scales to measure employees' appraisals of organizational-level stress management interventions. *Work & Stress*, 23: 1–23.

Shadish, W. R., Chacón-Moscoso, S., & Sánchez-Meca, J. (2005) Evidence-based decision making: enhancing systematic reviews of program evaluation results in Europe. *Evaluation*, 11: 95–109.

Ury, W. L., Brett, J. M., & Goldberg, S. B. (1988) *Getting Disputes Resolved. Designing Systems to Cut the Costs of Conflict*. San Francisco: Jossey-Bass.

Van de Vliert, E. (2010) Moving bullies and victims up on conflict-researchers' waiting lists. *Negotiation and Conflict Management Research*, 3: 87–90.

Zapf, D., & Gross, C. (2001) Conflict escalation and coping with workplace bullying: a replication and extension. *European Journal of Work and Organizational Psychology*, 10: 497–522.

Part IV

Other wisdoms

Chapter 16

Beyond the drama of conflict

Noreen Tehrani

> Knowing your own darkness is the best method for dealing with the darknesses of other people.
>
> (Carl Jung)

Introduction

This chapter explores the behaviours and relationships found in groups of people affected by conflict and bullying. It also examines social behaviours associated with positive values and attitudes including sensitivity, co-operation, empathy, justice and the appropriate use of power. The aggressive drive has long been regarded as an inherent aspect of the human condition (Freud, 1914) as is clearly demonstrated where the aggression is used to gain an increased access to food, shelter and sexual partners (Bueno, 2010). However, recent studies into the evolutionary, physiological and anthropological aspects of aggression have found that there are genetic and environmental underpinnings to this behaviour (Craig & Halton, 2009). Whilst conflict and aggression appear unavoidable in the individual's struggle to survive, there is also growing evidence to indicate the existence of innate predispositions which produce an engagement in co-operative and reconciliatory behaviours (Damasio, 2003).

Most people believe that what they perceive through their senses is tangible, reliable and accurate. They are confident in their ability to separate what is real from what is imagined. However, much of what they may regard as solid bricks and mortar is in fact a construction of the mind, open to errors and distortions as the sensory information is translated into unconscious neural patterns and dispositions rather than as the mirror images they imagine (Gilbert, 2006). Therefore, when looking at relationships it is important to question those things that appear obvious in order to identify the realities which reside hidden beneath.

Evolutionary preparedness

All organisms from the single-celled amoeba to human beings are capable of perceiving and responding to situations automatically without the need for conscious thought. This capacity has an evolutionary advantage, particularly when the organism encounters a threat to their life or well-being, due to the speed of the autonomic response which is significantly faster than responses involving conscious awareness and rational decision making. Indeed, because conscious thinking slows down effective responses, its involvement in information processing is blocked during times of danger, providing the unconscious with the opportunity to make the more rapid responses through the use of reflexes, habits and instincts (Van der Kolk, 1994). These innate bodily responses, particularly those related to homeostasis and survival, are extremely resistant to modification or extinction as even a small change in the fundamental functioning of the body chemistry or temperature regulation may have a catastrophic result (Carr, 2004). However, these automatic responses which may be essential to survival are a blunt tool and may require refinement when applied to circumstances where the needs are more complex. Over millions of years animals have developed a state of preparedness to respond automatically to particular stimuli, situations, features or objects. This preparedness has evolved as an innate response passed down as a genetic imprint (Buss, 2000). This genetically preparedness behaviour can be observed as common fear responses, such as the fear of snakes which is found in many animals and humans, even in parts of the world where snakes do not exist in the wild (Cantor, 2005). The ability for rapid recognition and response to negative stimuli has a significant evolutionary benefit. This is employed by all animals including primitive species such as the brittlestar, which, despite having no eyes and an extremely primitive nervous system, is successful in recognising and escaping from predators (Alzenberg *et al.*, 2001). This preparedness to respond to what are recognised as negative stimuli is relevant in interpersonal conflict and bullying where a particular stimulus may activate an innate response such as aggression, immobilisation, appeasement or withdrawal (Cantor, 2005).

Emotions and dispositions

Built upon the simple homeostatic reactions and preparedness to respond are emotions, the first level of which includes fear, anger, sadness and happiness which are exhibited in response to innately determined emotionally competent stimuli (ECS; Damasio, 2003). These primary emotions orchestrate a temporary change in the functioning of the body, brain and thinking with the aim of maximising pleasure and minimising pain. In addition to these primary emotions are a number of secondary social emotions that include shame/guilt, contempt/indignation, sympathy/compassion and gratitude/pride which are involved in social relationships. Whilst the primary emotions are mainly related to individual survival, social emotions are aimed at the survival and well-being of the family, tribe or social group (see Table 16.1).

As well as responding to current stimuli, emotion-related changes to body states can be achieved through recalling people, places, situations and events. However, memories are not held as multimedia archive files within our brains, but rather broken into their constituent elements and compressed to save memory space (Damasio, 2003). When an event is recalled the memory is reconstructed from its constituent elements so when we think about, for example, our cousin Jack who bullied us when we were children, we automatically scan the files of information about

Table 16.1 Impact of emotionally competent stimuli (ECS)

Basic need	Examples of ECS	Potential emotions	Desire
Relationship	• Exclusion • Betrayal • Sharing	Jealousy Compassion/ Sympathy Joy	To build and maintain supportive relationships
Recognition	• Isolation • Discrimination • Reward	Gratitude Envy Pride	To be seen as a worthy member of society
Control	• Coercion • Dominance • Power	Anger Indignation Fear	To have the freedom to pursue and achieve valued goals
Love/affection	• Coldness • Support • Care-giving	Desire Jealousy Hate	To have the commitment and affection of a partner, family and colleagues
Justice	• Truth • Unfairness • Dishonesty	Guilt Shame Contempt	To be treated fairly and with justice, seeing honesty rewarded and dishonesty punished

small boys, bullying behaviours, places and feelings of being upset. However, as each file holds conceptually similar information the reconstructed memory may be contaminated with information about other small boys, behaviours, places and feelings. Our dispositional processes determine and create a bias in what is collected during recall. When recalling a person or event the dispositional processes will select innate, physiological responses, drives and primary emotions together with the more flexible knowledge acquired through subsequent social interactions, learning and reasoning. Whilst the innate responses to stimuli do not undergo any significant change, the dispositional process can modify responses to some extent through subsequent experience and learning. Therefore when recalling a difficult relationship such as that involving Jack, our innate responses may cause our heart to start pounding, skin flush and facial muscles tighten. We may experience anger, disgust or fear as we recreate a sensory image of Jack, the situation and his behaviour. The neural networks in the pre-frontal cortex of the brain automatically respond to these constructed sensory images linking them to the acquired emotional responses experienced when exposed to similar situations and people. Depending on our dispositions for the selection of sensory information from the files (Canli, 2009) the emotional response may become more intensified should aspects of cousin Jack's behaviour become contaminated by other information such as being bullied at school, getting lost in a supermarket or being treated badly by one's boss. On the other hand the emotional response may be calmed or diluted if our dispositional process also includes Jack apologising for his behaviour, thus allowing our compassionate emotions to be activated. Although fear and aggression are the most studied primary emotions, other emotions have also evolved, including sadness, joy, shame and compassion, each with its own set of bodily responses.

Social cohesion

Whilst the innate homeostatic and primary emotional responses have been designed for dealing with emergencies, they are less effective at solving the complex problems faced by couples, groups and cultures (Keltner *et al.*, 2006). Emotions provide a means for assisting in the development of co-ordinated responses essential to forming and maintaining relationships and avoidance of conflict as well as the opportunity to create the circumstances in which scapegoating and mobbing may be used as a way of excluding people seen as different and not part of the group. For social groups to function peacefully there is a need to establish a state of reciprocal altruism in which each member of the group is prepared to devote some of their resources to the well-being of others and to avoid engaging in self-interested behaviours which may be harmful.

However, in order to develop reciprocal altruism individual members of the group need to be able to recognise their own emotional state and how it can affect their behaviours, as well as recognise and respond to the emotional state in others. This awareness has been called theory of the mind (Gilbert, 2005) and has evolved because of the advantages it gives in being able to predict how others are likely to behave. Whilst the underpinning of these social behaviours is innate, the expression of the emotions and the actions that follow are developed and refined through observation and experience. For example, the expression of the emotions of compassion, gratitude, embarrassment and shame is transformed into the power to increase co-operation within groups by reducing the levels of distress, recognising the contributions of others, accepting personal flaws and acknowledging one's own failings. Even emotions such as anger, envy, disgust and contempt can prove useful in maintaining individual and group coherence by motivating ourselves and others to repair relationships, highlight unfair differences, demonstrating displeasure towards those who violate group values and bringing the haughty down to size.

Child development

A theory of mind is found in children from around the age of 18 months at which time a child has a rudimentary understanding of the intentions of other people. This ability progresses until by the age of three or four children begin to assess what is occurring in other people's minds including their level of knowledge and emotional states. This use of our knowledge of our own minds as a means of deciding what may be going on in the mind of another is known as projection. It is this capacity which allows the development of our secondary social emotions including compassion, guilt and gratitude. Projection is also important since if we are unable to assume that other people are more or less like us then the world becomes highly unpredictable and alien (Nickerson, 1999). However, these theories of mind assumptions can cause problems when the child experiences a strong emotion which is not acceptable to other people. Carers frequently place requirements on the child to modify, deny or otherwise control their emotional responses. This is often the case for the more 'difficult' emotions such as anger, envy and fear.

Whilst the child experiences the physical and emotional responses to anger, envy, distress and fear, the outward behavioural manifestations of these emotions by the child are neither accepted nor rewarded. In order to maintain the love of the carer, the child will need to hide their 'unacceptable' emotions, only showing those aspects of themselves that are valued by their carer and by the social and cultural context within which they find themselves. To achieve this the child develops a shadow side into which they place and repress those aspects of themselves which they have learnt are not acceptable (Page, 1999). This can be observed in children who experience an innate fear of water. If the parent sees the reluctance of the child to dive into a swimming pool but forces the child to do so, the result may be that whilst the child is able to dive into the water they begin to express their unacknowledged fears by teasing other children whom they regard as anxious or fearful. The shadow is created without the child or its carer consciously recognising or understanding the importance of emotional expression as a mechanism for responding to and meeting the child's basic human needs.

The suppression of the child's emotional needs before the child has the opportunity to develop the capacity to meet these needs through other more refined or adaptive processes leaves the child in a state of unresolved distress. Instead of the child achieving a healthy understanding of all their deeper emotions, they develop a dispositional process which leads them to avoid any expression of some emotions through a mix of suppression, repression and denial. The child learns to release their emotional distress by exhibiting a range of behaviours which include projecting their unacknowledged emotions on to others, using passive aggressive behaviours, seeking recognition and love through making extreme demands, blaming and putting others down to make themselves feel better. These patterns of behaviour which are present in the shadow will continue into adult life with the earlier life experiences being added to and triggered by new events.

The shadow and the workplace

Unless we become able to recognise and meet our hidden needs, the shadows of childhood continue to affect us throughout life and emerge in automatic, compulsive, unwarranted, unacceptable and unexpected forms of behaviour. Most adults are unaware of the influence of these processes, and as a result their rational and sensitive responses to situations become mixed with compulsive, distress-driven reactions powered by a hidden inner distress. These displacement behaviours are often reinforced within the workplace where they may become valued and legitimised with the result that the rational and compulsive become intertwined. Employees become skilled at dressing up irrationally driven behaviours as being reasonable, for example, being driven to succeed in achieving career goals regardless of the cost to themselves or their families. They will justify their behaviour on the grounds of business need rather than recognising that this hyperactivity is a displacement of the distress or anger that they had experienced but not expressed when they did not achieve the recognition or validation they craved as a child. On the other hand where an employee has been found to have reported being a victim of bullying behaviours by colleagues or managers in every team or organisation they join, they will blame others for causing their distress whilst failing to recognise that their difficulty in establishing positive working relationships originates from a repressed destructive anger which followed the unexpressed feelings, for example, of the loss of a loved parent or sibling, and manifesting itself in an insatiable need for reassurance and support amidst feelings of being rejected.

We are able to develop emotional competence through understanding and accepting our drives, responses and reactions to our environment and our relationships. The emotionally competent individual can accept their emotions and is willing to recognise that their experience of distress is a mechanism which allows an increase in self-awareness and self-healing rather than providing evidence of their imminent psychological breakdown. Emotional competence requires people to recognise when emotional pain and distress from the past are being re-enacted in displacement or other forms of distorted behaviour, and then to attempt to recognise, understand and deal with the original hurt.

People differ in terms of their awareness of their emotions and in their ability to express these emotions appropriately to others. For some the identification and expression of emotions is almost impossible, whilst for others the experience of strong emotions can rule their behaviour and their lives. The ability to show emotional awareness is an important interpersonal skill which can help individuals and organisations to recognise and deal with workplace conflict and destructive relationships. Without some awareness of the difficulties that exist within the organisation, too much energy may be focused on resolving the problems of individual employees rather than those problems faced by the organisational system itself. Understanding the emotional dynamics at play within individual workers, teams and the larger organisation is not an easy task. However, it is essential if conflict and bullying are to be addressed.

The drama of bullying

Stories surrounding bullying are dramatic, involving high emotions, with references to acts of deceit, favouritism, humiliation, intrigue and undeserved punishments. It is important, however, to recognise that what is described by each of the players, particularly in instances of complex bullying, may be distorted and changed as it passes through the lens of unmet needs and unresolved life experiences. Identifying the true nature of the bullying drama is a skilled process requiring a detailed understanding of the life history of the client, an identification of the signs of emotional displacement observed during the interactions which take part within the therapeutic relationship and an awareness of the signals which provide an insight into what may be influencing the current perceptions and behaviours of the client, as abusive relationships involve interactions in which all the players play their part.

When a client tells his or her therapist 'I did nothing to cause this to happen to me', the therapist should be aware that this is unlikely to be the real situation and that their client may have failed to recognise, unwittingly or unknowingly, his or her part in the bullying drama. This does not mean that the target of abrasive or other bad behaviour has done anything intentional or wrong, but rather their behaviour or presence were perceived by the perpetrator as a threat to their power, position or self-esteem. Therefore, the true extent and complexity of the bullying drama may remain hidden unless the therapist has the opportunity to observe and work with all the players. Only by understanding the real causes of the conflict and by resisting the temptation to apportion blame and responsibility will it become possible for the therapist to address the underlying issues. This position of unconditional positive regard (Rogers, 1957) is essential prerequisite for all therapeutic relationships. Whilst the therapist may find the behaviours of their client unwise, irresponsible or cruel, in order to bring about any change in their behaviours the therapist must be prepared and able to form a working alliance (Satterfield & Lyddon, 1998) with their client, based on respect for them as a human being.

The drama triangle (Karpman, 1968) which describes a dynamic relationship between the persecutor, victim and rescuer is a useful way of looking at abusive relationships (Proctor & Tehrani, 2001). However, the drama triangle fails to recognise the importance of a fourth role which is common in bullying cases, that of the avenger. The avenger is typically someone who has experienced bullying in the past and attempts to deal with their unresolved distress by taking action on behalf of others.

In this new model it is proposed that the four roles interact with each other (see Figure 16.1). Each of the roles involves a compulsive maladaptive pattern of behaviour which is triggered by situations connected to an unresolved trauma from the past. Whilst occasionally a single individual will fulfil the characteristics of a single role, never moving into any of the other roles, this is a rare situation. More typically an individual will have a preference or feel comfortable in one or two of the roles and will alternate between roles as circumstances change. For the bullying drama to be played out, individuals will occasionally be forced to play roles with which they are less familiar. This situation may occur when there are changes in the balance of power within the system.

For example, an employee playing the victim role may seek the support of a colleague regarding what he or she believes to be bullying. The employee may feel that the oppressive behaviour of their manager could be unintentional and discusses this with a colleague with the aim of seeking support to raise the issue sensitively in a team meeting. However, the colleague may have had difficulties with the same manager and begins to push the victim to make a formal complaint against the manager. In this situation the colleague is using their avenger role created by their perceived 'victim status' coercively and as a result becomes an oppressor of the employee who has wished to take a more conciliatory action. The employee is now in a situation where he or she is faced with a decision on whether to collude with the avenger and take out a formal complaint against the manager or pursue their original decision which would involve them rescuing the manager from the aggression of the avenger. The bullying drama continues for as long as the players remain

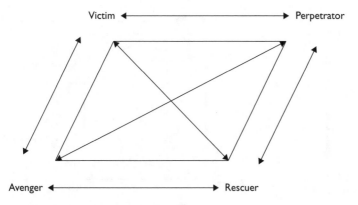

Figure 16.1 Roles within the bullying drama.

unaware of the true nature of the games that are being played and begin to recognise their part in sustaining the drama interactions. Self-awareness is essential as is the ability to recognise that only by moving beyond the game does it become possible to recognise the needs and frailties of all players which are so often obscured within these archetypal roles.

The restored self-model (see Figure 16.2) illustrates how the bullying drama, shown at the lower level, is connected to a higher level of understanding and meaning. It is by engaging with this higher level that the individual can become aware of their sense of vulnerability, power, responsiveness and wish for justice. Therapists need to encourage their clients to recognise that remaining within the bullying drama will not lead to justice and peace but rather a continuation of the game. Breaking the bullying drama requires the players to understand and operate at this higher level of functioning, freed from the negative feelings and fears found within the dynamics of the bullying drama. However, embracing vulnerability, power, responsiveness and justice requires determination and courage and considerable trust between client and therapist.

The role of the therapist is to demonstrate that whilst being vulnerable may make it easier for an individual to become a victim, true vulnerability is a strength when it enables the vulnerable person to recognise the reality of a difficult situation and encourage the seeking of support and understanding of others rather than trying to take control over everything on their own. Power can corrupt and lead to abuse, but it can also be used positively when it enables the powerful person to act with justice or compassion for others. Being overly responsive can turn a therapist and

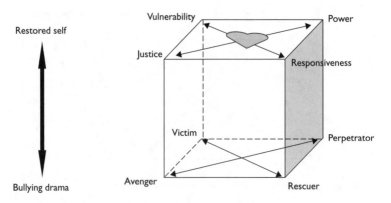

Figure 16.2 The restored self-model.

supporters into a compulsive carer, while the ability to listen and reflect without taking over can have a positive influence. Justice that is based on a lack of compassion and understanding can be experienced as punishing, whilst the helpful use of justice can assist to establish the right solution to the situation.

Discussion

In order to work with the bullying drama, therapists, coaches, supporters and managers must understand the nature of emotions and how the evolution of emotional competence is central to working with interpersonal relationships. There is a need to recognise the emotions that drive people to place blame outside themselves for their shortcomings and fallibilities. Unlike many of the current models used to address workplace bullying which tend to regard the victims and bullies as coming from fundamentally different positions, the approach adopted in this chapter recognises that whilst there are inappropriate behaviours which may be exhibited by one or more of the players in the bullying drama, the issue for all the players is essentially the same. Whilst harmful and punishing behaviours will always be unacceptable and need to be addressed, finding a solution that merely punishes the perceived wrongdoer whilst failing to recognise the purpose of the behaviours involved misses a major opportunity to bring about lasting changes to the way in which people relate.

For the therapist, coach or supporter there is not only the need to achieve an understanding of the patterns of behaviour being acted out in the bullying drama but to also recognise their own vulnerability to becoming caught up in that drama (Page, 1999). It is clear that when the content of the shadows is ignored or rejected due to discomfort, fear or anxiety, what follows will be an intolerance of the shortcomings and fallibilities of others. Everyone engaging in this work will have his or her own shadow containing their unexpressed emotional needs, faulty memories, projected feelings and introjected pain, but they may fail to recognise or deny their vulnerability to getting caught up in the complexity of the emotional quagmire which surrounds anyone working with bullying. For those who have worked in this field for a number of years there will be a familiarity of the experience of being pulled or seduced into the drama of the bullying by one or more of the players. Frequently this occurs when the therapist fails to recognise their own vulnerability within the bullying drama. This may be due to poorly defined contracts of working, a lack of recognition of their own shadows, inadequate supervision or pressure from the organisation or client to achieve a particular outcome.

References

Alzenberg, J., Tkachenko, A., Wiener, S. Addadl, L., & Hendler, G. (2001) Calcitic microlenses as part of the photoreceptior system in brittlestars. *Nature*, 412(23): 819–822.

Bueno, D. (2010) Aggressivity, violence, sociability and conflict resolution: what genes can tell us. Available at: http://journal-of-conflictology.uoc.edu/ojs/index. php/journal-of-conflictology/article/view/vol1iss2-tshiband (accessed December 27 2011).

Buss, D. (2000) The evolution of happiness. *American Psychologist*, 55: 15–23.

Canli, T. (2009) Individual differences in human amygdala function. In P. J. Whalen & E. A. Phelps (eds) *The Human Amygdala*. New York: Guilford Press.

Cantor, C. (2005) *Evolution and Posttraumatic Stress – Discourses of Vigilance and Defence*. London: Routledge.

Carr, A. (2004) *Positive Psychology – The Science of Happiness and Human Strengths*. Hove, UK: Brunner-Routledge.

Craig, I. W., & Halton, K. E. (2009) Genetics of human aggressive behaviour. *Human Genetics*, 126: 101–113.

Damasio, A. (2003) *Looking for Spinoza – Joy, Sorrow and the Feeling Brain*. London: Heinemann.

Freud, S. (1914) On narcissism: an introduction, Trans. J. Strachey. *The Standard Edition of the Complete Psychological Works of Sigmund Freud* (Vol. 14). London: Hogarth Press.

Gilbert, P. (2005) Compassion and cruelty. In P. Gilbert (ed.) *Compassion-Conceptualisation, Research and Use in Psychotherapy*. London: Routledge.

Gilbert, P. (2006) Old and new ideas on the evolution of mind and psycho-therapy. *Clinical Neuropsychiatry*, 3(2): 139–153.

Karpman, S. (1968) Fairy tales and script drama analysis. *Transactional Bulletin*, 7(26): 39–43.

Keltner, D., Haidt, J., & Shiota, L. (2006) Social functionalism and the evolution of emotions. In M. Schaller, J. Simpson, & D. Kenrick (eds) *Evolution and Social Psychology*. New York: Psychology Press.

Nickerson, R. S. (1999) How we know – and sometimes misjudge – what others know: inputting one's own knowledge into others. *Psychological Bulletin*, 125: 737–759.

Page, S. (1999) *The Shadow and the Counsellor – Working with the Darker Aspects of the Person, Role and Profession*. London: Routledge.

Proctor, B., & Tehrani, N. (2001) Issues for counselors and supervisors. In N. Tehrani (ed.) *Building a Culture of Respect – Managing Bullying at Work*. London: Routledge.

Rogers, C. R. (1957) The necessary and sufficient conditions of therapeutic personality change. *Journal of Consulting Psychology,* 21: 95–103.

Satterfield, W. A., & Lyddon, W. J. (1998) Client attachment and the working alliance. *Counselling Psychology Quarterly*, 11: 407–416.

Van der Kolk, B. A. (1994) The body keeps the score: memory & the evolving psychobiology of post traumatic stress. *Harvard Review of Psychiatry*, 1(5): 253–265.

Chapter 17

Building resilient workers and organisations

The Sanctuary® Model of organisational change

Sandra L. Bloom

Introduction

If we are to design, implement, and sustain workplaces that diminish and ultimately eliminate bullying we must have a clear, coherent, theoretically based and testable method for doing so. As has been illustrated in this book and well-described in the existing literature, bullying in the workplace is the result of complex and interactive individual, dyadic, group, organisational and societal factors (Hoel & Cooper, 2001; Tehrani, 2001; Einarsen *et al.*, 2011). The ideas described in this chapter have their genesis in the bullying that occurs between children and adults. We often learn about universal applications of theory by building systems that are responsive to those who have the most severe impairments. So it is in this case. We have learned about building workplace cultures of respect through learning about building those cultures for people who have been bullied the most, some of whom have become bullies themselves. Beginning in the 1980s my colleagues and I began what has become a long journey of over 30 years discovering how to be most helpful to traumatised and injured children and adults. Our approach has evolved into a model of organisational development that is now known as the Sanctuary Model (Bloom, 1997, 2010; Bloom & Farragher, 2010). In the following pages we will briefly describe what we have learned.

Background

In 1980 we began working within a general hospital based mental health setting in a suburban community. Early on we noticed that many of these adults had been bullied repeatedly throughout their lives in personal relationships, at school, at work, and even in treatment settings. This very fundamental abuse of power in relationships that were supposed to be nurturing and loving had severe, usually negative, developmental impacts. As children and now as adults, they had no safe refuge from the rigours of existence – no *sanctuary*. They had repeatedly experienced 'sanctuary trauma' defined as expecting a protective environment and finding only more trauma (Silver, 1986). From 1991 to 2001 we developed our Sanctuary programmes and specialised in treating adults who had been maltreated as children. The field of traumatic stress studies was just getting off the ground and we found gratifyingly effective methods to help our injured patients not just to improve but actually to recover from often life-long problems.

In 1998 the landmark Adverse Childhood Experiences Study (ACEs Study) was first released indicating that a high proportion of the subjects of the study – middle-class, middle-aged, Caucasian adults – had been exposed to significant adversity in childhood and those adversities were having negative impacts on their health, mental health, social adaption, and employment capacity across the lifespan (Felitti & Anda, 2010). We were not surprised by the outcome. These findings confirmed what we had been seeing in our clinical practices.

By this time we had begun to create training programmes for other organisations and we did informal ACEs surveys of exposure to childhood adversity of the training participants – all health, mental health, social service and administrative personnel. We found high levels of exposure to physical abuse, sexual abuse and other kinds of childhood adversity among the very people who were supposed to be helping children and adults most injured by these same kinds of exposure.

But while our work was proceeding in an exciting direction with much better results in care, the face of our industry was radically changing. Healthcare and mental healthcare delivery in the United States had become a profitable business and as a result business models and practices were applied to the profit-making and non-profit healthcare and social service industries. Little recognition was given to the bullying conduct and moral distress that subsequently arose when cost-saving measures and other business practices were applied to sectors dominated by the ethical demands of caregiving and 'doing no harm'. The result of these changes has been the widespread demoralisation of entire economic segments with systems 'in shambles . . . incapable of efficiently delivering and financing effective treatments' (President's New Freedom Commission on Mental Health, 2002).

We began to recognise that the combined effects of exposure to childhood adversity, individual stress and chronic organisational stress were having a widespread impact on our caregiving institutions and everyone within them, producing collective disturbances everywhere we looked. We began thinking about these complex interactions as 'parallel processes'.

Parallel processes

Parallel process at an organisational level has been described as that which happens 'when two or more systems – whether these consist of individuals, groups, or organisations – have significant relationships with one another, they tend to develop similar affects, cognition, and behaviours, which are defined as parallel processes'. As we experienced and these investigators recognised: 'Parallel processes can be set in motion in many ways, and once initiated leave no one immune from their influence' (Smith *et al.*, 1989: 13). As a result of these interactive processes, the symptoms of our clients were often mirrored in our own behaviour and in the attitudes and behaviour of every level of organisation within which we were all embedded. As we began consulting with other health, mental health and social service programmes, we began to recognise that the stressful experiences we had experienced, as well as the consequent demoralisation and interpersonal dysfunction, was widespread and could not be attributed solely to individual causes. We have now trained over 200 organisations, some small group homes or shelters, others that are large, multi-service agencies, in our model of organisational change – the Sanctuary Model. We saw that as a result of widespread changes in service delivery, human service workplace environments in the United States had become fertile ground for bullying behaviour. We also began reviewing the business literature in other industrial settings only to discover that the multiple effects of economic shifts, deindustrialisation, and globalisation appeared to be having similar negative impacts in other economic sectors. The picture that began to emerge we called 'systems under siege'.

Systems under siege

The practice-based evidence we have garnered through formal research and informal observation supports the conclusion that chronic workplace stress results in organisations that are chronically hyperaroused so that they are unable to determine what is and what is not a true crisis and over time become unable to mobilise an effective crisis response when one exists. We view this as a loss of the capacity to manage emotions institutionally, which makes new organisational learning difficult and sometimes impossible. Under such circumstances, the most emotionally charged information becomes 'undiscussable' and organisations develop 'alexithymia' – the inability to give words to the most pressing internal and external conflicts. In this way, caregiving organisations can develop 'learning disabilities', usually accompanied by 'organisational amnesia' for problem solutions that have been tried and either succeeded or failed in the past. Under these circumstances, formal and informal leaders are likely to become more bullying, authoritarian and punitive, while workers respond with counter-aggression and passive-aggressive behaviour and the social norms within the entire institution become progressively more aggressive, unjust and less democratic. When bullying and authoritarian behaviour are substituted for true leadership, conflicts do not get resolved, learning does not occur, innovation decreases, and creative problem solving comes to a halt. Despite this apparent deterioration, the likelihood is that chronically stressed organisations will be unable to perceive what is happening and instead simply continue to repeat the past, thereby engaging in re-enactment with each other and with their clients.

When this sequence is unfolding, staff members at every level of the bureaucratic hierarchy become ever more crisis-oriented, punitive, disempowered, and demoralised, often living in the present moment, haunted by the past, and unable to plan for the future. Complex interactions among traumatised clients, stressed staff, pressured organisations, and a social and economic climate that is often hostile to recovery efforts recreate the very experiences that have proven so toxic to clients in the first place. The resulting chronic organisational stress both mirrors and magnifies the trauma-related problems from which our clients seek relief. Just as the lives of people exposed to chronic trauma and abuse can become organised around traumatic experience, in this way our caregiving systems also become organised around the recurrent stress of trying to do more under ever-increasing pressure. The result are patterns of attitude and behaviour that we have described at length; parallel processes that at an organisational level self-replicate in uncanny ways creating more of the very problems we are supposed to help (Bloom & Farragher, 2010; Bloom & Farragher, in press).

Parallel process of recovery

Because of our experience working with thousands of very injured clients over the course of two decades, we know that healing is possible. Similarly, our experience of the last decade has demonstrated to us that healing is possible for chronically stressed and traumatised systems as well.

The first attempt to apply what we had learned in our original programme to traumatised children and adolescents was done under the auspices of a research grant from the National Institute of Mental Health. We found positive changes in the staff as well as the children in that initial study (Rivard *et al.*, 2003; Rivard, 2004; Rivard *et al.*, 2004; Rivard *et al.*, 2005). As part of developing a specific training and certification programme we are continuing to study the organisational impact of implementing whole-system change.

We now know that organisations can change just as individuals can, but such change requires a shift in our basic mental models for understanding the way organisations work, particularly in viewing organisations as living systems rather than machines. The organisational motivation behind such a shift often arises from the need to recognise the advances in our scientific understanding about the impact of trauma, adversity and disrupted attachment that challenges existing ideas about what constitutes illness. But organisational change also requires what amounts to a 'rediscovery' of unconscious dynamics, particularly the power of compulsive re-enactment and a recommitment to the power and possibility of creative change.

Shifting mental models

The process of 'creating sanctuary' begins with getting everyone on the same page – surfacing, sharing, arguing about, and finally agreeing on the basic values, beliefs, guiding principles and philosophical principles that are to guide decisions, decision-making processes, conflict resolution and interpersonal behaviour. Trauma-informed change as we define it requires a change in the basic mental models upon which thought and action are based and without such change, treatment is bound to fall unnecessarily short of full recovery or fail entirely. This change in mental models must occur on the part of the clients, their families, the staff and the leaders of the organisation.

Mental models exist at the level of very basic assumptions, far below conscious awareness and everyday function and yet they guide and determine what we can and cannot think about and act upon (Senge *et al.*, 1994). In any new experience, most people are drawn to take in and remember only the information that reinforces their existing mental models. Mental models thus limit people's ability to change.

There has long been a tension in the mental health field generally, and the psychiatric field in particular, between those who favour doing whatever it takes to stabilise a patient – drugs, restraint and punishment – and those who see strategic and creative possibilities within the individual chaos of the disturbed psyche. Defining what it is we are actually doing and illuminating the basis of the assumptions we make is critical to achieving meaningful goals. If the goal is 'stabilisation' or 'controlling behaviour' then bullying behaviour on the part of those in control becomes virtually inevitable. There is no way to control another person's thoughts, feelings, and behaviour without some form of coercion. The Sanctuary Model is a method to help shift the mental models of enough people within an organisation that true change in attitude and subsequently in behaviour can occur because people choose to change.

Living organisations

The first mental model shift that we promote in the Sanctuary Model is in helping organisational participants to realise that their organisations are not machines, but instead are living collective entities that emerge out of the combined individual identities of everyone within the organisation. As such, living systems are complexly interrelated and interdependent and therefore change in one part of the system is likely to affect every part of the system. Because they are alive, organisations cannot be successfully 'engineered' but they can evolve, change and grow. The dimensions of that growth, how long it takes, as well as the form it takes, will be determined by the intentions, will and behaviour of all of the living entities that comprise the whole. Therefore, training and education must involve everyone in the system – from the board of directors to the people that work in the kitchen.

Trauma-informed and attachment-based

Science has helped humanity to shift our understanding away from superstition and simple causal explanations of events and probe far more deeply into the complex nature of reality. If we are to solve the multiple crises facing human service delivery systems – and all of humanity for that matter – we need a different way of understanding human nature and human dysfunction, one that incorporates 150 years of accumulated scientific knowledge and clinical wisdom. That requires yet another shift in mental models through developing a working knowledge about the psychobiology of trauma and adversity, what it does to individuals, particularly when trauma is repetitive, occurs in early development, and is a result of interpersonal violence.

In order to understand the profound impact of trauma and adversity, we need to understand the way in which trauma disturbs the human operating system by disrupting attachment relationships – what the grandfather of attachment research, Dr John Bowlby termed the internal working model. What we know now is that trauma and adversity create toxic stress (McEwen, 2002; McEwen & Gianaros, 2010). When toxic stress exposure begins in childhood it does to the human operating system what a computer virus does to the computer operating system. It wreaks havoc with the attachment system and does so unpredictably, contagiously, virulently and intergenerationally. Trauma disrupts attachment.

Organisations have operating systems as well. The operating system for the organisation is embedded within the organisational culture. Organisational culture arises spontaneously whenever groups of people come together for any length of time and focus on tasks long enough to create common traditions, rites and history. It is binding in that it determines how people enter the organisation, survive within it, and learn to solve problems. There are close and interactive relationships between individual identity and organisational identity. Just as attachment is the basis of the individual operating system, social relationships are the basis of organisational functioning as well. We believe that in a parallel way, traumatic experience and adversity can profoundly disrupt the operating systems of organisations. The scientific basis for the Sanctuary Model is a thorough understanding of the ways in which chronic stress, adversity, toxic stress and traumatic stress impact individuals, families, groups, organisations and whole cultures.

Injury instead of illness

A very fundamental shift occurs when people begin truly to reckon with the impact of adversity, trauma and toxic stress on the developmental trajectory of the young. For us this represents a mental model shift from thinking about the subjects of our work as 'sick' or 'bad' to thinking of them instead as people who have suffered a wide range of injuries and subsequent disabilities. In common parlance, when we hear that someone is 'sick' we usually think of a cause that lies within the individual – a weakness, a deficit, a genetic problem. Whatever it is, unless it is an infectious disease, sickness is largely decontextualised and located solely in the person – although there is a social acceptance that they are largely not responsible for their illness. In contrast, an injury model connects the injured person to their environment – injuries always occur within an interpersonal, social and political context. Injury implies recovery and rehabilitation, even with a possible long-lasting handicap. Injury requires the active participation of the injured party – they must do what they can to help themselves heal and not do anything that will make their injuries worse. They are personally and socially accountable for the healing of their injuries, although the social context within which the injuries occur may make it impossible to fairly locate 'blame'.

In an injury model we should pay a great deal of attention to injury prevention and universal precautions that prevent injury. Injury can be physical, psychological, social and moral, and all these forms of injury are recognised as being interactive and complex. Injuries can result from too much of something or too little – as in neglect, deprivation and developmental insult. An injury model implies a process of recovery and rehabilitation that is mutual and may require a long-term commitment to that recovery. And such a commitment requires an actively collaborative relationship between the helper(s) and the injured party. It leads interactive exploration away from that sickness/badness dichotomy expressed as 'What's wrong with you?!?' to a very different question, 'What happened to you?' (Bloom, 1994).

Conscious and unconscious

Due in large part to the biological reductionism of the past few decades, we find that many people working in healthcare, mental healthcare and other caregiving institutions fail to comprehend the reality of unconscious motivation. But living beings have both conscious and unconscious processes. For a living organism to be consciously aware all the time of everything that is going on would require brain power not available to individuals. Similarly, every organisational culture has both conscious and unconscious components and both elements get transmitted to new organisational members. Their ability to translate these elements – to read and respond to the 'visible and the invisible group' – then determines whether or not they are able to survive in the organisation (Agazarian & Peters, 1981).

Over time, and in the course of individual and organisational development, much activity that may at one point have been conscious, deliberate and strategic takes on a life of its own, outside of conscious awareness. The longer an organisation has been in operation, the more likely it is that much of what occurs in the organisational culture is happening at the level of unconscious norms and basic assumptions, built on mental models that are completely out of view. Any challenges to these basic assumptions – which provide our individual and shared organisational minds with stability and security – are likely to give rise to anxiety and to 'social defence mechanisms' (Menzies, 1975).

The collective result of this natural inclination to contain anxiety becomes a problem when institutional events occur and produce uncertainty, particularly those events that are associated with insanity, injury, death or the fear of death. Under these conditions, containing anxiety may become more important than rationally responding to the situation. But this motivation is likely to be denied and rationalised. As a result, organisations may engage in behaviour that serves to immediately contain anxiety but that is ultimately destructive to organisational purpose. Especially important is the tendency of organisations under threat to become increasingly totalitarian, authoritarian, punitive and aggressive, and thereby diminish their capacity for innovation and creativity (Menzies, 1975; Lawrence, 1995; Pyszczynski et al., 2003; Pyszczynski, 2004).

Creating and sustaining non-bullying, therapeutic cultures

The Sanctuary Model is a method for reorganising whole organisational cultures. Becoming a 'trauma-informed' culture requires a shift in the very foundations of the way we think, what we feel, how we communicate, and how we practice. The Sanctuary Model represents a trauma-informed method for creating or changing an organisational culture in order to more effectively provide a cohesive context within which healing from psychological and socially derived forms of traumatic experience can be addressed.

The philosophy of a therapeutic community is central to the Sanctuary Model (Bloom, 1997; Haigh, 1999; Norton & Bloom, 2004). The basic tenets expressed by the therapeutic community movement represent what all human beings need to function effectively. Given the widespread exposure to trauma and adversity that exists in the general population, we make the case that all workplace environments should be inherently therapeutic, meaning, 'restoring to health' and 'promoting healing'. The Sanctuary Model challenges organisations to re-examine their basic assumptions concerning the extent to which workplace environments promote safety and non-violence across physical, psychological, social and moral domains. As such, the intervention is aimed both at strengthening the therapeutic community environment and at empowering people to influence their own lives and communities in positive ways. Workplace communities can adopt the therapeutic community's core values by recognising that every workplace is a community and that being social creatures we are extremely susceptible to the influence of the group for good and for ill; that adult human beings are responsible for their own lives; that we tend to function more effectively in demo-cratic rather than authoritarian settings; and that people can help each other to grow and to learn (Kennard, 1998; Kennard & Lees, 2001).

Some of the critical questions we address in the Sanctuary Model are these:

- How do we create treatment cultures that promote and support posi-tive change in adults, families and ourselves?
- How do we maximise each other's strengths and minimise each other's weaknesses?
- How do we create workplace cultures that buffer us from the impact of repetitive stress so that we can be effective in helping our clients to recover?

These tasks are too large to approach from an individual position. We have to make greater efforts to shape our organisational cultures to achieve more. Organisational culture matters because cultural elements determine strategy, goals and modes of operating, and because the organisational culture plays such an important role in determining whether or not bullying is encouraged as a social norm (Schein, 1999). Organisational factors are clearly important in the emergence, maintenance, prevention and response to bullying behaviour (Brodsky, 1976; Tehrani, 2001; Vaughan, 2011). Bullying will only occur if the offender believes he has the overt or more usually covert support from superiors for his or her behaviour. Organisational tolerance for or lack of sanctions against bullying serves to give implicit permission for the bullying to continue. Unhealthy environ-ments lend themselves to the emergence of what have been described as 'toxic leaders' (Lipman-Blumen, 2004). Toxic leaders are subtly or overtly abusive, violating the basic standards of human respect, courtesy and the rights of the people who report to them. They tend to be power hungry and appear to feed off the use and abuse of the power they have.

In the Sanctuary Model, we recognise that in order to create and sustain a healthy, non-bullying normative culture, the desired culture must be explicit, consciously and deliberately planned to promote the objectives of the organisation. It must be continually monitored both directly and indirectly, while any evidence of a weakening of the culture must produce an immediate, co-ordinated response by the entire organi-sation. There must be a mechanism to regularly familiarise all members with the social norms and it will probably be necessary to manipulate member pressures to ensure that high status in the organisation is closely associated with conformity to positive prosocial norms.

The astonishing power of re-enactment

One of the most important challenges to any therapeutic environment is the successful management of traumatic re-enactment. Trauma demands repetition. Clients come into treatment exhausted after a lifetime based on repeating an overwhelming and humiliating past. Trauma produces a fragmentation that results in the accentuation of a non-verbal and a verbal split in memory, affect, perception and identity. The language of the non-verbal self is behaviour and in the presentation of their symptoms our clients tell the story of their most terrible experiences. The role of the social environment is to engage enough with the story to understand the script, but then to change the automatic roles that are being cued for by the client so that the story changes instead of being repeated. Traumatic re-enactment can be seen in the shifting roles that clients and staff assume on the 'rescuer–victim–persecutor' triangle (Karpman, 1968).

In the Sanctuary Model, the group-as-a-whole is conceptualised as having a life different from, but related to, the dynamics of the individuals within the group. In other words, groups are seen as living systems and the individuals in the group are subsystems of which the group is comprised. The group-as-a-whole concept implies that individual behaviour in groups is largely a result of group forces that channel individual action. From this perspective, when a person speaks, he or she does so not only for themselves but also voices the unconscious sentiment of the group.

An organisation that cannot change, that cannot work through adversity, trauma and losses so as to move on will, like an individual, develop patterns of re-enactment, repeating past ineffective strategies without recognising that these strategies may no longer be effective. Re-enactment patterns are most likely to occur when events in the past have resulted in behaviour that arouses shame or guilt in the organisation's representatives. Shame and guilt for past misdeeds are especially difficult for individuals and organisations to work through. If a group-as-a-whole can be a repository of hopes and fears, then it can also become a repository of secrets, of what is fragmented, denied, cast off and suppressed (Ettin, 1993). Such a dynamic system paves the way for individual re-enactment behaviour. So too does it pave the way for group re-enactment. The way an organisation talks to itself is via communication between various 'voices' of the organisation. If these voices are silenced or ignored, communication breaks down and is more likely to be acted out through impulse-ridden and destructive behaviour (Bloom, 2005). This can easily lead to organisational patterns that become overtly abusive and bullying. With every repetition there is further deterioration in functioning. Knowledge about this failing is available but it tends to be felt before it is cognitively appreciated. If the capacity to put words to feelings is lacking, a great deal of deterioration may occur before the repetitive and destructive patterns are recognised. Healthier and potentially healing individuals enter the organisation but are rapidly extruded as they fail to adjust to the re-enactment role that is being demanded of them. Less autonomous individuals may also enter the organisation and are drawn into the re-enactment pattern. In this way, one autocratic and abusive leader leaves or is thrown out only to be succeeded by another, while those who have been involved in the hiring process remain bewildered by this outcome (Bloom, 2005).

The counteractive power of the creative

Because of the powerful, largely unconscious aspects of compulsive individual and organisational re-enactment, we need the unlimited power of human creativity to counteract the pull toward repeating the past. Any environment that hopes to facilitate the healing of trauma survivors must be able to recognise and respond creatively to repetitive patterns. The capacity for innovation cannot solely reside within the most creative individuals simply because when they individually leave or grow tired they take their innovative skills within them. The Sanctuary Model is designed to promote the processes that encourage what has been called 'group genius'. The most effective improvisational genius groups are self-managing and have an ability to restructure and regroup in response to unexpected events without being directed by a leader and are particularly effective in rapidly changing environments (Sawyer, 2007).

The Sanctuary Model: an operating system for organisations

'Creating Sanctuary' refers to the shared experience of creating and maintaining physical, psychological, social and moral safety within a social environment – any social environment – and thus reducing systemic violence. The Sanctuary Model emphasises the creation of a 'living-learning environment' that is physically, psychologically, socially and morally safe for both clients and staff (Jones, 1968).

Establishing and maintaining a therapeutic community in the Sanctuary Model requires an active process of breaking down institutional, societal, professional and communication barriers that isolate administrators, staff and clients. Simultaneously, the rebuilding process involves consciously learning new ways to relate as interdependent community members, creating and modelling healthy and supportive relationships between individuals, and developing an atmosphere of hope and non-violence.

In order to train other organisations in a specific model we have had to clearly define what was originally simply good interpersonal practice. The value system of the Sanctuary Model is embodied in the seven Sanctuary Commitments. These commitments are tied directly to trauma-informed treatment goals.

The Sanctuary Commitments

The seven Sanctuary Commitments represent the guiding principles for implementation of the Sanctuary Model – the basic structural elements of the Sanctuary 'operating system' – and each supports trauma-related goals for clients and for staff. For organisational change to be effective, the Sanctuary Commitments must become internal commitments for each organisational member and the organisation as a whole. None of these commitments can stand alone. If an organisation fails to be equally committed to them all, it is not likely that they will get traction with any of them. Likewise, there is and always will be a tension between the real and the ideal. The Sanctuary Commitments in their totality describe an ideal environment to promote health and human welfare while minimising the abusive use of power. A picture may best describe how these values fit together (see Figure 17.1).

As an organisation begins to hold itself accountable to these commitments, mental models of individual members and the organisation-as-a-whole begin to shift. Awareness of the importance of grappling with trauma, adversity and disrupted attachment represents the beginning of this shift. But quickly organisational representatives begin to grasp the reality of both conscious and unconscious group dynamics. As this occurs, they deepen their understanding and ability to respond to the chronic stress and the way it has affected and often injured individual and group effectiveness. Truly comprehending the ways in which repetitive but ineffective strategies form the core of present reality eventually compels programme managers and staff to engage in creative problem solving as the only way of getting out of the binds of re-enactment

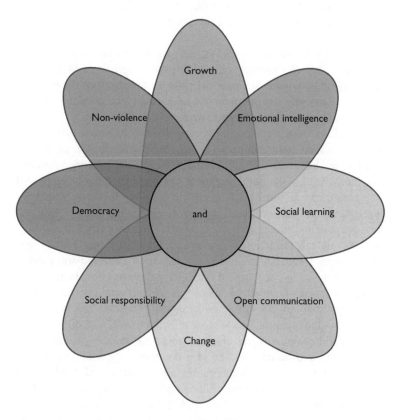

Figure 17.1 The seven Sanctuary Commitments.

behaviour. When this happens, significant treatment gains are made and staff job satisfaction improves.

S.E.L.F. and the Sanctuary toolkit

The four key domains of healing from just about anything include:

- *S = Safety* (attaining safety in self, relationships and environment)
- *E = Emotional management* (identifying levels of various emotions and modulating emotion in response to memories, persons, events)
- *L = Loss* (feeling grief and dealing with personal losses and recognising that all change involves loss)

- $F = Future$ (trying out new roles, ways of relating and behaving to ensure personal safety and help others).

This accessible language demystifies what sometimes is seen as confusing and even insulting clinical or psychological terminology that can confound non-clinical personnel while still focusing on the complex aspects of problematic interpersonal adjustment that pose the greatest problems for any working environment.

S.E.L.F. provides a non-linear, cognitive behavioural therapeutic approach for facilitating movement – regardless of whether we are talking about individual clients, families, staff problems or whole organisational dilemmas. S.E.L.F. is useful because it can simultaneously be employed in a parallel process manner to deal with problems that arise within the workplace setting between staff and clients, among members of staff, and between staff and administration. Applied to such issues as staff splitting, poor morale, rule infraction, administrative withdrawal and helplessness, and misguided leadership, S.E.L.F. can also assist a stressed organisation to conceptualise its own present dilemma and move into a better future through a course of complex decision making and conflict management.

The Sanctuary toolkit comprises a range of practical skills that enable individuals and organisations to more effectively deal with difficult situations, build community, develop a deeper understanding of the effects of adversity and trauma, and build a common language. The present toolkit includes staff training in community meetings, safety plans, red flag reviews, S.E.L.F. planning, Sanctuary team meetings, and S.E.L.F. psycho-educational groups. Along with the hundred-plus organisations that are co-evolving this model with us, we have also developed an implementation manual, a direct care staff training manual, an indirect care staff training manual, and several S.E.L.F. psycho-educational manuals as well as a Sanctuary certification process. For more information about our publications, training programme, the Sanctuary Institute, the Sanctuary network and Sanctuary certification, please visit www.sanctuaryweb.com and www.andruschildren.org.

References

Agazarian, Y., & Peters, R. (1981) *The Visible and Invisible Group: Two Perspectives on Group Psychotherapy and Group Process*. London: Routledge Kegan Paul.

Bloom, S. L. (1994) The Sanctuary Model: developing generic inpatient programs for the treatment of psychological trauma. In M. B. Williams & J. F.

Sommer *Handbook of Post-Traumatic Therapy: A Practical Guide to Intervention, Treatment, and Research.* Westport, CT: Greenwood Publishing.

Bloom, S. L. (1997) *Creating Sanctuary: Toward the Evolution of Sane Societies.* New York: Routledge.

Bloom, S. L. (2005) Neither liberty nor safety: the impact of trauma on individuals, institutions, and societies. Part III. *Psychotherapy and Politics International,* 3(2): 9111.

Bloom, S. L. (2010) The Sanctuary Model: an operating system for living organizations. In N. Tehrani (ed.) *Managing Trauma in the Workplace: Supporting Workers and Organizations.* London: Routledge.

Bloom, S. L., & Farragher, B. (2010) *Destroying Sanctuary: The Crisis in Human Service Delivery Systems.* New York: Oxford University Press.

Bloom, S. L., & Farragher, B. (in press) *Restoring Sanctuary: A New Operating System for Organizations.* New York: Oxford University Press.

Brodsky, C. M. (1976) *The Harassed Worker.* Toronto: Lexington Books.

Einarsen, S., Hoel, H., Zapf, D., & Cooper, C. L (2011) The concept of bullying and harassment at work: the European tradition. In S. Einarsen, H. Hoel, D. Zapf, & C. L. Cooper (eds) *Bullying and Harassment in the Workplace: Developments in Theory, Research, and Practice.* London: CRC Press.

Ettin, M. R. (1993) Links between group process and social, political, and cultural issues. In H. I. Kaplan & B. J. Sadock (eds) *Comprehensive Group Psychotherapy.* Baltimore, MD: Williams and Wilkins.

Felitti, V. J., & Anda, R. F. (2010) The relationship of adverse childhood experiences to adult medical disease, psychiatric disorders, and sexual behavior: implications for healthcare. In R. Lanius & E. Vermetten (eds) *The Hidden Epidemic: The Impact of Early Life Trauma on Health and Disease.* New York: Cambridge University Press.

Haigh, R. (1999) The quintessence of a therapeutic environment: five universal qualities. In P. Campling & R. Haigh (eds) *Therapeutic Communities: Past, Present and Future.* London: Jessica Kingsley Publishers.

Hoel, H., & Cooper, C. L. (2001) Origins of bullying: theoretical frameworks for explaining workplace bullying. In N. Tehrani (ed.) *Building a Culture of Respect: Managing Bullying At Work.* London: Routledge.

Jones, M. (1968) *Beyond the Therapeutic Community: Social Learning and Social Psychiatry.* New Haven, CT: Yale University Press.

Karpman, S. B. (1968) Fairy tales and script drama analysis. *Transactional Analysis Bulletin,* 7(26).

Kennard, D. (1998) *An Introduction to Therapeutic Communities.* London: Jessica Kingsley Publishers.

Kennard, D., & Lees, J. (2001). A checklist of standards for democratic therapeutic communities. *Therapeutic Communities,* 22(2): 143–151.

Lawrence, W. G. (1995). The presence of totalitarian states-of-mind in institutions. Paper read at the inaugural conference on Group Relations of the Institute of Human Relations, Sofia, Bulgaria. Available at: http://human-nature.com/freeassociations/lawren.html (accessed November 23 2006).

Lipman-Blumen, J. (2004) *Allure of Toxic Leaders: Why We Follow Destructive Bosses and Corrupt Politicians – and How We Can Survive Them*. New York: Oxford University Press.

McEwen, B. (2002) *The End of Stress As We Know It*. Washingon, DC: Joseph Henry Press.

McEwen, B. S., & Gianaros, P. J. (2010) Central role of the brain in stress and adaptation: links to socioeconomic status, health, and disease. *Annals of the New York Academy of Sciences*, 1186: 190–222.

Menzies, I. E. P. (1975) A case study in the functioning of social systems as a defense against anxiety. In A. D. Colman & W. H. Bexton (eds) *Group Relations Reader I*. Washington, DC: A. K. Rice Institute.

Norton, K., & Bloom, S. L. (2004) The art and challenges of long-term and short-term democratic therapeutic communities. *Psychiatric Quarterly*, 75(3): 249–261.

President's New Freedom Commission on Mental Health (2002) *Interim Report*. (accessed September 17 2005).

Pyszczynski, T. (2004) What are we so afraid of? A terror management theory perspective on the politics of fear. *Social Research*, 71(4): 827.

Pyszczynski, T., Solomon, S., & Greenberg, J. (2003) *In the Wake of 9/11: The Psychology of Terror*. Washington, DC: American Psychological Association.

Rivard, J. C. (2004) Initial findings of an evaluation of a trauma recovery framework in residential treatment. *Residential Group Care Quarterly*, 5(1): 3–5.

Rivard, J. C., Bloom, S. L., Abramovitz, R., Pasquale, L. E., Duncan, M., McCorkle, D., *et al.* (2003) Assessing the implementation and effects of a trauma focused intervention for youths in residential treatment. *Psychiatric Quarterly*, 74(2): 137–154.

Rivard, J. C., McCorkle, D., & Abramovitz, R. (2004) Implementing a trauma recovery framework for youths in residential treatment. *Child and Adolescent Social Work Journal*, 21(5): 529–550.

Rivard, J. C., Bloom, S. L. *et al.* (2005) Preliminary results of a study examining the implementation and effects of a trauma recovery framework for youths in residential treatment. *Therapeutic Community: The International Journal for Therapeutic and Supportive Organizations*, 26(1): 83–96.

Sawyer, K. (2007) *Group Genius: The Creative Power of Collaboration*. New York: Basic Books.

Schein, E. H. (1999) *The Corporate Culture Survival Guide*. San Francisco: Jossey-Bass.

Senge, P., Kleiner, A., Roberts, C., Ross, R., & Smith, B. (1994). *The Fifth Discipline Fieldbook: Strategies and Tools for Building a Learning Organization*. New York: Currency/Doubleday.

Silver, S. (1986) An inpatient program for post-traumatic stress disorder: context as treatment. In C. Figley (ed.) *Trauma and Its Wake, Volume II: Post-Traumatic Stress Disorder: Theory, Research and Treatment*. New York: Brunner/Mazel.

Smith, K. K., Simmons, V. M., & Thames, T. B. (1989) Fix the women: an intervention into an organizational conflict based on parallel process thinking. *Journal of Applied Behavioral Science*, 25(1): 11–29.

Tehrani, N. (ed.) (2001) *Building a Culture of Respect: Managing Bullying At Work.* London: Routledge.

Vaughan, S. (2011) The influence of organizational culture in dealing with workplace conflict: an ethical and cultural perspective. In N. Tehrani (ed.) *Managing Trauma in the Workplace: Suppporting Workers and Organizations.* Hove, UK: Routledge.

Chapter 18

Systematic suffering

Andreas Liefooghe and Siriyupa Roongrerngsuke

Introduction

Bullying, the systematic abuse of power in interpersonal relationships, has been a topic that has attracted considerable attention in the academic press over the last few decades. Originally a cause for concern in a school environment, gradually places of work have also emerged as the stage where similar negative behaviours have been observed. The aims of this chapter are twofold. First, a concise overview of the research traditions of school and workplace bullying will be presented, mainly focusing on the links between these two fields. Second, three points will be highlighted that are of particular interest: the notion of intent, the role of coping, and viewing schools as organisations. From this, an agenda for future direction in these two fields will emerge, based on a systematic cross-fertilisation between these two similar yet distinct areas.

School and workplace bullying

In Scandinavia in the 1970s, Olweus (1978) was the first scholar to systematically examine the phenomenon of school bullying. Since then, numerous papers and books have been published on the topic, showing that this is an issue that echoes around the globe. In a relatively recent book, Smith *et al.* (1998) provide a concise summary of research into school bullying in over 19 countries. The relative homogeneity of the phenomenon is striking: while differences in incidence do vary, it is clear that similar negative behaviours are experienced regardless of national context. It was not until 1993, however, that Heinz Leymann published research that bore striking resemblances to school bullying – with the main difference that the context was the workplace rather than the school playground. Since this early work, publications in this field have flourished, and have attracted so much media attention that several countries are now at the point of introducing or have introduced legislation to counteract and prevent these occurrences. Einarsen *et al.* (2003) brought together for the first time all leading researchers in the bullying at work field, discussing comprehensively issues such as the nature, incidence and cause and effect of this phenomenon.

But are both research domains investigating the same topic? This question has been preoccupying scholars for some time, and there is scant empirical evidence to support the notion. If one assumes a developmental perspective, then it holds that perpetrators' and victims' experiences may shape their future life trajectories: in other words, the school bully becomes tomorrow's bullying boss. Some research indicates (Smith *et al.*, 2003) that there may be links for victims or targets of bullying, but there is insufficient data available on the perpetrators.

Against this backdrop, we want to raise some specific issues that are salient at present in these fields. It is beyond the scope of this chapter to present an exhaustive history of bullying, and the reader is referred to the above publications for further background information. What we want to raise here are specific problematics that manifest themselves in both fields of inquiry. Whether or not school experiences and those at work are developmentally linked, there are nevertheless important lessons that these two fields can learn from each other. As the field is now so big, most researchers are not sufficiently exposed to each other's particular echelon. This is why we decided to join forces in authoring this chapter to present debates around intent, coping and the role of organisation. We chose these topics because they give a comprehensive overview of the bullying phenomenon, investigating motivations for the behaviours, the reactions to them, and the context in which they occur. These vignettes will give the reader an insight into the issues faced when researching and trying to understand bullying.

The notion of intent

Whether intent to harm should be included in a definition of bullying or not is disputed. While some researchers have included the notion of intent, others decided that this was not appropriate. For instance, in schools Tattum and Tattum (1992) argue that bullying is a wilful and conscious desire to hurt. This is echoed by Olweus (1978), but he does not always consistently apply this view. Bjorqvist *et al.* (1994) consider intent to harm as a key feature of bullying.

The role of intent applies in two ways: whether or not the act was intentional and whether or not the harmful outcome of the act was intentional. Nobody denies, however, that perceived intent, whether real or not, can increase or enhance the feeling of being bullied. Distinctions with regard to the intentionality of harm doing have been made. Harm to the victim can be the main objective of the perpetrator (reactive harm) or it may be simply 'collateral damage' suffered by the victim, as the perpetrator is trying to achieve other goals (instrumental harm). For example, Keashley and Jagatic (2003), quoting Buss (1961), and Neuman and Baron (1997) show that reactive harm can be anger related (wanting to get one's own back or punish), while instrumental harm may come as a side effect of wanting to achieve promotion or heighten one's own self-image. This is a useful distinction, as it may account for the discrepancies in overall reported frequencies of victimisation and self-reports of bullying others. Generally, self-reported victimisation is higher than self-reported bullying. This could be explained by arguing that victims do not make the distinction between these two forms of harm, but the perpetrators do. The perpetrators of instrumental harm doing may not classify this as bullying because it is not intentional, while the victim may regard the same incident as intentional. Whilst behaviours may be the same, intent differs.

The usual argument against including intent in a definition of bullying centres on the unlikelihood of verifying the presence of intent (Einarsen *et al.*, 2003). While we agree with this claim in the context of the contemporary literature, we would argue that this notion of verification is only impossible because scant attention has been paid to other parties involved in data collection on bullying, notably the perpetrator. We consider investigating intent as an important route to further understanding of the motives playing a role in any bullying scenario. What explains some of the confusion in this area is that most research has focused on victimisation rather than bullying. Of course, it is quite right that it was the victim's plight that provided the initial impetus to conduct research into bullying. Yet without a fuller understanding of the motivational aspects involved in the process of bullying, it will not be possible to construct a more comprehensive map of this phenomenon. This should on no account be taken as being an apologist for perpetrators – rather, it is a clear acknowledgement that we are dealing with 'shades of grey' rather than black and white phenomena.

Zapf and Einarsen (2003) identify three potential areas of motives for the perpetrator of bullying: to protect self-esteem; to compensate for lack of social skills (in particular emotional control); and micro-political behaviours (to ensure own career goals are met, possibly at the cost of others). At present, however, these are theoretical notions and have not been empirically researched. Work in schools has some data on this with two studies being particularly important. Craig and Pepler's (2007) work, using participant observation, showed that alleged perpetrators do not necessarily intend to harm, but are trying out different ways of being in a social group.

Using focus groups and questionnaires Olafsson *et al.* (1999) asked pupils how they explained the behaviour of bullies. These lay theories revealed a plethora of different explanations, including engaging in behaviours to entertain the group, playing, as well as causing harm. It is therefore difficult to sustain the notion that perpetrators are solely 'evil' individuals intent on causing harm on innocent bystanders – at times, behaviours experienced as negative by some are not necessarily intended as such by the actors.

We can therefore conclude that while certain behaviours are no doubt experienced as harmful by the target, perpetrators do not regard themselves as bullies, and in many cases have no awareness that this is how they are perceived by others. In other words, we could argue that victims and perpetrators inhabit different, possibly incompatible, psychological worlds, where no shared meaning takes place. For instance, O'Moore *et al.* (1998) found on the basis of victims' reports that those who bullied them are often managers new to a role. As in schools, we could postulate that for these managers the shift to a new role heralds a period of discovery, where new techniques need to be tried and tested. To them, their behaviours and their intent for these behaviours are within the framework of 'coming to grips with a new task' – recipients may experience this as bullying. Important here is the work of Baumeister *et al.* (1993) which analysed biographical accounts of being angered and of angering someone else and found that only a few perpetrators did not understand their own motives, but a substantial number of victim accounts referred to the incomprehensibility of the perpetrator's motives and actions. Victims were significantly more likely to see the perpetrator's acts as arbitrary, incoherent, contradictory and senseless. Thus, the incompatible perspectives lead to a situation of conflict which is ultimately unsatisfactory for all parties involved.

The implications for practice are vast. If we are able to tease out the different functions that bullying-like behaviours hold in a social context, much more refined interventions at an organisational level can be applied. Clearer rules, guidelines and more specific training, and even the redesign of jobs, could lead to an environment where shared meaning is created (see also Liefooghe & Olafsson, 1999, for a further discussion). However, we equally firmly believe, echoing Zapf and Einarsen

(2003), that the focus on these different individual antecedents in the development of bullying does not undermine or change the responsibility of those who have a duty of care in either school or workplace in the prevention and management of these social problems.

Coping with bullying

We argued that different motivations and intentions are likely to be involved in bullying. Equally, we will argue that people have a variety of ways in which they cope with the situation. We will now look at research on how people cope with bullying, that is, the coping strategies used in such extremely stressful circumstances, and speculate on the determinants of these coping strategies. Recent attention has been devoted to coping strategies used in bullying situations in both schools (Bijttebier & Vertommen, 1998; Olafsson et al., 1999; Cowie, 2000; Olafsen & Viemerö, 2000; Smith et al., 2001) and the workplace literature (Hogh & Dofradottir, 2001; Zapf & Gross, 2001).

We shall now describe Olafsson et al.'s (1999) study of coping strategies used in school bullying, and show how a reference to three contributions from the workplace context help interpret and extend its findings (Glasl, 1994; Zapf & Gross, 2001; Leather, 2003). Based on these studies in conjunction, elements towards a model will be presented to account for coping strategies used in bullying-type experiences. First, a brief overview of the study by Olafsson et al. (1999) will be presented.

In a national study of school bullying, pupils were asked in focus groups to discuss 'What can be done if one is being bullied?' On the basis of these discussions, 31 statements about coping strategies were identified (e.g. 'tell the teacher', 'cry', 'just continue what I was doing') and written in a questionnaire, which was subsequently administered to a larger cross-sectional sample. Participants rated the degree to which they had (or would) use each strategy if bullied. The coping strategies were then classified on the basis of factor analysis and multidimensional scaling. The main dimension identified positioned the active and assertive items to one side (e.g. 'show them they had better not mess with me' and 'get my revenge') and, on the other side, the passive or submissive items (e.g. 'cry', 'feel helpless', 'tell the teacher'). The use of these strategies was compared between groups who had been subjected to different amounts of bullying. Some had not been bullied at all, while others had been bullied extensively. It turned out that those who were not bullied much had a tendency to use more the active/assertive strategies (like 'stand my ground') compared with those who were bullied more who used more passive/submissive strategies like 'cry', 'feel helpless' and 'try to get away'. In fact, the use of the assertive strategies decreased linearly as people were bullied more, and the contrary was true for the more submissive strategies.

At least two interpretations are possible to account for this relationship between use of coping strategies and the amount of bullying suffered. The cross-sectional nature of this data does not, however, allow us to choose between them. It could be that pupils have a preferred coping style (some active, others passive), and that these strategies differ radically in terms of effectiveness, which would explain why the users of one type of strategy are much less bullied than the users of other strategies. Alternatively, one could adopt a more process-oriented view, claiming that all pupils are able to use different types of strategies (active or passive), but that the choice of coping strategy depends on the situation, mainly the intensity and duration of the bullying, and the outcome of earlier attempts to deal with it. According to this latter interpretation, the victims of bullying would initially use a more active/assertive strategy, but if the bullying continued, and if attempts to deal with it were ineffective, victims would adopt more passive strategies. The former interpretation is more trait oriented, while the latter is process or situation oriented. Both these interpretations are consistent with the finding that those who are bullied more tend to use passive strategies, while those who are bullied less use more active strategies.

Here, research on workplace bullying provides useful insights regarding the validity of these interpretations. Zapf and Gross (2001) interviewed 19 victims of bullying and were able to trace, based on victims' retrospective accounts, the changes in their strategy use, as the bullying history progressed. They classified the coping responses using successively two models of conflict management strategies: the EVLN-model (Withey & Cooper, 1989) and the Rahim and Magner's (1995) model. These two analyses led essentially to the same conclusion. We will focus here on the EVLN-model.

The EVLN-model presupposes four main coping strategies: *Voice* (trying to improve the situation by active and constructive problem solving); *Loyalty* (passively support the organisation with the hope of problem solving); *Neglect* (reduction of commitment to the organisation); *Exit* (i.e. quit the job, active but destructive from the point of view of the company). Zapf and Gross (2001) found that the majority of victims started with Voice, but ended with Exit (i.e. they left the company). In between, they used a variety of other strategies and typically shifted several times between strategies. These results also confirm

Niedl's (1996) earlier results. Analysis of the Zapf and Gross data showed that the majority of victims started with 'integrating' (i.e. aimed for collaboration and showed concern for the interests of the other party as well as for their own) and ended with 'avoidance' (i.e. withdrawal and ignoring the conflict).

Overall, the workplace studies support a more process-oriented interpretation of Olafsson *et al.*'s (1999) school data. Victims of workplace bullying start with an active coping strategy, but shift to more passive strategies if the bullying persists. The role of coping strategies in perpetuating or ending bullying remains, however, and needs to be studied further. Why do bullying-type experiences never go beyond a certain stage for some people, but escalate and intensify in other cases? To what extent is this process related to the target's skill in the use of the active/assertive coping strategies which are associated with early stages (Zapf & Gross, 2001) or to low levels (Olafsson *et al.*, 1999) of bullying – and to what extent is this determined by factors outside the 'control' of the victim or target?

Another insight provided by workplace bullying research concerns the content of the coping strategies suggested by the pupils in the focus groups (Olafsson *et al.*, 1999) There is a distinct lack of typical 'problem-solving' strategies, or 'integrating' strategies in Rahim and Magner's terms like 'openness, exchange of information, and examination of differences' (p. 123) in the school data. A useful clue towards an explanation of this deficiency comes from Glasl's (1994) conflict escalation model, described and applied by Zapf and Gross (2001) to the workplace bullying data. Zapf and Gross point out that bullying is a 'severe social stressor', which should be located towards the sixth stage of Glasl's nine-stage model of conflict escalation. At such advanced stages of a conflict 'confrontations have become very destructive. The other party is viewed as having no human dignity, and any attempt to achieve positive outcomes is blocked' (Zapf & Gross, 2001: 502). The intervention of a third party is necessary to find a solution, and the initial problem-solving approach, which may be appropriate at lower levels of conflict, is no longer useful. With reference to Glasl's conflict escalation model, the lack of 'problem-solving' strategies in bullying makes sense: The pupils, who would see bullying as a highly escalated conflict, did not see traditional 'problem-solving' strategies as helpful in bullying situations, and therefore did almost exclusively suggest strategies suitable for more advanced stages of conflict. The lack of co-operative problem-solving strategies among the suggestions of schoolchildren as responses to bullying reflects their understanding of the bullying situation as a case of highly escalated conflict, where such strategies are no longer appropriate.

Interestingly, in Olafsson *et al.*'s (1999) study, the social support items are located in different areas of the active–passive dimension. These differences do not marry well with the practice of grouping social support items under one hat (or factor) in mainstream classification systems (e.g. Causey & Dubow, 1992), on the assumption that they are measuring the same thing: social support. The difference in location observed in the school study, however, reflects a subtle contrast in meaning and content of these items. The more aggressive, power-oriented social support items are located toward the 'active' side of the dimension. These include coping strategies about mustering help from other pupils in aggressive counterattack against the bully. Conversely, towards the 'passive' end of the dimension are located social support items from adults, e.g. 'tell my parents' and 'tell the teacher'. Why are the social support items not grouped together? It is likely that those who are able to get help from their peers to defend them against bullies have a stronger social network among peers at school, and therefore do not need to go to parents or teachers for help. It may also be that more benign instances of bullying can be handled without the intervention of adults. In any case, it seems that seeking help from peers is associated with a more assertive, independent choice of strategy, while seeking help from parents and teachers is associated with a weaker position, i.e. crying and feelings of helplessness. It is likely that the help provided by adults is more emotionally oriented than the help provided by peers, and the fact that the participants should need this, betrays a weaker position in the dispute.

Leather's (2003) research could be supportive of this interpretation. He found that among work employees faced with violence at work, help sought *outside* the organisation was associated with less success in solving the problem than seeking help *inside* the organisation. Here, parallels can be drawn in the interpretation of these studies. It is likely that the help provided by people outside the company (e.g. by spouse) is different in nature from help sought inside the company (e.g. from co-workers) and that the help from the latter is probably more action oriented, while the spouse would give emotional support, for example. In both studies, the data suggests that help sought from peers/co-workers is associated with a more benign or solvable problem, while help sought from the outside (parents/teachers or spouse) is associated with a problem that has reached a stalemate, is provoking anxiety and is perhaps more intense than the former. Future research on social support should give consideration to the nature of the help provided by these different sources, and link this to the severity and nature of the bullying conflict.

Jointly, the studies drawn on here are consistent with a model that views coping strategies not only as a trait or characteristic of the individual but as largely determined by the intensity of the bullying experience, and the outcome of earlier attempts to deal with it. As the bullying intensifies, and if no solution is found (from lack of skill of the victim or the rigid persistence of the bully), there is a tendency to move from active to submissive/avoiding coping strategies. Future research needs to assess how much each of these factors explains the choice of coping strategies.

Schools as organisations

While research into school bullying has been conducted systematically since the 1970s, and copious attention has been focused on the individuals involved (be they perpetrators, victims or bystanders), little attention has focused on the school environment. Granted many interventions to counteract bullying advocate a 'whole school approach', meaning that everyone, from teachers to dinner ladies to pupils and parents, should be involved in putting a stop to bullying. However, we would argue that this insufficiently addresses the type of organisation a school is. We will use this section to explore this idea further.

From research into bullying at work, we know that the structure and design of an organisation plays an important role. Leymann (1993), for instance, argued that personality should not even be considered in explaining bullying at work. He singles out issues such as organisational design and leadership as key factors. Other bullying at work researchers have backed this up to a certain extent, although the main thrust of the bullying at work literature also follows a predominantly individualistic approach. In a 1994 study, Einarsen et al. showed that workplaces with the highest bullying incidences were those that had the lowest levels of autonomy. Bringing this back to schools, we could view schools as organisations with a low autonomy environment combined with autocratic leadership. While there are of course individual differences between teaching styles and school environments, it is generally not surprising that bullying would be rife in this context. An often overlooked study by Rivers and Soutter (1996) into Steiner schools supports this argument. The authors' article focuses on the effect of school ethos upon levels of bullying behaviour. Whereas it may be said that all schools have an ethos, in the case of this study the term refers to a particular educational philosophy which underpins the teaching of academic subjects. This article discusses the Steiner or Waldorf education system as an example of a system with a strong ethos. It looked at three classes of 30 pupils in one school in the south of England and found a very low level of bullying, despite the fact that many pupils came to the school because they had been victimised elsewhere. Rivers and Soutter suggested that bullying is a situational problem rather than one due to the fact that some young people are so-called 'natural' victims. We also know that these types of school are characterised by participative leadership or teaching styles and a higher level of autonomy for students (Rivers & Soutter, 1996).

Other research by Berdondini and Genta (2001) gives further evidence to suggest that a move from individual to organisational characteristics is necessary. By filming groups of five- and seven-year-old pupils, she observed that the role of victim or bully is not static. Instead, she found that the same person can play different roles in different contexts – an assumption that is the cornerstone of work that aims to tackle bullying at school. In other words, the intervention is to reinforce positive alternative relational strategies and behaviours, more pro-social and co-operative than those to which all pupils, bullies, bystanders and sometimes even victims are accustomed. This assumes that everyone has the potential to access and become accustomed to positive social behaviour. The way this is achieved is not solely by focusing on interpersonal behaviour, however. Of crucial importance is a redesign of the school and teaching structure. By applying an intervention called co-operative group work, which emphasises autonomy and participative teaching, Berdondini and Genta (2001) found that bullying incidence reduced drastically. The important conclusion from this is that at times both fields of inquiry have overly relied on individual and interpersonal explanations for the bullying phenomena under investigation. It can no longer be ignored that in schools and workplaces the 'way that we do things around here' in terms of organising work flows, how we teach/manage and how work (be it teaching or specific work tasks) is organised, has a significant effect on bullying incidences.

We can even take this one step further. Liefooghe and Mackenzie Davey (2001) found that when employees used the term bullying to denote their experiences, they were not referring to 'bad' individuals making their life miserable. Instead, they were referring to institutionalised practices such as performance appraisal and systems of surveillance that were proscribed by the organisation, and the solving of industrial disputes. Importantly, employees used bullying as a metaphor to describe their behaviours, because they felt they were treated as if they were at school. Lack of autonomy due to strict procedural adherence and direct control mechanisms produces a context where employees feel powerless, systematically abused over a long period of time – all the ingredients for a bullying definition.

This institutionalised bullying is rife in organisations – yet the perpetrator cannot be found at an individual level of analysis, but at an organisational one. At times, the discipline of psychology (where most of the work on bullying is located) has a tendency to be overly preoccupied with the analysis of variables located at an individual level. Context, and in particular the role and function of the principles of organising and controlling, are often overlooked. It is time to fundamentally redress this balance if we genuinely seek to understand the high bullying incidences reported in both schools and workplaces.

Conclusions and future directions

The above discussions about intent, coping and the role of organisation in contemporary life lead to some important conclusions for bullying research. First, we would argue that the field is now sufficiently mature to move away from an exclusive perspective on the victim or target of bullying. While we do not deny that the latter perspective is crucial, a maturing field needs to apply itself to understand as well as to limit harm. Investigations centring on motives and intent of perpetrators is an important next step in the research agenda.

Second, a review of coping has shown remarkably similarities between the two fields, adding value to the argument that school and workplace bullying should co-operate more thoroughly. Finally, in viewing schools as organisations and organisations as at times infantilising places due to lack of autonomy and autocratic leadership styles, we held that the role of organising structure and design can both facilitate bullying and could form institutionalised bullying.

This snapshot of the literature in this field is inevitably limited and incomplete. However, we hope to have raised awareness of some issues that simply cannot be ignored, and worked towards setting an agenda for future inquiry and investigation to further our understanding of both school and work bullying.

References

Baumeister, R. F., Heatherton, T. F., & Tice, D. M. (1993) When ego threats lead to self regulation failure: negative consequences of high self esteem. *Journal of Personality and Social Psychology*, 64: 141–156.

Berdondini, L., & Genta, M. L. (2001) Perception of internal and external family boundaries by well-adjusted children, bullies and victims. In T. M. Gehring, M. Debry, & P. K. Smith (eds) *The Family System Test (FAST): A New Approach to Investigate Family Relations in Clinical Research and Practice.* Hove, UK: Psychology Press.

Bijttebier, P., & Vertommen, H. (1998) Coping with peer arguments in school-age children with bully/victim problems. *British Journal of Educational Psychology*, 68: 387–394.

Bjorqvist, K., Osterman, K., & Hjelt-Back, M. (1994) Aggression amongst university employees. *Aggressive Behaviour*, 20: 173–184.

Buss, A. H. (1961) *The Psychology of Aggression.* New York: Wiley.

Causey, D.L., & Dubow, E. F. (1992) Development of a self-report coping measure for elementary school children. *Journal of Clinical Child Psychology*, 21: 47–59.

Cowie, H. (2000) Bystanding or standing by: gender issues in coping with bullying in English schools. *Aggressive Behavior*, 26: 85–97.

Craig, W. M., & Pepler, D. J. (2007) Understanding bullying: from research to policy. *Canadian Psychology*, 48: 86–93.

Glasl, F. (1994) *Konfliktmanagement. Ein Handbuch fur Fuhrungskrafte und Berater* [Conflict Managment: A Handbook for Managers and Consultants], 4th edn. Bern: Haupt.

Einarsen, S., Hoel, H., Zapf, D., & Cooper, C. L. (2003) *Bullying and Emotional Abuse in the Workplace: International Perspectives in Research and Practice.* London: CRC Press.

Hogh, A., & Dofradottir, A. (2001) Coping with bullying in the workplace. *European Journal of Work and Organizational Psychology*, 10(4): 485–495.

Keashley, L., & Jagatic, K. (2003) By any other name: American perspectives on workplace bullying. In S. Einarsen, H. Hoel, D. Zapf, & C. L. Cooper (eds) *Bullying and Emotional Abuse in the Workplace: International Perspectives in Research and Practice.* London: CRC Press.

Leather, P. (2003) Violence at work. In A. P. D. Liefooghe (ed.) *Proceedings of the ESRC Seminar Series of Bullying at Work.* Swindon: Economic and Social Research Council.

Leymann, H. (1993) *Mobbing – Psychoterror am Arbeitsplatz und wie man sich dagegen wehren kann.* Reinbeck bei Hamburg: Rowohlt.

Liefooghe, A. P. D., & Olafsson, R. F. (1999) Scientists and amateurs: mapping the bullying domain. *International Journal of Manpower*, 20: 39–49.

Liefooghe, A. P. D., & Mackenzie Davey, K. (2001) Accounts of workplace bullying: the role of the organization. *European Journal of Work and Organizational Psychology*, 10: 375–392.

Neuman, J. H., & Baron, R. A. (1997) Aggression in the workplace. In R. A. Giacalone & J. Greenberg (eds) *Antisocial Behaviour in Organizations.* Thousand Oaks, CA: Sage.

Niedl, K. (1996) Mobbing and well being: economic, personal and development implications. *European Journal of Work and Organizational Psychology*, 5(2): 239–249.

Olafsen, R. N., & Viemerö, V. (2000) Bully/victim problems and coping with stress in school among 10- to 12-year-old pupils in Aland, Finland. *Aggressive Behavior*, 26: 57–65.

Olafsson, R. F., Olafsson, R. P., & Björnsson, J. K. (1999) *Umfang og eðli eineltis í íslenskum skólum*. Reykjavík: Rannóknarstofnun uppeldis-og menntamála.

Olweus, D. (1978) *Aggression in the Schools – Bullies and Whipping Boys*. Washington, DC: Hemisphere Press.

O'Moore, M., Seigne, E., Mcguire, L., & Smith, M. (1998) Victims of bullying at work in Ireland. *Journal of Occupational Health and Safety – Australia and New Zealand*, 14(6): 569–574.

Rahim, M. A., & Magner, N. R. (1995) Confirmatory factor analysis of the styles of handling interpersonal conflict: first-order factor model and its invariance across groups. *Journal of Applied Psychology*, 80: 122–132.

Rivers, I., & Soutter, A. (1996) Bullying and the Steiner school ethos – a case study analysis of a group-centred educational philosophy. *School Psychology International*, 17(4): 359–377.

Smith, P. K., Morita, Y., Catalano, R., Jungen-Tas, J., Olweus, D., & Slee, P. (1998) *The Nature of School Bullying*. London: Routledge.

Smith, P. K., Shu, S., & Madsen, K. (2001) Characteristics of victims of school bullying: developmental changes in coping strategies and skills. In J. Juvonen & S. Graham (eds) *Peer Harassment at School: The Plight of the Vulnerable and Victimised*. New York: Guilford Press.

Smith, P. K., Singer, M., Hoel, H., & Cooper, C. L. (2003) Victimisation in the school and the workplace: are there any links? *British Journal of Psychology*, 94: 175–188.

Tattum, D., & Tattum, E. (1992) *Social Education and Personal Development*. London: David Fulton.

Withey, M., & Cooper, W. (1989) Predicting exit, voice, loyalty and neglect. *Administrative Science Quarterly*, 34: 521–539.

Zapf, D., & Gross, C. (2001) Conflict escalation and coping with workplace bullying: a replication and extension. *European Journal of Work and Organizational Psychology*, 10(4): 497–522.

Zapf, D., & Einarsen, S. (2003) Individual antecedents of workplace bullying: victims and perpetrators. In S. Einarsen, H. Hoel, D. Zapf & C. L. Cooper (eds) *Bullying and Emotional Abuse in the Workplace – International Perspectives in Research and Practice*. London: CRC Press.

Index